PURE
EVIL

PURE EVIL

THE BAD MEN OF
BOLLYWOOD

BALAJI VITTAL

HarperCollins *Publishers* India

First published in India by
HarperCollins *Publishers* 2021
A-75, Sector 57, Noida, Uttar Pradesh 201301, India
www.harpercollins.co.in

2 4 6 8 10 9 7 5 3 1

P-ISBN: 978-93-5489-318-6
E-ISBN: 978-93-5489-319-3

Cover illustration: Wasim Helal
Cover design: Saurav Das

Typeset in 10.5/15.2 Adobe Caslon Pro at
Manipal Technologies Limited, Manipal

Printed and bound at
Thomson Press (India) Ltd.

🅕🅘🅞🅞 HarperCollinsIn

This book is produced from independently certified FSC® paper
to ensure responsible forest management.

I dedicate this book to the doctors, paramedics, nurses and others in the medical fraternity, the law and order personnel, and the caregivers in India, who risk their own lives every day in the valiant war against the invisible villain.

I salute you all.

Contents

VI
TUM LOG MUJHE DHOOND RAHE HO ...
The Anti-heroes

VII
JAANE BHI DO YAARO ...
Crime and Punishment   275

Foreword

The first 'villains' in my movie journey were the strict cinema-hall managers in Poona, who kept a hawk's eye on kids trying to sneak into 'Adults Only' films. Imagine spending two hours in the advance-booking line, another three hours anticipating the movie and then not being allowed to enter Rahul Cinema to watch *Enter the Dragon* (1973). A friend even nicknamed his strict father Han after the villain in the film!

One Saturday afternoon, another classmate called me up, saying he had got an extra ticket for the 3 p.m. matinee show of a film playing at Sonmarg. Since my Dad was in the room and within earshot, I told my friend, 'Yes, I will come and collect the Maths tutorial notes right away.' As it was already 2.30 p.m., I cycled furiously towards the cinema hall. I glanced back instinctively and, to my horror, glimpsed my Dad following me on his scooter at a discreet distance. He had obviously smelt a rat. I cycled right past the cinema hall and led Dad on a wild goose chase until I finally lost him. I returned home brandishing a notebook which I'd hidden under my shirt before leaving home. I survived the day, though my friend didn't forgive me for making him waste a ticket, and worse, miss the beginning. Quite aptly, the film in question that incident-filled afternoon was titled *Paap aur Punya* (1974).

It was in 2019 that Balaji Vittal met me as part of his research for this book. After three excellent works dealing with music in Hindi films, a book about Hindi film villains was a wicked and delicious departure, I thought. And soon we were flashbacking into our childhoods, discussing our favourite baddies and revisiting many forgotten gems and guilty pleasures. Yakub in *Paying Guest* (1957), Jeevan in *Kohinoor* (1960), Prem Chopra in *Do Anjaane* (1976), Bindu in *Dastaan* (1972) (my favourite), Lalita Pawar as a Chinese spy in *Ankhen* (1968) and Om Prakash as Seth Dharamdas, who, along with his coterie in *Apna Desh* (1972), murder an upright schoolmaster ... What fascinated us most about the last film was the murder weapon: walking sticks. I also remember a newspaper ad for *Dharma* (1973) starring Pran which said 'where there's Pran there's life'. Suddenly we realized that two whole hours had passed in discussing these bad men. Boy, these villains were memory magnets, we both agreed.

The bad men 'taught' me a lot. I didn't know what 'catharsis' meant but remember experiencing it when Shakaal's (Ajit) foot in *Yaadon ki Baaraat* (1973) gets trapped in the changing lines of the railway track and Shankar (Dharmendra) watches as Shakaal gets mowed down by a speeding train. In *Deewar* (1975), when Vijay (Amitabh Bachchan) barges into Samant's (Madan Puri) bedroom, tears him away from the arms of a woman and throws him down five floors ... for that moment, I was Vijay.

A few years ago, while researching for a film on Raman Raghav, my meeting with the serial killer's psychiatrist made me chuck what I had considered my killer script and make an entirely different film. 'Don't treat him like a criminal. Remember he was a sick man,' he had said to me. It's something I will never forget.

Of course, nobody is a villain in their own story. Take a look at a few of mine: Saif Ali Khan's character Karan in *Ek Hasina Thi* (2004), a charming but lethal character; Neil Nitin Mukesh in *Johnny Gaddaar* (2007) was a reluctant villain, both tormented and emboldened by his crimes—we consciously decided not to give him a dying close-up in the end. In *Badlapur* (2015), the hero becomes the villain and vice versa. (In fact, Massimo Carlotto's novel, *Death's Dark Abyss*, on which *Badlapur* was based, fascinated me because it went against the grain of every revenge story I had loved.) And Simi in *AndhaDhun* (2018)? I still wonder if she was a villain or a victim.

In *Apna Desh*, the villain Dharamdas's catchphrase was '*Narayan Narayan*'. He invokes this chant as he goes about his heinous deeds. Those were innocent times. Villains in films today have tough competition from real life.

Why do villains fascinate us? Because they needn't follow any rules. And wouldn't we all like that? Whereas the hero always needs to play by the book.

Balaji's book is a colourful canvas against which we get to see through the workings of these accursed minds. It talks about the changing social milieu down the decades and how it gave birth to different villains in Indian cinema, ones who made many a moviegoer excited to watch the films on the big screen. It explores how the image of the villains and the nature of their villainy have changed with time. It blends research and our love for the movies—especially its bad men and women—to bring to readers, the film buff, the student, the researcher, and anyone remotely interested in Bollywood, the stories behind and a deep understanding of what makes our villains so alluring. It does so, however, in a language that is easily relatable.

Here you'll meet a range of thugs and femme fatales—segregated and classified into various sections based on their brand of villainy; their sources and inspirations; and the great actors behind these characters. For example, the chapter '*Dhoom Macha Le*' is all about the technology-savvy, handsome trickster-thieves in the new millennium in films like the

Dhoom series, *Players*, etc., in which the hero and the thief match each other's intelligence and smartness.

Like Balaji's other books, this one too is meticulously researched and peppered with anecdotes and insights. For example, in his conversation with actor Boman Irani, Balaji discovered how Irani, in preparation for his role of Lucky Singh in *Lage Raho Munna Bhai*, visited a motor dealer's shop owned by a sardarji in Mumbai's Lamington Road, and simply sat in his shop and observed him closely. And sometimes, he would also mind the shop when the sardarji would be on a loo break! Also, did you know that the first rape scene in Indian cinema was way back in 1929 in a V. Shantaram film? And that the censors had objected to the scene?

There are some sharp observations around the sartorial details and mannerisms of the villains that breathed life into those characters when we watched them on screen. Reading about those in print rekindled my nostalgia. For example, how Amrish Puri zeroed in on his black and shocking pink costume for the role of Mogambo in *Mr India*. And how the blonde-coloured duke-wig was needed to create that foreigner look. The book also touches upon the anti-heroes that arrived in the early 1970s, and the 'dark ensembles' represented by classics like *Jaagte Raho* and *Jaane Bhi Do Yaaro*.

In this book I was glad to see a mention made of the villains' foot soldiers like Shetty, Dan Dhanoa, Mac Mohan, too. A few actors whose iconic villain roles are covered in depth are no longer with us. This book can serve as a fitting homage to those actors.

'After all, crime is only a left-handed form of human endeavour,' says a character from John Huston's noir classic *The Asphalt Jungle*, which is one of the first films to be told from the criminal's point of view. How true. I totally enjoyed *Pure Evil*. I am sure it will send you on a quest for some rare and obscure classics. Be warned, though, it is a ticket to a den of vice!

Sriram Raghavan

Introduction

'*Kaanon aur police kee to madad karna mai apna farz samajhta hoon* (I consider it my duty to help the law and the police),' smuggler J.K. Verma (Amrish Puri) tells Deputy Commissioner of Police Ashwini Kumar (Dilip Kumar) in *Shakti* (1982).

Laughing sarcastically, Ashwini Kumar replies, '*Bahut nek jazba hai. Sach poochiye to, aap jaise "shareef" logon ke wajah se hee hum police waalon ka kaam chalta hai. Agar aap log na ho, to hamara to yeh department hi band jaaye* (Very noble emotions. Frankly, we policemen owe our livelihood to 'decent' individuals like you. Without you, our department would shut down).'

The night show is over. The vehicles in the parking lots gun back to life, impatiently honking their way out. Quick 'how-was-it?' glances get exchanged between the viewers while milling out through the staircases and elevators. Soon, seated in their cars or on their bikes, they discuss the plot and the characters of the Hindi film they have just seen. Arguably the most hated on-screen character is discussed in the greatest detail.

And that is the way it has been for the past ninety years of Hindi talkie cinema. This book too traces the most memorable and magnetic villains and dark characters in Bollywood, going back almost a hundred years.

In any ecosystem a few people are more powerful than the others. And this power places these few people in a position to influence, dominate, dictate, bend (or break) rules and gain disproportionate benefits. They may be in our homes, in our workplaces, in the bihad (ravines), in cities, in our villages … indeed, in our societies. Their vices range from land grabbing, narcotics, counterfeit currency, smuggling, mercenary contracts, prostitution—anything and everything that nurtures cheats, smugglers, terrorists, pimps, goons and killers on contract, spies, drug-peddlers, pickpockets, black marketeers, bootleggers and dacoits. And then there are those who are born with a proclivity to torment their loved ones. Who knows? Some are zealots, megalomaniacs or even psychopaths.

This thing called power is like a drug, with a tendency to corrode public figures on whom great responsibility and trust are imposed. In other words, with great power comes great (ir)responsibility. Corrupt politicians, greedy policemen and unscrupulous lawyers shrouding themselves in various shades of grey while officiating in their uniforms— all fall into this category. To this same list one can add the 'businessmen' doctors, ready to write up a hasty death certificate to hush up a botched, illegal abortion or needlessly detain patients in expensive nursing homes in order for the hospital to earn some extra revenue.

Such characters inhabit this world in flesh and blood, and we have often seen them on celluloid. That's no surprise, given that Indian cinema has always mirrored both the society and the individual, following as it has, the course of our history; in terms of the socio-economic and political changes we have sustained; the wars, pogroms, genocides, civil disturbances and terrorist attacks we have endured. In fact, cinema could be described as the most tangible portrayal of the paradox of good and evil. In it, the villain is the entity symptomatic of the evil that besets society. In the history of Indian cinema, one could say, films have been a replay of the *Ramlila*. Despite being well aware of the denouement, people come in hordes to see the burning effigies of Ravana every year. He is the embodiment of all that stands for 'bad' in the eyes of the public, the source of torment, oppression and torture, of unforgivable lust, and he must, therefore, be destroyed. The spectators cheer in celebration, as the fiery arrow finds its mark many feet above the ground, its locus lighting up the night sky in a resplendent arc.

Likewise, for the villains in Bollywood, in the end, there is no escape from justice. They are beaten up to an inch of their lives while the audience cheers the heroes on. Like spectators in a Roman coliseum, we walk out of the cinema happy that justice has been served. We need villains to experience the satisfaction of comfortably externalizing the bad elements within ourselves and then witnessing their exorcism in public.

There has been a wide range of Bollywood villains portrayed on-screen through the years. There is the sly urbanite and the crude village man, the outsider and the traitor, the evil father–son combo, and the twins. There has been the comical duo in khakis at the quay and the effeminate rapist. Among the women villains, we have seen wily mothers-in-law on the one hand and rebelling bahus wanting their in-laws out of and off their turfs; scheming wives of wealthy old men and evil young brides; a megalomaniac heiress who imprisons a blind painter like a parrot and an acrobatic countess trying to steal a jewel. We have also seen them as sexy molls, clutching the villain's arm, fetching him a drink, serving as a bait for some ulterior motive of their boss ….

They have ridden stallions and driven in limousines. They have dwelt in hideouts under the sea, as well as baked in the hot sun of the ravines. Villains on-screen also have a distinct style. From chequered blazers, white gloves and cigarette holders to riding breeches, whips, bowler hats and walking sticks that turn into bayonets—fashion is an expression and extension of their character.

Contrary to the popular but bland 'Vijay' and 'Rahul' for heroes, the on-screen names of villains have been more colourful: Dr Dang

(*Karma*), Teja (*Zanjeer*), Mogambo (*Mr India*), Shakaal (*Yaadon ki Baaraat*), Topiwala (*Meri Aawaaz Suno*), Loin (*Kalicharan*, though he meant 'Lion'), Gabbar (*Sholay*), Supremo (*Parvarish*), Bhaktawar (*Hum*), Chappan Tikli (*Sir*), Poppy Singh (*Kaala Sona*), Gama Maatin (*Yudh*), 'Danny Boy' (*Sharara*), Makhan Seth (*Qayamat*), Master (*Warrant*), Kancha Cheena (*Agneepath*) and Wong (*CID 909*). No hero's image could have afforded a name like Drona. But there he was in Kathmandu (in *Hare Rama Hare Krishna*). There have been the Shera Daku or Daku Shamsher Singh with their cruel laughter, the cryptic JK, or the deliberately pronounced K ... D ... Narang, not to forget the perennial Prem (Prem Chopra had the screen name 'Prem' in no fewer than eighteen films) or the dubious Dharamatma. Some had surprisingly innocuous names like Satish (*Pyar Hi Pyar*), Mukesh (*Om Shanti Om*), Sharmaji (*Bombay to Goa*) and Raghavan (*Aks*). There was an aptly named Sir Judas (*Karz*) whose actions spoke louder than his words; in fact, he could not speak at all. And there was *Don*—one each in 1978, 2006 and 2011.

And of course, there were the worthy deputies—the faceless (almost generic) Raabert (Robert), the butcher Martin, the hitman Shetty and Daaga faithfully assisting their bosses. Some, like Sunam from Sikkim, shunned villainy and returned to the quotidian. But the rest remained incorrigible.

Good and bad will continue to coexist on earth as long as there is night and day. As DCP Ashwini Kumar in *Shakti* puts it aptly, it is the evil in the world that creates the need for all that is good and great. So, long after we have forgiven our screen villains for their misdeeds, we can't but admit that their lives exist as if only to justify the presence of justice. Besides, a big part of the entertainment in cinema could not have been without them.

The chapters that follow do not purport to glorify or justify the actions of our film villains. Take it as a stroll through the rogues' gallery, where villainy, in all its colours, is showcased. It is like the spectacle of a man-eater stunned by a tranquilizer gun. We can watch them fearlessly.

They can't bite now.

I

MERA BHARAT MAHAAN
United against the Outsiders

They are the enemies against whom we fight to either ensure the freedom of our country or safeguard the independence of another country. They are the terrorists who infiltrate our borders, bomb our property, assassinate our leaders, steal our scientific secrets, hijack our aircraft and terrorize our people.

They have been the British, the Chinese, the Pakistanis—the 'foreigner villains' of Hindi cinema.

How did it all start? And when?

1

Angrezi Hukumat
The Colonizer as Enemy

During the 1920s and 1930s, with the Indian freedom movement gathering momentum, the enemy of the people—the British—were the most obvious choice of villains in films. But needless to say, the British Indian Censors would generally not permit the release of films depicting anything patriotic, let alone show the British as the villains. Here is a classic example of censorship roadblocks ....

It was a fine morning in Bombay, sometime in 1931. The film being premiered that day at Majestic Cinema was V. Shantaram's *Swarajyache Toran* (Thunder of the Hills), starring Shantaram himself in the role of Chhatrapati Shivaji. When the head of the British Indian Censor Board (who also happened to be the Commissioner of Police in Bombay) arrived at the theatre along with the rest of the Censor Board members—all Indians, he was enraged because the title of the film contained the word 'Swaraj' and a poster of the film depicted Chhatrapati Shivaji hoisting a flag. No surprise that he exclaimed, 'No! No! This can't be passed!' As the screening ended, the Indian members of the Censor

Board conveyed to Shantaram with their heads bowed, 'The picture is banned.' Shantaram, swamped by a welter of emotions ranging from disappointment to shock, sat down in a heap outside the Majestic while his friend and film distributor, Baburao Pai, walked the officials to the exit gate, conversing with them.

The censors urged that the film's title be changed, a few scenes modified and the flag-hoisting scene in the climax be deleted in its entirety. Although reluctant to yield to such demands at first, Shantaram eventually gave in. *Swarajyache Toran* was renamed *Udaykaal* and released.[1]

In a discussion with the author, documentary film-maker and V. Shantaram's daughter, Madhura Jasraj, shared, 'Incidentally *Udaykaal* portrayed the only beardless Chattrapati Shivaji in Hindi film history. Historically, Shivaji was just sixteen years old during this conquest. Perhaps they would have thought that a beard would have been inappropriate. This was the kind of attention Shantaram lent his scripts.'

Given these clampdowns by the British Censor Board, the British foreigner villain in the pre-1947 Hindi films was at best implicit, and often metaphorical. For instance, the character of Vidur in Kanjibhai Rathod's silent film *Bhakta Vidur* (1921) is a mediator between the two warring mythological cousin camps (symbolically the Congress and the Muslim League, in all likelihood). But the telltale topi (cap) of the lead actor, Dwarkadas Sampat, and the use of a charkha (spinning wheel) led to the film being banned, with the 1928 Indian Cinematograph Committee (ICC) report terming it 'A thinly veiled resume of political events in India'.[2] 'We know what you are doing. It is not Vidur, it is Gandhiji, we won't allow it', said the report. Unverified accounts also state that Bhalji Pendharkar's *Vande Mataram Ashram* (1926), which questions the British system of education and carried overtones of Madan Mohan Malaviya and Lala Lajpat Rai's sentiments, was also censored and briefly banned.

Bhakta Vidur *was rereleased as* Dharma Vijay *in 1922, probably in a much-truncated form.* Bhakta Vidur *was also remade as* Mahatma Vidur *in the early 1940s by P.Y. Altekar starring Vishnu Pant Pagnis. However, film historian Sanjit Narwekar disagreed that* Mahatma Vidur *was a remake of* Bhakta Vidur.

Despite the censorship restrictions at the time, a few cheeky film-makers were able to slip veiled messages to their compatriot viewers that the Censors would have scissored out, had they been able to decipher them.

Film historian Sanjit Narwekar talked about how it was 'an insider joke. People knew that when Shivaji was talking about Purna Swaraj in *Udaykaal*, it meant Purna Swaraj [complete independence] of India.'

A few films emphasized the need to be united and socially progressive in order to fight the British. *Duniya Na Mane* (1937), based on the Marathi novel *Na Patnari Goshta* by Narayan Hari Apte, advocates widow remarriage. Master Vinayak's *Brandy ki Botal* (1939) criticizes liquor consumption while *Ghar ki Rani* (1940) highlights the dire consequences of aping Western traditions. The messages put out by these films began receiving the attention and support of the country's nationalist leaders. For example, even before the release of *Achhut* (1940), director Chandulal Shah had secured the public blessings and support of Mahatma Gandhi and Sardar Patel. And the British censors poked their noses once again, ordering the removal of the library footage of Vallabhbhai Patel's speech about abstinence from *Brandy ki Botal*.[3]

Communal harmony was another potent weapon in fighting the British. For instance, *Padosi* (1941), remade from Shantaram's Marathi original *Shejari* (1940), is about an outsider (read Britisher) attempting to divide two good neighbours, Thakur and Mirza. Interestingly, the film's cast itself made the point: the role of Thakur was played by Mazhar Khan (not to be confused with another actor of the same name in the 1980s) and the role of Mirza by Gajanan Jagirdar, i.e., a Hindu playing a Muslim and vice versa.

But surprisingly (or maybe, not so surprisingly), not all native Indians were supportive of the Indian film-makers. V. Shantaram's *Dharmatma* (1935), originally titled *Mahatma*, had to be renamed because of objections not from the British censors but from Kanaiyalal Maneklal Munshi, the then Home Minister of Bombay State, who was also a Congressman. According to Madhura Jasraj, Munshi charged Shantaram with '… exploiting the name of Mahatma Gandhi for [his] selfish purposes.' Shantaram argued that there was nothing wrong in calling the protagonist, Sant Eknath, a mahatma, since he had taken up the cause of eradicating untouchability. But Munshi would have none of that.

———

There were films that contained songs which, while upholding the sentiment of the struggle, were overlooked by censors given the Britishers' unfamiliarity with Hindi. *Apna Ghar* (1942), *Naya Tarana* (1943) and *Amar Jyoti* (1936) feature lyrics the Angrezi hukumat (British Raj) would have termed inflammatory, had they gotten a whiff of what the words mean. There is, for example, '*Charkha chalao bahno* (Spin the wheel, sisters)' in *Aaj ka Hindustan* (1940), '*Chal Chal re naujawan* (March on, youth of the nation)' from *Bandhan* (1940) and the cheeky '*Door hato ae duniyawalon, Hindustan hamara hai* (Back off, o world! India belongs to us)' from *Kismet* (1943). This last, however, incurred arrest warrants against poet and songwriter Kavi Pradeep, and composer Anil Biswas. 'Both my father and Pandit Pradeep had to go underground to escape arrest,' said Shikha Biswas, daughter of Anil Biswas. 'They could resurface only when it was pointed out to the government that the lyric "*Tum na kisike aage jhukna, German ho ya Japani* (Supplicate to none, be it the Germans or the Japanese)" were directed against the Axis powers, Germany and Japan. Therefore, it was pro-Allied (and hence pro-British) rather than anti-British,' she added.

The Second World War led to a few red-tape issues as well. Films with a patriotic undertone—*Desi*, Brit or otherwise—had to be specifically cleared by a central body in Delhi. Filmistan Studios, which was formed in 1943, had to lobby hard for getting their film *Shikari* (1946) cleared, with director Gyan Mukherjee having to camp in Delhi for quite a length of time. Ironically, *Shikari* was anti-Japanese—and hence pro-British. And yet …. The British Indian Censors obviously had no problems with non-British villains in Hindi films. In Sohrab Modi's *Sikandar* (1941), the villain is a Greek invader—Alexander the Great, played by Prithviraj Kapoor. *Sikandar* was ahead of its time in its portrayal of the villain, showing the villain's romantic side as well as his vulnerabilities in the face of mutiny by his army. He is both the protagonist and the villain of the film. Prithviraj Kapoor essayed this contrast brilliantly, bringing to the fore his stately screen presence, showing that an enemy of the country can still command an ambassadorial status rather than that of a mere dictator.

The battle scenes of Sikandar *were shot in Kolhapur, with the help of Her Highness Maharani Tarabai Saheba of Kolhapur and the State Officials of Kolhapur.*

Meanwhile, the Empire struck back. As a counter-strategy to patriotic Hindi films, the English film *The Drum* (1938) portrays Indians as untrustworthy, always scheming against their British masters. Bombay city rose in revolt against the screening of the film, with the Frontier Gandhi, Khan Abdul Gaffar Khan, demanding the film be banned. In the September 1938 edition of *Film India* magazine,[4] celebrated journalist Baburao Patel called it a 'shameful fling at the Frontier Pathans', suggesting that 'Dr Khan Saheb (Khan Abdul Gaffar Khan, the Frontier Gandhi) ought to take notice of this dirty propaganda that is being carried on against his men ….' And it did happen. Within a week of its release on 1 September 1938, there was wide-scale agitation against *The Drum*, which brought the uptown business and commercial areas of Bombay to a virtual halt, creating a severe law and order situation.[5]

Another film that met with resistance in India was the 1939 *Gunga Din*, in which Gunga Din (played by Sam Jaffe) is a water bearer who is loyal to the British Army. Then there was *The Lives of a Bengal Lancer* (1935) which was met with protests in Lahore for its disrespectful portrayal of the Muslim community.[6]

But, come the early 1940s, with World War II draining all resources, India became too expensive and difficult for the British to manage. The call for freedom was in the air. Busy packing their bags, the British censorship's grip began to slacken. 'The titles of the films did not matter to them now,' pointed out Narwekar. There was a kind of new-found audacity in the content of the cinema posters too. 'Bringing Light to a Vexed Nation' was the tag line in the poster of *Chal Chal Re Naujawan* (1944) while 'Turn East—and Hear India Speak! Is Today's Tip To The West' was the tag line for Prabhat's *Hum Ek Hain* (1946) poster that appeared in the *Times of India* edition dated 17 August 1946.[7] A twenty-three-year-old actor, who made his debut in *Hum Ek Hain*, would go on to play several successful negative characters in the years to come. His name was Dharamdev Anand—better known as Dev Anand.

As Independence Day drew nearer, Indian film-makers took the Empire head-on with in-the-face titles like *1857* (1946), about the eponymous first war of Indian independence, in which the villain is the East India Company. The film begins with the Company's siege of Rahmatpur in March 1857, leading to the subsequent 1857 mutiny and the war against the British led by the combined forces of Rani Laxmibai, Tantia Tope and Nana Saheb Peshwa. True, *1857* still had to fall in line with censorship rules, as is evidenced by its ending, which showed the Indians welcoming the news of Queen Victoria taking charge of India, but the heroes of the film are still the freedom fighters.

Indian film-makers may not have been allowed to depict the British as outright villains, but now they could at least celebrate their *heroes*. This was progress.

And finally, India achieved freedom. The British left, never to come back. A few years later the Portuguese too left Indian shores forever.

2

Videshi Haath
Foreign Villains in a Free India

Surprisingly, even in free India, Bollywood scriptwriters have hardly given us a memorable British or Portuguese villain. In most cases it has been the colonizing country *as a whole* that became the villain, represented film after film by white-skinned men, their intimidating whips, their ramrod straight backs with palms clasped behind their backs, their seething *'You bloody Indian'* expletives in accented Hindi. There are hardly any nuances or differentiations. If you've seen the British general (played by Tom Alter) in *Kranti* (1981), the British officer (played by Bob Christo) in *Palay Khan* (1986), General Douglas (Brian Glover) in *1942: A Love Story* (1994) and the Portuguese invader of the Malabar coast General Barborosa (K.N. Singh) in *Baaz* (1953), you've probably seen them all. Films in which the colonizer is the villain are actually biopics, celebrating the lives of Indian freedom fighters with scripts that focus more on patriotism, its symptoms and consequences, and physical conflict. Or there were costume dramas like *Shokhian* (1951) in which the Portuguese villain is merely incidental. As film historian Kaushik

Bhaumik stated, 'Foreign influence on India was masked. We never saw it explicitly.' And thus, the colonizer villains are no more than the proverbial skin-deep. Actor Anupam Kher, who played the British General Bonz in *Palay Khan* (1986), which was loosely based on *Lion of the Desert* (1981), said, 'The role of Bonz in *Palay Khan* was a typecasting according to me. I did not put on any accent because that would have been idiotic.'

Some of the biopics in which the *country of Britain* as a whole is the villain include Bimal Roy's *Pehla Aadmi* (1950), which includes rare footage of Netaji himself; *Samadhi* (1950); Shyam Benegal's *Bose: The Forgotten Hero* (2005), which highlights lesser known episodes of Netaji's journey; Srijit Mukherjee's *Gumnaami* (2019), which revolves around the mystery of Netaji's disappearance in the Saigon plane crash; Manoj Kumar's *Shaheed* (1965), which is the best known biopic of Shaheed Bhagat Singh; Phani Majumdar's *Andolan* (1951), which is about Sardar Vallabhbhai Patel's Bardoli satyagraha (a little essayed fact in Hindi cinema history); K.A. Abbas's *Saat Hindustani* (1969), based on the real-life struggle of a band of satyagrahis in the Goa liberation struggle against the Portuguese and Ashutosh Gowariker's *Khelein Hum Jee Jaan Sey* (2010), about the life of Surya Sen of Chittagong (Chattagram, now in Bangladesh) who led an armed ambush into the British armoury in the early 1930s.

Khelein Hum Jee Jaan Sey was adapted into the award-winning book Do and Die: The Chittagong Uprising 1930-34 *by Manini Chatterjee, daughter-in-law of Kalpana Dutta, one of the associates of Surjya Sen. The film made news for a dubious reason: it was alleged that Amitabh Bachchan had influenced the release of Bedabrata Pain's* Chittagong, *also based on the Chittagong Uprising, to promote his son Abhishek Bachchan. Finally released in 2012,* Chittagong *won the best film by a debut director at the National Film Awards in 2013. Gowarikar's* Khelein Hum Jee Jaan Sey, *with its disjointed screenplay and make-believe Bangla diction, turned out to be a dead duck at the box office.*

Benegal's film Bose: The Forgotten Hero *attracted controversy for stating that Netaji died in the Saigon plane crash, whereas history says that nothing was known of the fate of the passengers in that ill-fated airplane. Benegal himself defended the petition in court and won.*

Actor Prem Chopra, who played Sukhdev in Shaheed, *recalled: 'Manoj gave me that role and it helped me rise in my career. After leaving my job at the* Times of India, *I had no other means to earn a livelihood. Post* Shaheed, *I was there in almost every film of Manoj's.'*

A few film-makers took liberties with history. For example, *The Legend of Bhagat Singh* (2002) shows Bhagat Singh forecasting an India of the future burning in communal chaos and religious strife. Also, Ketan Mehta's *The Rising: Ballad of Mangal Pandey* (2005) resulted in public protests (including protests from Mangal Pandey's hometown, Baliya) as well as from political parties for the way Mangal Pandey is portrayed.

But memorable British villain characters remained far and few.

———

It took someone of the stature of Satyajit Ray to give us two of the most memorable British villains in Indian films. Ray's *Shatranj ke Khilari* (The Chess Players) made in 1977, based on a short story of the same name by Munshi Premchand, is a period drama set in 1856, when the British are about to annex the Indian state of Awadh. The principal villains are Captain Weston (played by Tom Alter) and General Outram (played by Sir Richard Attenborough, who cook up a premise to oust the weakling Nawab Wajid Ali Shah from Awadh. Outram's incisive political strategy in spotting the Nawab's weaknesses and Weston's shrewd execution was the first successful example in Hindi cinema of the British 'divide-and-rule' formula. Outram goes beyond mere whip wielding. In fact, there is not a trace of violence in him. His villainy lies in his strategy—he is the khilari (chess player) and the Nawab and his council of ministers are the shatranj (chess pieces). Outram is also acutely aware of the unfairness in the way the British were going about disposing the Nawab, a fact he privately shares with a colleague in the film. But then, Outram has a job to do.

In producer Suresh Jindal's book on the making of *Shatranj ke Khilari*, titled *My Adventures with Satyajit Ray: The Making of Shatranj ke Khilari*, Jindal stated, 'While researching his part as General Outram, Richard Attenborough found that the man smoked cheroots and wore a pince-nez. He not only began practising a Scottish accent but also brought the props with him (to Calcutta).'[8]

A reasonably good attempt at creating an interesting on-screen foregner villain was the Portuguese policeman Captain Gomes (Shakti Kapoor) in *Armaan* (1981). Captain Gomes is part comic, part evil, dancing with semi-clad women in carnivals and bars even while he is in his policeman's uniform. This role of Captain Gomes, the equivalent of Captain Renault (Claude Rains) in *Casablanca* (1942), from which *Armaan* was adapted, was a significant one in Shakti Kapoor's career. It was one of his first comic villain roles, the likes of which he which he would go on to essay consistently for the next twenty years.

The other purported Portuguese villain around the same time—Police Chief Montero (Prem Chopra) in *Pukar* (1983) looks no different from any of the bribe-hungry rogue policemen that frequent Hindi films. The 'foreigner' factor is missing in his characterization altogether. In the absence of this differentiation, coupled with the presence of routine ingredients of dance, fights and comedy, *Pukar* turned out to be just another expensive masala dish with the Portuguese liberation angle thrown in as a mere excuse.

Lagaan: Once Upon A Time In India (2001) has a British villain who was arguably the most unique in the genre—Captain Russell, who challenges the poor villagers to a game of cricket. If they lose, they are to pay triple the tax to their colonial masters. But if they win, the taxes for three years for the entire province will be waived. Captain Russell has the familiar trademarks of megalomania and oppression of the colonizers.

But he is more than a tyrannical ruler. He loves to taunt the Indians—be it Raja Puran Singh's vegetarianism or the villagers' unfamiliarity with cricket. Russell is loathed by the Indians and disapproved by the British alike. By the way, *Lagaan* is incorrectly believed to be based on a true story. Answering questions from the audience at National Film and Television School (NFTS) London, producer Aamir Khan clarified, 'It (*Lagaan*) has no link to any true story.' Khan further adds, '… 1893 was when no Indian had played cricket.'[9] *Lagaan* was pure fiction.

In a chat with the author, veteran actor Kulbhushan Kharbanda, who played Raja Puran Singh in Lagaan, *he recalls: 'Director Ashutosh Gowariker went through the script thoroughly. He held eight to ten meetings with the entire cast. While reading the script, all of us knew that if the last forty-five minutes stuck, the film would stick. And how it stuck! Everyone knew the hero would win, but the thrill lay in how close to the wire the fight would go.'*

In The Spirit of Lagaan, *author Satyajit Bhatkal writes how 'Robert Croft' (name changed), the actor originally chosen to play the role of Captain Russell in Lagaan, was rejected by Aamir Khan after the contract was inked, and Aamir had to placate the livid agent by compensating Croft for the full contractual amount despite the fact that he would not be shooting at all. Bhatkal discloses that the Reserve Bank of India (RBI) smelt a rat at this very curious transaction in which a foreigner got paid for a contract he never fulfilled. After much questioning, the forex was reluctantly released…*[10]

The actor chosen to play the wicked Captain Russell was Paul Blackthorne. Blackthorne did not know any Hindi and struggled with the Hindi dialogues written phonetically in Roman script. Blackthorne's initial reaction on seeing the script was, 'After fifteen minutes of reading my first line in Hindi, I could remember barely three syllables. I put my head in my hands and thought, "I've made a terrible mistake. I must call the whole thing off."'[11] Bhatkal further states in his book that

Aamir Khan turned to author Rachel Dwyer of the School of Oriental and African Studies (SOAS) at the University of London for help. Dwyer drafted one of her students, Samin, a young Pakistani girl, to handle the challenge of teaching Paul Blackthorne and Rachel Shelley (who played Elizabeth) Hindi in a month.[12]

Another problem that came up with Blackthorne was that despite his British origin, he wasn't very familiar with the game of cricket. Stated Bhatkal, 'But Paul (Blackthorne) playing Captain Russell, is a stranger to cricket and though every member of the unit has volunteered advice and coaching, Paul continues to be a novice.'[13]

> *Procuring nineteenth-century cricket equipment cricket gear was a major impediment.[14] Aamir and his (then) wife Reena combed London but couldn't find what they were looking for. Finally, a dealer suggested to them that one Shawn Arnold's shop may be the right destination. Aamir and Reena arrived at Shawn Arnold's just before closing time and found an array of old 'stitched' cricket balls and genuine nineteenth-century cricket bats. Mr Arnold was persuaded by Aamir Khan to sell him the entire range of vintage bats, stumps, pads and gloves—and also a book full of nineteenth-century photographs of cricket.*

About his experience shooting for *Lagaan*, Kulbhushan Kharbanda said, 'The village was one unit. We stayed there for six months. The village and its people had "adopted" us.' And Kharbanda has no regrets about *Lagaan* not winning the Oscar. 'The Foreign Films section is a very small piece of the entire show. We getting excited about it is like *begani shaadi mein Abdullah diwana*. We have our own National Awards. Those are more important.'

Another of those rare British villain characters worthy of recall is Major General David Harding (played by the Scottish actor Richard McCabe) in Vishal Bhardwaj's *Rangoon* (2017), a period movie set in 1943. Like other colonial masters, Harding's villainy too is about quelling the Indian freedom movement, including the Indian National Army's march. But Harding is the Indian that even many native Indians are not. He is comfortable quoting Ghalib in banquets and the battlefield alike. Clad in a kurta and immersed in his early morning riyaz with his harmonium, Harding makes his deputy wait at the doorstep till he has got the precise swar of the song '*Kaa karoon sajni*' right. Harding has all of Captain Russell's imperialistic arrogance, coercion and cruel humour—just that Harding is a man of the arts whereas Russell was into cricket. Russell's gaunt face and cold eyes makes his villainy more predictable but Harding, with his round, ever-smiling face is deceptive—the mask could slip any moment to reveal his naked face. Other factors like a weather-beaten storyline and a drawn-out climax let *Rangoon* down, robbing history of a potential cult villain character brilliantly played by Richard McCabe.

A couple of British villains are noteworthy because of the conflict within a conflict they were caught in. In Sohrab Modi's *Jhansi ki Rani* (1952), Henry and Manu are childhood playmates in the gullies and bazaars of Jhansi. When they grow up, Manu becomes Rani Laxmibai and Henry becomes Lieutenant Henry Dowker (played by a young and handsome Anil Kishore). Dowker, by definition, is the foreigner villain pitted against the Rani, executing the orders of the Governor General to bring to the Rani the news of the East India Company's directive to annex Jhansi. But throughout, there is an undercurrent of mutual respect between Dowker and the Rani. In the ensuing war, Dowker gets mortally wounded by the Rani in the battlefield and dies in her arms. Like Outram, Dowker too had a job to do as the villain. Likewise, the British character of Jailor McKinley (played by Steve Macintosh) in *Rang De Basanti* (2005) is a layered character and not a cardboard villain. Tasked with meting out torture to the revolutionaries, McKinley lights a candle at the church and screams at Jesus Christ, 'How can this be the will of God?!' He breaks down and weeps bitterly. The British too were humans, after all.

Unfortunately, due to the commercial failure of Jhansi ki Rani *at the box office, Modi had to give up the ownership of the prestigious Plaza Cinema hall in Delhi.*[15]

These were the types of nuances that were missing in most other films with British or Portuguese villains.

———

In the aftermath of the 1962 Sino–Indian war and the 1965 Indo–Pak war, the Chinese and the Pakistanis became the new foreigner villains.

In the case of Pakistanis, it was war films and more than that, war films blended with romance and layered with patriotic emotions, therein leaving very little face time for any specific villain to develop. Little wonder that many ambitious films with Pakistanis as villains, e.g., Dev Anand's *Prem Pujari* (1970), Chetan Anand's *Hindustan ki Kasam* (1973), J. Om Prakash's *Aakraman* (1975), flopped. Chetan Anand's war-romance theme had, however, worked very well in his earlier film *Haqeeqat* (1964), the first film to portray China as the treacherous villain.

Regarding the failure of Hindustan ki Kasam, *maybe Chetan Anand's originally conceived ending of the IAF blowing up Pakistan Television and the Indian spy getting killed would have helped. 'But then the distributors pressurized my father to change it to a happy ending. He resisted but gave in to their wishes as his money was involved', disclosed Ketan Anand, son of Chetan Anand, in a chat with the author.*

Said Ketan Anand, son of Chetan Anand, 'The Chinese betrayal in 1962 affected my father a lot.' And thus germinated the idea of making a film around the 1962 war. 'The then Chief Minister of Punjab, Partap Singh Kairon, jumped at the idea and told my father, "*Tu Punjab da puttar hai. Bana picture.* (You are the son of Punjab. Make the film.) We want the reality to come out." That idea became a reality—*Haqeeqat*, with the

Punjab Government financing the project', he added. Chetan Anand, who had chronic asthma, led his cast and crew in the harsh conditions of Ladakh, all the while taking the support of his breathing pump.

Punjabis, with their large frames, broad features and strong voices are perhaps furthest from the small-statured Chinese as far as physique is concerned. But somehow, film-makers felt that Madan Puri, a quintessential Punjabi, would make a good Chinese villain. Tao Ki Chen (Madan Puri) in *Humsaya* (1968) and Mr Chang in *Prem Pujari* (1970) were two Chinese villains portrayed by him. Coincidentally, the villainy of both Chen in *Humsaya* and Mr Chang in *Prem Pujari* was about planting impostors to spy on India. Chen asks a Chinese Colonel, Lin Tan, to undergo plastic surgery to resemble the Indian Squadron Leader Shyam Singh (Joy Mukherjee in a double role) while Mr Chang plants a captured Indian soldier, Ramdev Bakshi, as his own country's spy by giving him a fake Tibetan passport. *Prem Pujari* met with widespread backlash (including a mob attack) because of its portrayal of the Chinese. This backlash took place in India, in Calcutta to be precise, where the film had to be withdrawn from theatres.

Better cinematographic technology brought classier cinematic adaptations of true-life war incidents involving India and Pakistan—J.P. Dutta's *Border* (1997) is about the Battle of Longewala of the 23rd Punjab Regiment in the 1971 war with Pakistan, while his interminably long *LOC Kargil* (2003) is about the 1999 Kargil war. Set within the backstory of Pakistan intrusion into Batalik and Dras by crossing the LoC, Farhan Akhtar's romantic war story *Lakshya* (2004) is a fictionalized account about the reclamation of Peak 5179 at Kargil. All three are patrioritic war-films, with the enemy being Pakistan— and not any specific Pakistani portrayed as the villain. Another film in which Pakistan as a country is the villain is *Sarbjit* (2016). Though it isn't about war, it shows the 1999 Kargil war as one of the reasons that scuttled the release of an Indian prisoner unlawfully detained in a Pakistan jail. *Sarbjit* is based on a real-life story of an Indian villager whose identity and existence gets pitilessly destroyed by the Pakistan Police and judiciary.

The idea of Prem Pujari, *the first film to portray Pakistan as a villain, is said to be an outcome of a conversation between Dev Anand and General Pargat Singh at Nathu-La pass during the making* of Jewel Thief.[16]

In war movies, the enemy is stationed so far away that we can hardly see any of them, unless the camera zooms in on their camps. There were a few fleeting Pakistani villains in these war-movies that had the potential to be developed into something more significant. But the film-makers failed to spot the opportunity to develop strong subplots around these characters. The loud-mouthed Pakistani Army Colonel (played by Shatrughan Sinha) in *Prem Pujari* (1970) in a two-scene appearance was one such lost opportunity. Likewise, in *Hindustan ki Kasam*, the promise of a riveting espionage/counter-espionage subplot involving Pakistani Squadron Leader Amjad Qadalbash (Amjad Khan's debut in an adult role) and an Indian spy posing as his girlfriend, fizzles out. Another such lost opportunity was in *Lakshya* in which Pakistani Major Shahbaz Humdani (played by Parmeet Sethi) is a shrewd military counter-strategist who out-thinks the Indian Army's ambush strategy of climbing the vertical cliff face and almost manages to upset Indian Col. Sunil Damle's (Amitabh Bachchan) plans. Director Farhan Akhtar missed a trick; more face time to Humdani could have brought in the much-needed variety and contrast to the story.

Prem Pujari *was also Shatrughan Sinha's first signed film. Sinha, who went on to become a major villain in the years to come, had practised the art of throwing a cigarette and grabbing it with his lips. Dev Anand took a prominent shot of the same, and this cigarette jugglery, apart from being a rage, inspired another actor—not a villain—to perfect the art: Rajnikant.*

Conversely speaking, films which were *not* war-films helped present a more close-up view of the villains. For example, *1971* (2007) is a post-war story about Indian Prisioners of War (PoWs) detained in Chaklala, Pakistan, for six years after the 1971 Indo–Pak War (and a few PoWs of the 1965 war too who have gone insane). Pakistani Major Karamat Ali (Sanjeev Wilson), Pakistani Colonel Shakoor Akhtar (Maj. Bikramjeet Kanwarpal), Pakistani Colonel Shahryar Khan (Vivek Mishra) and a host of others in Pakistan's PoW camp are the villains of the story. In a storyline with obvious resemblance to John Sturges's *The Great Escape* (1963), the villainy of the Pakistani captors is their flouting of the PoW detention norms agreed to in the Geneva Convention, hiding the PoWs and denying the presence of PoWs to the International Red Cross. These human rights violations bring in a flavour of villainy different from the standard gun-firing Pakistani soldier from somewhere far away.

In Avijit Ghosh's 40 Retakes, *Amrit Sagar says that the film was based on a story called '6 Qaidi' (Six Prisoners) written by Sagar's father Moti Sagar. According to Avijit Ghosh, the shooting was completed in a single seventy-one-day (numeric coincidence!) schedule in a Himachal winter that had continued till April. 'Sometimes it rained, sometimes it was snowy and sometimes sunny. Maintaining a consistent look in the film was a major problem,' said cinematographer Chirantan Das.*[17]

Young film-makers brought in refreshing dimensions to wartime stories. Meghna Gulzar's *Raazi* (2018) and Sankalp Reddy's *The Ghazi Attack* (2017) revolve around specific Pakistani flesh-and-blood characters shown up close. What makes their characters realistic and complex is the fact that they challenge the Indian protagonists with their intelligence. In *Raazi*, based on Harinder Sikka's novel *Calling Sehmat*, the home of Pakistani Brigadier Parvez Syed (Shishir Sharma) is something of a 'war zone' with capable, shrewd antagonists like Brig. Syed's domestic help Abdul (Arif Zakaria) whose sharp instincts sniff out an Indian spy in the household. Spying on critical war documents, cryptic communications and close shaves between Sehmat and her Pakistani in-laws' family holds more menace than missiles. *The Ghazi Attack* is a mental game of war strategies between Pakistani Commander Razzaq Khan (Rahul Singh) of the Pakistani submarine *PNS Ghazi* and his enemy commanders of India's submarine *S21*. All through the underwater cat-and-mouse game of torpedoes and water mines, Razzaq Khan is a thinking adversary who earns admiration from his counterparts in the Indian camp.

A few foreigners discovered alternative means of harming India. In the films of the 1970s, the foreigner villains in Indian cinema are likely to be customary white-skinned men with flaxen hair nursing a drink at a smuggler's party, or the Arab in a white flowing robe whose vocabulary never seems to go beyond '*Subhan Allah*', or a Mr Wang with stereotypically slanted eyes. These foreigners are the clients of desi smugglers (more of which, in a following chapter) who need to be entertained by girls in sparkly, short dresses and pillbox hats, or a Miss Kitty dancing in scanty clothes and a blonde wig. A rare example of a foreigner villain of South African origin is Williams (Prem Nath) in *Chhupa Rustam* (1973) in that typical light-coloured wig. Williams is desperate to unearth thousands of tons of gold from the now-buried 3,000-year-old Golden Age civilization somewhere in the snow-clad Nangla Valley located beyond the Himalayas close to the No Man's Land between India and a fictional neighbour Tibut. Funded by ten other investors from Europe, Africa and other continents, Williams has built tunnels underneath the sovereign Indian land space to unearth the Nangla gold, but without success. And then two 'desi' smugglers—a father and son duo, Vikram Singh and Bahadur Singh (Ajit and Prem Chora respectively), step in to suggest an alternate diabolical plan. Prem Chopra shared an incident during the making of *Chhupa Rustam* that caused a misunderstanding between the Anand brothers—Dev and Vijay. 'Dev Anand had only one song and he asked Vijay, "What am I doing in this picture, yaar? You are doing everything!" Being the director, Vijay Anand had cornered a bigger share of screen time for himself.'

Also, terrorism on the ground was becoming a huge concern in India, providing a mouth-watering business opportunity to international suppliers of arms and ammunition. An international outfit led by Captain (Madan Puri) and Doctor X (Jeevan) in *Aankhen* (1968) keeps sourcing, assembling and then providing lethal arms to Indian terrorists to blow up railway bridges in Assam. Captain and Doctor X are one of the first instances of a foreign villain enabling terrorist activities in India. In the late 1970s and early 1980s, these international outfits came with villains modelled on those in James Bond films, e.g., Dr Shiva (played by South Indian actor Balaje) in Ravee Kant Nagaich's *Surakksha* (1979) who plans to destroy cities and countries using his atomic reactor that he had built in his underwater hideout. *Raksha* (1982), again by Nagaich, is also about a foreign villain, Big Hardy (Prem Chopra), keen on scuttling India's atomic power programme by assassinating and abducting Indian scientists. Director Nagaich seemed to relish this 'atomic power' theme as well as the James Bond genre equally. Iftekar plays the equivalent of 'M', James Bond's boss, in both *Surakksha* and *Raksha* while the towering, steel-toothed villain 'Jaws' in the James Bond film *The Spy Who Loved Me* (1977) was lifted for *Raksha*, the 6 feet, 8 inch-tall Olympian and Asian Games champion Praveen Kumar Sobti playing 'Gorilla', the villain with iron teeth.

———

By the mid-1980s, things were getting too serious on the foreigner villain and the audience could do with some lightening up of the mood. How about a character with an outlandish costume and weird hairdo who the kids would laugh at? Mogambo of *Mr India* (1987) brought in the families, children, popcorn and laughter. Mogambo is a watershed character in Bollywood history. He is a synthesis of all the manifestations of villainy till date—drug peddling, distribution of spurious medicines, food adulteration, smuggling stolen artefacts, bribery, goondagardi, supply of arms and terrorist activities. And yet, he isn't entirely debauched. For one, he isn't into prostitution. Nor does Mogambo indulge in any violence towards women. He is childlike in that he is attention-seeking, forcing his gang members to salute him with a 'Hail Mogambo!'. He refers to himself in the third person, a sign of his pompousness. After every heinous act of crime or conspiracy, his punchline 'Mogambo khush hua' (Mogambo is pleased) instantly neutralizes his evilness and invites loud cheers and claps from the audience. Mogambo looks to be a blend of two venomous villains from the good old comics. One was the cold and ruthless Cobra with a mad desire to rule the world (from the Mandrake the Magician series); the other was the gregarious, colourful Rastapopoulos from the Tintin series.

In his autobiography, *The Act of Life*, Amrish Puri shared his insights.

> *Mogambo was conceived as a Hitler-like character. He was vicious and so very eccentric, because he wanted to rule the world and build his empire. Since his nationality wasn't clear and the foreign origins weren't specified, though he definitely looked like an invader, the name had to be unusual, mysterious and hard-hitting. And Mogambo was derived from a 1953 Hollywood film of the same name, starring Clark Gable.[18]*

About the costume for the role, he writes:

> *And this time round I picked a black and shocking pink, and black and striking golden yellow contrasts, because the character was outlandish. One thing was sure that black is associated with negative and garish colours embellished with golden embroidery would have a shocking value. So the outcome was regality and reality of evil.[19]*

Given the indeterminate nationality of Mogambo, there had to be some feature about him that would establish his foreign origin. The actor revealed: 'Initially, I thought he should be bald, but after some thought we decided to give him a look of a foreigner with duke-like blonde wigs.'[20]

That topped it. Another actor—Anupam Kher—had initially been chosen for the role. After nearly sixty per cent of the film had been shot (as per Anupam Kher, he had shot for two months), Amrish Puri was brought in, perhaps after his role as Mola Ram in *Indiana Jones and the Temple of Doom* (1984) became a major success. Anupam Kher, the perfect gentleman, gracefully acknowledges, 'When I saw *Mr India*, I thought Mr Puri was brilliant. I would never have been able to manage those nuances because Mr Puri was a larger than life person and those came easily to him.'

This storyline of a scientific invention turning a man invisible was however seen in many more films before Mr India. *Prominent among them are* Mr X *(1957),* Mr X in Bombay *(1964), and the relatively lesser known* Elaan *(1971) with Madan Puri as the underworld boss and Vinod Khanna as the other bad guy.*

Surfing the wave of success after *Mr India*, Amrish Puri played the terrorist Dong in Anil Sharma's *Tahalka* (1992), loosely based on *Where Eagles Dare* (1968). Dong is a terrorist and dictator in a far-off kingdom called Dongrila, who constantly attempts to breach India's borders. Unlike Mogambo, Dong is a rotten pervert who runs prostitution rackets and dismembers young girls to sell their organs. Dong looks distinctly Mongoloid whereas Mogambo's nationality is ambiguous. Dong's character is unpredictable, as we see him suddenly laughing out loud while talking. Puri writes about Dong: 'His *takiya kalam* [signature line] in the film "*Dong kabhi wrong nahi hota*", (Dong is never wrong) was an extension of the eccentricity of the character that emerged as the director made me portray it despite my reservations.'[21]

If we permit ourselves the luxury to include Non-Resident Indians (NRI) in the 'foreigners' category then we need to talk about Don Quixote (Amrish Puri) in *Oh Darling Yeh Hai India!* (1995). There is some ambiguity over whether Don Quixote really is the country's richest NRI as he claims to be or is a Bombay underworld don as his activities suggest. Anyway, he has this mad plan to capture India by kidnapping the President of India and installing an impostor Nathuram (Anupam Kher) whose face has been altered by plastic surgery to look like the president (Anupam Kher in a double role). True to the Spanish fictional character of the same name, Don Quixote (pronounced Kee-ho-tay) is convinced that his ridiculous ideas are actually clever ones. '*Ghazab khopdi Don Quixote* (The incredible brain of Don Quixote),' he laughs out loud, standing in front of an ensemble of twenty mirrors. And '*Ghazab khopdi Don Quixote*' is his takiya kalam in the film that he keeps repeating. Quixote has not a strand of hair on his face. His other marked characteristic is that he never blinks.

Thus, between 1987 and 1994, Amrish Puri had created a niche for himself in these caricature, harlequin-type foreigner villains. Despite the comic element embedded in these characters, Amrish Puri essayed these roles with great command and poise. He was never the clown unlike, say, Shakti Kapoor.

Another international terrorist character that set the cymbals and bells clanging was Dr Michael Dang (Anupam Kher) in *Karma* (1986). Dr Dang's agenda is pretty much the same—terror and disruption in India. Unlike the loud and flamboyant Mogambo, Dr Dang is cold, clinical and soft-spoken. He looks like someone from the scientific field or from the corporate world. Said Anupam Kher, 'The whole credit for the brilliant conceptualization and interpretation of Dr Michael Dang as an international figure goes to Director Subhash Ghai, not to me. True, Dr Dang's character was an exaggeration because he was moving around openly and demanding boiled food and flowers. But my job as an actor was to give flesh and blood to the character that Mr Ghai had conceived and make it look believable. Mr Ghai had a friend in Dubai whose name was Dr Michael Dang. My character in *Karma* was named after that person. In fact, I met the real Michael Dang in a flight later. The name had an oddity to it like Gabbar, Mogambo.'

International terrorism continued in the new millennium too. Jamwal (Pankaj Kapur) in Anubhav Sinha's *Dus* (2005), is another one of these international mercenaries. Unlike the typical Bollywood villain who makes the earth rumble under his feet, Jamwal has no screen presence at all because, for the better part of the film, Jamwal hides in broad daylight as an impostor to fool the Indian Anti Terrorist Cell. Sinha's selection of the diminutive Pankaj Kapur, and his unobtrusive make-up and costume for the role of the terrorist plotting to kill thousands in a football stadium in Canada, made perfect sense. Pankaj Kapur proved more than equal to the task, contributing to *Dus*'s box office bounty. The legacy of professional arms suppliers like Captain (Madan Puri) and Doctor X (Jeevan) in *Aankhen* (1968) who source, assemble and supply arms to terrorists was carried on by villains like Mikhail (Prithviraj Sukumaran) in *Naam Shabana* (2017). While Captain and Doctor X restrict their activities to Indian terrorists, the suave and charming arms dealer Mikhail is the one-stop shop for Jaish, Lashkar and the Indian Mujahideen for all their arms requirements. He is believed to have a 75 per cent market share of arms supplies in India, Bangladesh, Pakistan and Afghanisthan. All that Interpol, the Research and Analysis Wing (RAW) and Inter-Services Intelligence (ISI) have on Mikhail is a solitary, two-year old photograph. Mikhail has been elusive for the past ten years with no fingerprints or voice samples of him available. In such films, professional terrorist outfits would get hired by the jihadis to carry out terror attacks on India. *Mission Kashmir* (2000) is one such instance, with Hilal Kohistani (Jackie Shroff), a professional assassin and terrorist who gets hired by a group of jihadis who want Hilal to carry out a major terrorist attack in Kashmir.

But then, Captain, Dr Shiva, Big Hardy Mogambo, Dr Michael Dang, Mikhail, Jamwal and Hilal Kohistani were leaders of *independent* terror outfits of a foreign origin. It gets so much worse when a foreign country and its government-owned intelligence agency actively promote terror. Pakistan has been the single most notorious on-screen villain on this count. They have been portrayed as sponsors of cross-border terror, gun-running, infiltration and interferences in India. As opposed to the war-films in which the overall country of Pakistan was the villain, now we started seeing *specific* Pakistani spies, terrorists and infiltrators. In *Sarfarosh* (1999), Pakistani ghazal singer Gulfam Hassan (Naseeruddin Shah) is sent to India by Pakistan as their spy and liaison man in the country's quest to arm the local mafia with AK-47s and other sophisictated firearms. In *Dil Pardesi Ho Gaya* (2003) it is not just the Pakistani Army but a Muslim clergyman (played by Prem Chopra) who colludes with the jihadi Tabrez Baig (Mukesh Rishi) to kidnap Indian Army Major Ram (Ashutosh Rana), thereby coercing the Pakistani Brigadier Sarfaroz Khan (Amrish Puri) to deny Major Ram's presence in Pakistan.

At the turn of the millennium, Pakistan's secret agencies became the new villain of Bollywood, especially in films centred around Pakistan's age-old grumble over Kashmir. *Border Kashmir* (2002), *Lamhaa—The Untold Story of Kashmir* (2010), *Zameen* (2003), *The Hero: Love Story of a Spy* (2003), *Asambhav* (2004), *Agent Vinod* (2012) are all about spying, insurgency or assassination conspiracies by militant and terrorist groups harboured by Pakistan. *Lamhaa—The Untold Story of Kashmir* shows seven-to-eight-year-old boys being indoctrinated into anti-India sloganeering in a Lashkar Training Camp in Pakistan Occupied Kashmir (POK). In this film we also see Pakistan's ISI HQ funding and controlling local leaders like Haji Sayyed Shah (Anupam Kher) who are wielding a jihad for an Azaad Kashmir. In *Zameen* (2003), Pakistani outfit Al Tahir hijacks an Indian civilian plane with 107 passengers and crew to the POK and demands the release of their leader, the dreaded terrorist, Baba Zaheer Khan (Mukesh Tiwari). In *Zameen*, Pakistan's direct involvement is so explicit that the Pakistan Army actually congratulates the hijackers and deploys troop to protect them. Even Pakistan's Ambassador to India (played by Arun Bali) refuses to help India. *Asambhav* (2004) is about the kidnapping of the President of India from a hotel in Brissago Islands in Switzerland by a mercenary, Rafiq Mabroz (Shawar Ali), to be handed over to Youssan Baksh (Mukesh Rishi) of the Al Hamaz Kashmiri militant group who, in turn, intends to hand over the President to ISI's General Ansari (Milind Gunaji). ISI's assurance deal to Youssan is that he would head Kashmir once it became independent. In *The Hero* (2003), ISI's Additional Head Chief General Isaq Khan (Amrish Puri) is the principal villain who masterminds Operation Nishaan which is about the ISI clearing the way for the jihadis to steal the Islamic nuclear bomb, while the Pakistan government would pretend that they had nothing to with the bomb being stolen. With the help of the bomb, the religious militant would win back Kashmir from India. The difference between these films and earlier war movies was evident—being undercover ISI agents or militant group leaders, the villains are specific, identifiable individuals.

In *Escape from Taliban* (2003), Director Ujjwal Chatterjee presented a different flavour of a foreigner's villainy—the ultra-radical Taliban in Afghanistan that liquidates anyone that is not an orthodox Muslim. Abdul Malik (played by Pakistan born actor Alyy Khan) and his gang of Talibs is but one of the thousands of other Taliban activists in Afghanistan. The film is based on the true story of Calcutta-based Sushmita Bandopadhyay's 's six-year travail (1988–1994) in Taliban riddled Afghanistan and her fortuitous escape from that land. Bandopadhyay documented all this in her bestselling autobiography, *Kabuliwalah r Bangali bou* (A Kabuliwalla's Bengali Wife, published by Bhasa o Sahitya, 1998).

Tragically, the real-life Sushmita Bandopadhyay died in 2013, after she returned to Afghanistan. She was reportedly killed by the Taliban.[22]

Agent Vinod (2012) presents a galaxy of foreigner villains with several layers of subplots of bomb attacks on India. There is an ISI Chief (played by Rajat Kapoor), a rogue ISI colonel, Huzefa, as well as a good-bad ISI undercover agent, Iram Parveen Bilal (Kareena Kapoor), the Lashkar-e-Taiba as well as the LTTE ... way too confusing to even write here, let alone for the audience to comprehend. Director Sriram Raghavan agreed, '*Agent Vinod* was more inspired by *Octopussy*. Our film didn't do well because there was too much of plot to narrate; too serious and too fast. The audience didn't have enough time to breathe. I should have had added some fun but then I really had no time to make the changes. We were fire-fighting all the time.'

> *But* Agent Vinod *didn't lack the trademark detailing that one would expect from Sriram Raghavan. A few hitherto unheard terms in Hindi films like 'selling short' and 'handler' were part of the dialogues. Said Sriram, 'I had heard this term "shorting the market" in* Casino Royale. *I knew it meant something. The other "culprit" film that I was inspired by was* The Bourne Ultimatum.'

In the post 9/11 world, international terror had taken a turn for the worse with the likes of Lashkar-e-Taiba and the Mujahideen making daily front-page news. Neeraj Pandey's *Baby* (2015) is about the unofficial war between the Indian Intelligence and Anti-Terrorist Squad (ATS) on one side, and Pakistan's ISI, LeT, Indian Mujahideen and the lesser heard of Nanhe Mujahid on the other. A series of aerial strikes in various cities of India is being planned by Lashkar and Indian Mujahideen using Lashkar's 'Jumbo Jet Room' based in Karachi. This operation is led by Pakistan-backed terrorist Bilal Khan (Kay Kay Menon) currently incarcerated in Mumbai. But the IM and ISI help Bilal Khan escape from Mumbai and flee to Saudi Al-Dera (perhaps a veiled name for Saudia Arabia) to plan and execute these aerial attacks. Bilal needs to be neutralized. *Baby* was banned in Pakistan for purportedly showing Pakistan and Muslims in a bad light. The other prominent villain in *Baby* is the Pakistani clergyman Maulana Mohammed Saeed Rahman (ironically played by Pakistani actor Rasheed Naz) screaming anti-India rhetoric from the rooftop (literally). Said Kay Kay Menon who played terrorist Bilal Khan in the film, 'Neeraj wanted me to look like a cool guy who can blend anywhere and at the same time, look like someone that can create an apocalyptic situation. In the end, he does nothing—but the chase was more frightening than the kill. Apart from Neeraj's brief I did not have any other reference point for the role. Incidentally, I had long hair at the time that came in handy.'

Terrorist attacks also provided opportunities to make biopics. One of the worst terrorist attacks that took place on Indian soil was at the Bombay Stock Exchange on 12 March 1993. Anurag Kashyap's *Black Friday* (2004), based on crime reporter and writer Hussain Zaidi's *Black Friday: The True Story of the Bombay Bomb Blasts* (Penguin, 2002), brought to the fore, in an authentic way, Pakistan's undeniable role in the Bombay serial blasts of March 1993. Although in reality, the blasts were perpetrated by Don Tiger Memon (and Dawood Ibrahim denied any role in it), *Black Friday* doesn't strictly belong to the mafia genre of films. Zaidi explained: 'Mafia and terror are two different things. Mafia guys have nothing to do with terror. Mafia are violent but they want to work in a company.'

Pavan Malhotra, who plays the terrorist villain Tiger Memon in the film, said: 'When Anurag told me about the film, I read the script before deciding to do the film. After doing my research I placed a request with Anurag—that every time he would narrate the story to a group of people or another member of the cast, I would like to hear it because I wanted to hear the narration as many times as I could. On the first day of shoot, post briefing me on the scene, Anurag said, "Now you go ahead; do what you think is right. If you do only what I tell you to do, I'll never get you to give me your best as an actor."'

Another principal character in the March 1993 blasts was DCP Rakesh Maria of the Bombay Police. Kay Kay Menon, who played Rakesh Maria in Black Friday, told the author that he had never met Rakesh Maria. All his inputs, i.e., the archival material and reference photographs were provided by the production. That, combined with the script and Menon's imagination of how that person would be and what he might have gone through when he heard of the Bombay Stock Exchange blowing up, formed the character seen on screen.

Rakesh Maria was fictionalized onscreen once again—the second time being in Ram Gopal Varma's *The Attacks of 26/11* (2013) by Nana Patekar, based on the terrorist attacks that took place across south Mumbai on 26 November, 2008 (referred to as the '26/11' attack). The role of the Pakistani terrorist Ajmal Kasab, who wreaked havoc the night of 26 November, was played by actor Sanjeev Jaiswal. Said Jaiswal, 'After spending four years looking for a good break, I auditioned for this role in early 2012. A few days after the audition, I got a call saying that I had been shortlisted. One of the next steps was a meeting with Ram Gopal Varma who asked me to speak a few lines of dialogue. He was quite impressed with me and it was almost sealed. He then made me go through a "look test" in the get-up and make-up and seemed convinced that I had come very close to the character Kasab. To my surprise, they conducted another look-test. But I cleared that too and on 17 March 2012, the front page of *Hit List* magazine announced "RGV has found his Kasab."'[23]

About his experience of working with Nana Patekar, Jaiswal, at the time a newcomer, said, 'I met Nana sir once very briefly, for just thirty seconds, during which he shook my hands and left. The interrogation scene in the film was my first shot with him. Now, I could not afford to get overawed. I had to tell myself that the person sitting opposite me was Rakesh Maria and not Nana Patekar. That interrogation scene was a four-page script but I completed it in a single take.'

But playing the role of the dreaded Kasab would have needed a lot of research. Agreed Jaiswal: 'For days I pored over the available video footage, read Rommel Rodrigues's book *Kasab: The Face of 26/11* (published by Penguin India in December 2010) as well as the material which the assistant director shared with me. The delay in permissions to shoot meant that the film was shot over almost a year, giving me ample research time in between the shooting schedules.'

Consistent with the trend of films inspired by real-life terror attacks, Sri Lanka's LTTE (Liberation Tigers of Tamil Eelam), responsible for the assasination of Indian Prime Minister Rajiv Gandhi, was fictionalized as the LTF (Liberation of Tamils Front) in *Madras Café* (2013). In the film, LTF supremo Anna Baskaran (played by Ajay Ratnam) was a thinly veiled portrayal of Velupillai Prabhakaran. In an interview with *India Today,* director Shoojit Sircar denied that the film was based on the assassination of Rajiv Gandhi.[24] But the plot resembled the incident too closely for Sircar's denial to be credible.

But what about the countries farther west? Contrary to what one would have expected in a Nehruvian socialist India, there hasn't been a single prominent film in Bollywood that has an American villain. Partly because the average Indian generalizes in their perception of Americans, Frenchmen and Englishmen: for them, all three fall under a generic 'angrez'. Secondly, we cannot realistically show a war with the Americans because we have never fought one with them. 'The Americans would be the villains for Iranians and Iraqis, not for us,' observed film writer Sanjit Narwekar.

So, for the Indian, 'Amreeka' is a bad place and the American villain is the all-corrupting culture of that country. In *Doli* (1969), Prem Kumar (Prem Chopra) visits a nightclub upon landing in the USA, a visit that proves to be a one-way street into immoral abyss. Similarly, in *Pardes* (1997) and *Aa Ab Laut Chalen* (1999), the villain is not any specific gum-chewing Texan or mugger in downtown Bronx in New York. The villain in such films was the American lifestyle itself—one that consisted of multiple sexual partners, and the concomitant ills of drinking and gambling, and, therefore, the antithesis of what we understand to be Bharatiya sanskar or Indian culture and values.

The tendency to deride anything that is Western has always persisted, thus making a villain out of anything Western. So much so that in *Purab aur Pashchim* (1970), the hero Bharat refuses to acknowledge anything outside of makki ki roti, sarson ka saag and pudiney ki chutney as khana (food). In *Andaz* (1949), Rajan (Raj Kapoor) blames his wife's Westernized upbringing for her alleged infidelity. Pointed out Shyam

Benegal, 'Western values were considered inimical and threatening to Indian familial social tradition. In the hero versus villain situation, it was always the villain who was Westernized and therefore, depraved and perverse.'

Director Abhishek Sharma, on the other hand, showed far more nuance in his *Parmanu—The Story of Pokhran* (2018). In the film, the US is the villain for a specific reason—Bill Clinton and the CIA were trying to systematically thwart India's nuclear testing programme. Or take the example of NASA's caustically cynical Indian-American scientist Rupert Desai (Dalip Tahil) in *Mission Mangal* (2019) who, after failed attempts to discourage ISRO's mission, keeps hoping, at every step, that the Mars mission would fail.

Have foreigner villains exhausted their ideas? What novel villainy can they now conceive of? What about an invisible, man-made virus in a laboratory in China that is contagious enough to bring India's social and economic machinery to a halt? This, in turn, leads to the creation of an economic cartel against that country. But then, China's deep-rooted investments in Indian companies makes it hard for India to impose those sanctions.

Yes, that could be the next big flavour of villainy.

II

MERE HUMDUM MERE DOST
The Enemies Within

Villains needn't always be foreigners. Some of them are present in our homes, in the form of vile uncles and greedy nephews, the hazy 'door ke rishtedaar', the jealous brother-in-law, the aptly called 'saala', and the deceitful brother of the sauteli maa (stepmother) who pops up from vilayet (abroad) with a single suitcase, needy and waiting to strike when you least expect it. There is also the dishonest employee, the disloyal friend who sweeps your wife off her feet from right under your nose, cheating wives and ungrateful children. Sometimes competitors in a business, profession, science, art, music or sports wanting to win at any cost make for villains of the story.

The motives behind such cruel acts of deceit are quite simple, really—wealth, women or power—sometimes one or the other and sometimes, ideally, all of these.

1

Vishwasghaat
The Back-stabbers

'*Mai to pehle bhi tumhare dimaag aur mehnat ka parkhi tha. Aur aaj bhi hoon. Isiliye maine yeh faisla kiya hai ki aaj se tum is company me 5 per cent ke partner ho.* (I have always admired your intelligence and hard work. That is why I've decided that, from today, you will be a 5 per cent partner in this company),' says Vishwanath Sharma (Ananth Mahadevan) to his employee, Madan Chopra (Dalip Tahil), in *Baazigar* (1993).

Out of earshot, Madan Chopra mutters, '*5 per cent! (mocks) Bewaqoof, mai yahan ka 100 per cent maalik bankar tujhe laat marne aaya hoon.* (Five per cent! You idiot. I am here to become the 100 per cent owner of this company and kick you out.)'

Back-stabbing employees, business partners, friends and ex-fiancées have constituted the most common kind of villain in films. They plant impostors, forge cheques, abuse legal documents, manipulate people and circumstances, and even resort to kidnapping and murder.

In *Mere Sanam* (1965), Shyam Kumar (Pran) takes advantage of his employer's absence and converts the family mansion into a hotel and a gambling den while Ratanlal (Madan Puri) in *Aayee Milan ki Bela* (1964) pilfers company goods, betraying the trust of his employers. Avinash Babu (Madan Puri again—yes, his very presence guaranteed cheating) in *Charitraheen* (1974) is hired by Indrajeet (Sanjeev Kumar) on compassionate grounds as Avinash is unemployed and claims that he is unable to even feed his children and pay their school fees. But Avinash 'repays' the largesse by encashing blank cheques and ruining his employer Indrajeet's business in no time.

They needn't necessarily be violent or even scary. *Mr Sampat* (1952, the titular role played by Motilal) is the habitual conman who, with his gentlemanly charm and gift of gab, manages to travel on trains without tickets, keeps defaulting on house rent and keeps eating meals on credit in restaurants. Mr Sampat is the quintessential consultant who convinces a ghee factory owner, Seth Makhanlal (Kanhaiyalal), to open a bank, a restauranter, Bajranglal (Agha), to open an account in it and a theatre star, Malini (Padmini), to open a theatre company. The bank and the theatre company soon go bankrupt. But Mr Sampat has extracted his consultancy fee, has kept his hands clean throughout and steers clear of any business risk or liability. He walks away leaving them in ruins. Makhanlal is reduced to a wandering ice-cream vendor, Bajranglal becomes a tangewala (horse-carriage driver) and Malini's house and personal effects are up for auction.

Bashu Bhatt (Farooq Shaikh) in *Katha* (1982) is a modern-day version of Mr Sampat. He bags a job with a leading footwear company by lying to the CEO Mr Dhindoria about his background. And then plays truant from work, has simultaneous affairs with Dhindoria's gorgeous second wife Anuradha (played by Mallika Sarabhai) *and* Dhindoria's teenaged daughter Jojo (Winnie Paranjape) from Mr Dhindoria's first wife. It is revealed that Bashu had got fired from his previous employer too, barely escaping getting handed over to the police. In the current job, Bashu's lack of integrity is exposed and he gets fired again. But just like

Mr Sampat, Bashu manages to sweet talk another unsuspecting victim into an employment and takes off to his next destination.

———

In Bollywood, these business partnerships and agreements never quite worked out, it seems. In *Naseeb* (1981), four friends, Damodar (Amjad Khan), Raghuvir (Kader Khan), Namdev (Pran) and Jaggi (Jagdish Raj), come to an agreement by a draw of playing cards that Jaggi would get to keep the lottery ticket (and the money too if the ticket won) that the four of them had bought. But when Jaggi wins the lottery, Damodar and Raghuvir murder Jaggi and frame Namdev as the culprit. In *Buddha Mil Gaya* (1971), the kind-hearted employer Giridharilal Sharma (Om Prakash) makes a few of his employees partners in his business. But, taking advantage of the simpleton Giridharilal, the partners, led by their 'leader' Bhagat (Brahm Bhardwaj), appropriate Giridharilal's wealth and frame a case against him for which he is jailed for twelve years. Bad begets bad. There are three smuggling partners in *Gumnaam* (1965): Madanlal (Tarun Bose), Khanna (Hiralal) and Sohanlal. Madanlal gets betrayed by the other two. And Khanna gets Sohanlal run over by a vehicle. And then, Madanlal, in turn, kills Khanna. But Madanlal isn't quite done. He picks out five individuals who were partners to Khanna, lures them to an uninhabited terrain .... *And Then There Were None*.

'Trust and betrayal are central to human existence' is the message in Sudhir Mishra's directorial debut, *Yeh Woh Manzil To Nahi* (1987).[25] The film, with Uttar Pradesh politics at its core, portrays betrayal at two levels. Many years ago, during British rule, three student freedom fighters, Shamsher Singh (Manohar Singh), Akhtar Baig (Habib Tanwar) and Murlimanohar Joshi (B.M. Shah) betray their comrade Srikant (Lalit Tiwari) to the British police in return for a pardon for having attempted to assassinate a member of the British Police. The years pass but those three are unable to get rid of the trauma of a guilty conscience. Forty years later, at a college reunion, they come face to face with the past. But now, another betrayal is staring at them—that of the youth of their college being betrayed by the nation. It is an exact replay of what had happened forty years earlier except that it was happening in an India ruled by Indians. A student leader Rohit (Pankaj Kapur) gets shot to death the same way that Srikant was shot dead by the British policeman forty years ago. Said Director Sudhir Mishra, 'In my growing up days on the campus in the early 1980s, the Jai Prakash Narayan movement was dying, things were fading, brutal politics was taking over again. The storyline of the young students in *Yeh Woh Manzil* ... was based on a lot of real incidents that happened on campuses. The old men part was partly fictional. You always go back to an area you know. You can hold on to that world much easier.'

An amount of INR 2.5 crores (25 million) as profit is too mouth-watering an amount for partners to remain honest with each other. And that was the exact price of temptation in *Johnny Gaddar* (2007). Five partners are involved in a drug deal in which each member is to pocket a profit INR 50 lakhs (5 million). Their intentions turn ugly immediately as Shardul (Zakir Husain) suggests to the boss Seshadri (Dharmendra) that the deal remain just between the two of them, thereby increasing their share of the INR 2.5 crore pie. One of the five, Vikram (Neil Nitin Mukesh) goes ahead and executes the plan that had merely germinated in Shardul's mind. Vikram knocks out Shiva (Dayanand Shetty) and pushes him out of a speeding train. Next, Vikram kills the boss Seshadri himself and, in a game of cat-and-mouse among the three surviving members, Vikram kills both Prakash (Vinay Pathak) and Shardul. Said Director Sriram Raghavan in an exclusive interview, '*Johnny Gaddar* was all about shady guys with no hero. The kingpin had this unusually harmless name Seshadri, which was the name of one of my uncles. And because Neil Nitin Mukesh was new, nobody could predict what he was up to.'

Some of these scheming back-stabbers took creative ways to wangle out what they wanted, e.g., recourse to the supernatural. In Raj Khosla's *Woh Kaun Thi?* (1964), which was partly inspired from Wilkie Collins's

The Woman in White, (a story Khosla later remade in 1989 as *Naqab)*
Dr Ramesh (Prem Chopra), a close friend and cousin of Dr Anand
(Manoj Kumar), uses a pair of twins (both played by Sadhana) to make
it appear to Dr Anand as if he is seeing the same girl in two different
places at the same time. The motive is to prove Dr Anand insane so that
the family property can pass on to the next legal claimant—Dr Ramesh
himself. *Ab Kya Hoga?* (1977) was something of a remake of *Woh Kaun
Thi?* Young Ram Sinha (Shatrughan Sinha) runs a textile company and
is quite happy in life. Suddenly unnatural things start happening around
him. For example, Ram sees his wife Chitralekha in two different places
at the same time. Gradually, it gets established that Ram is of unsound
mental health. It later transpires that a trusted friend had constructed
these incidents to make the wealthy Ram Sinha appear insane with a
motive to take control of Ram's company. Only that in this case, instead
of a twin, the girl was a moll hired by the treacherous friend of Ram.
She could imitate other's voices very well and was made to wear a mask
to make her look like Chitralekha, Ram's wife. This treacherous friend
of Ram, i.e., the villain of the story, was played an actor who is better
known for comedy roles.

Over time, one thing became clear about the 'ghost' sub-genre—in
most cases these 'ghosts' were make-believe ones—a prop that the bad
guy would use as a part of his scheme. But it gave an opportunity for the
film-makers to adapt classics like *Rebecca*, *The Hound of the Baskervilles,
Vertigo* and others. *Yeh Raat Phir Na Aaygi* (1966) was inspired by Alfred
Hitchcock's *Vertigo*, in which the villain Rita (Mumtaz) is once again a
friend of the hero Suraj (Biswajit). Rita connives with Rakesh (Sailesh
Kumar) who engineers a yarn of a 2,000-year-old spirit of a woman called
Kiranmayee wanting Suraj to fall to his death so that his soul may be
reunited with the spirit Kiranmayee. Kiranmayee (Sharmila Tagore) is, in
reality, a poor village girl forced by Rakesh to act as a ghost—part of Rita
and Rakesh's trick to get rid of Suraj so that Rita may inherit Suraj's wealth.

——

We have discussed the 'impostor' angle used by villains in films like *Woh Kaun Thi?* and *Ab Kya Hoga?*. This trope of planting an impostor to extract benefit unethically (and even illegally), is leveraged by Nasir Hussain in *Tumsa Nahi Dekha* (1957) in which Sohan (Pran) assumes the fake identity of Shankar, the long-lost son of the wealthy Sardar Rajpal. Sohan's agenda was to usurp Rajpal's wealth. The 'impostor' trope continued to feature in quite a few films of Nasir Hussain right till *Manzil Manzil* (1984).

Other film-makers picked this impostor angle up, too. In *Zameer* (1975) Ram Singh (Ramesh Deo), the ingrate servant of Maharaj Singh, is privy to the fact that Maharaj Singh's son Chimpoo has a tattoo of a trishul on his left shoulder. Chimpoo gets kidnapped and, twenty years later, Ram Singh plants a thief Badal (Amitabh Bachchan) as Maharaj Singh's long-lost son. Ram Singh's game plan is to make Badal siphon out money from Maharaj Singh and for Badal to share 50 per cent of the spoils with him. These freak-of-nature lookalikes ended up giving contemptible ideas to villains. In *Satte Pe Satta* (1982), Ranjit Singh (Amjad Khan), the guardian of the heiress Seema (Ranjeeta Kaur), hires an assassin Babu and plants him in the place of Ravi (both Amitabh Bachchan), the latter being the head of the family where Seema is stationed. Babu, masquerading as Ravi, is contracted to kill Seema. If Seema died, Ranjit Singh would inherit the ancestral property.

Similar to ethical internet hackers, there were a few good Samaritan impostors too like Madhu in *Kati Patang* (1971) and Amrit in *Bade Dil Wala* (1983)—both assume a fake identity to alleviate a bereaved family's trauma of losing a loved one. Both these films had identical storylines and were borrowed from *I Married a Dead Man* by Cornell Woolrich. Unfortunately, both Madhu and Amrit fall prey to dirty blackmailers like Kailash (Prem Chopra) and Bhagwat Singh (Amjad Khan), respectively, who, on knowing the impostors' true identity, keep blackmailing them for money. In these films, the blackmailers Kailash and Bhagwat, and *not* the impostors, are the villains.

On the subject of blackmailing, it was easy for a villain like Brij Bhushan (Ranjeet) in *Uljhan* (1975) to blackmail his ex-fiancée Kamla (Farida Jalal) to get into bed with him one last time—else he would share with Kamla's husband the love letters exchanged between Brij and Kamla during their relationship. *Uljhan* was a remake of *Kangan* (1959) in which Iftikar plays the blackmailer Ramesh, who demands INR 5,000 in lieu of the scandalous letters exchanged between Ramesh and Kamla (Purnima). Rakhal Babu (Kalipada Chakravarty) in *Mamta* (1966) is another example of an astute blackmailer who keeps wringing money out of his estranged wife Devyani (Suchitra Sen) who had left Rakhal as he was a debauched drunk. But Rakhal tracks Devyani down in Lucknow and threatens to take her to court demanding Restitution of Conjugal Rights (as per the Hindu Marriage Act). Or else, Devyani needs to part with her hard-earned money. For blackmailers, these dirty secrets concerning marital histories of others could be like sweepstakes at Las Vegas. For instance, the dirty Seth (Om Prakash) in *Kanoon* (1960) has in his possession the certificate of a woman's second marriage while she was still legally married to her first husband. And Seth keeps using it to blackmail her for money.

While blackmailing as a form of villainy thrived, somewhere in the early 1990s, impersonation lost its zeal. With electronic verifications and other systemic checks in place, it increasingly became less credible a trope with the young audience. It continued to surface as part of comic subplots in *Hum* (1991), in which a nautanki actor replaces a kidnapped army general (both played by Kader Khan). By the turn of the millennium, the impostor angle was officially dead.

———

When these villainous employees were not planting impostors, they were planting something else—mistrust. In *Dil Deke Dekho* (1959) employee Harichand (Surendra) fakes his own death by dressing up a dead man in his clothes. And then Harichand plants his own 'suicide' note suggesting that he had been in a relationship with his wealthy employer Jamuna, thus sowing suspicion in the mind of Jamuna's husband Rana Jagat Narayan about his wife's fidelity. This was Harichand's way of venting his frustration at not having been able to marry Jamuna and losing her to Rana Jagat Narayan. Rana believes the fake suicide note to be true and deserts his good wife.

Sometimes, back-stabbing the employer and planting mistrust between the members of the employers' family members runs as a composite strategy for these vishwasghaat employees. In *Charitraheen*, Avinash keeps poisoning the mind of his boss Indrajeet's wife that her husband is having an affair with a prostitute, Rosy. It is untrue. But Avinash's nefarious plan almost succeeds in breaking up Indrajeet's home. In *Chacha Bhatija* (1977), another 'trusted' employee Lakshmidas (Jeevan) has an even better idea. By fabricating a scene showing his boss Teja's (Rehman) wife partially undressed and intimate with another man, he convinces Teja that the latter's pious wife is cheating on him. That woman isn't Teja's wife at all. It is Laxmidas's sister Sonia in an identical sari. But Laxmidas's plan succeeds. Teja throws his wife out of the house. And Laxmidas convinces Teja to remarry Sonia, to be able take control of Teja's wealth. 'Caeser's wife must be above suspicion', runs the idiom. But men are vulnerable to Judas-like friends such as Langda Tyagi (Saif Ali Khan) in *Omkara* (2006), an adaptation of Shakespeare's *Othello*. Peeved at having lost out the post of the gang's capo regime to Kesu (Vivek Oberoi), Langda hatches a plot to ease Kesu out by planting suspicion in Omkara's (Ajay Devgn) mind that Kesu and Dolly (whom Omkara loves) are having an affair. In parallel, Langda sullies Kesu's image in Omkara's eyes by needling Kesu into a drunken brawl. One can't help but accept that Langda, despite his betrayal, is a brilliant strategist with an incisive brain and exceptional execution skills. Omkara may have paid for his critical error of not explaining to Langda the rationale of his decision to promote Kesu over him, but Langda's heinous plan succeeds enough for Omkara to murder Dolly.

———

When mistrust doesn't work, try marriage. To be part of one is a legitimate and cost-effective way to sneak in and wrest wealth. In *Dulhan Wahi Ji Piya Man Bhaaye* (1977), Ms Saxena (Shashikala) is very keen to get her gorgeous daughter Rita (Shyamalee) married to young Prem, the sole scion of the extremely wealthy Seth Harikishan (Madan Puri). When Seth Harkishan disapproves his grandson's Prem's choice of Rita, Prem walks out of the mansion, ready to give up the money and comforts he has grown up in, just to marry Rita. But utter shock awaits Prem when Rita and her mother discloses that Prem sans his wealth was of no use to them. Rita goes to the extent of wishing that Prem's grandfather Harkishan were dead so that Prem could become the owner of Harkishan's empire.

Being part of a marriage doesn't always work, though. Never mind, for there's always murder. This is what Mukunda (Anwar Hussain) resorts to with Seth Bholaram sethji in *Ab Dilli Door Nahi* (1957). Mukunda's lorry is mortgaged with the moneylender Bholaram and Mukunda breaks into Bholaram's house to steal Bholaram's money. In the scuffle, Mukunda strangles Bholaram to death. But why bother murdering when kidnapping is good enough? The dismissed ex-employee Raj Singh (Amjad Khan) kidnaps his ex-boss Haridas Chowdhry's (Shreeram Lagoo) son in *Inkaar* (1977) as an act of revenge against Chowdhry who had fired Raj Singh for misbehaving with a female employee.

Not that the employers were very clean either. In *Baat Ek Raat Ki* (1962), is Ranjan (Chandrashekhar) in love with Neela (Waheeda Rehman) or her property? And why does Neela allegedly shoot Ranjan dead when he is about to confess the name of the mastermind behind all this? Beware the man in white.

———

Where there is a will, there is a kill. Lawyers in Hindi films were not known for using their common sense while drafting their clients' wills. Taking advantage of a badly drafted will in *Phandebaaz* (1978), the estate diwan Bunny (Prem Chopra) whips his boss Rana Shantidas (Dharmendra) into marrying a woman of Bunny's choice within a fortnight because the will stated that Rana's bride would become the owner of the estate only if the wedding happened before that deadline. Bunny's obvious plan was to kill Rana after the wedding and become the virtual owner of the estate. In the comedy *Maalamal* (1988), the villain Chander Oberoi (Aditya Pancholi) actually tries to *prevent* Rajkumar Saxena (Naseeruddin Shah) from blowing up INR 30 crores in 30 days because a bizarre family will decreed that, if Rajkumar were to succeed in spending the amount, he would inherit INR 330 crores. Else, Chander and the pair of duplicitous lawyers that he was colluding with would get the INR 330 crores.

In the 1992 *Khiladi*, the rogue 'uncle' (Ananth Mahadevan)—an ex-employee of Neelam's (Ayesha Jhulka) dad's business—tries to murder Neelam before she turns eighteen. The motive was that he would become the sole owner of Neelam's property if she were to die before she turned eighteen. The whodunnit question tantalizingly points at many suspects, including Neelam's friends, till the real killer is revealed. And the stepfather Oberoi (Raj Babbar) in *Barsaat* (1995) tries to poison his stepdaughter just *after* she turned eighteen because the will said that Oberoi would inherit the property if the girl died after the age of eighteen!

Ananth Mahadevan credited director-duo Abbas–Mustan for choosing someone like him for a villain's role and making him look convincing as a killer in *Khiladi*. 'We had a fleet of usual villains like Prem

Chopra and Shakti Kapoor in the cast. So there had to be a red herring. Abbas–Mustan had to get in a person who did not have the image of a villain. Those days I was doing the role of a good man in the TV serial *Tipu Sultan*. And hence I was chosen.'

———

Professional jealousy is a big catalyst in turning perfectly ordinary men into villains. Buddies, stung by jealousy, can turn traitors. In *Ab Tak Chappan* (2003), Yashpal Sharma plays the role of the black-sheep policeman Imtiyaz who is jealous of his superior, Sadhu Agashe (Nana Patekar), an inspector of the Crime Branch who is well known for killing members of the mafia in fake encounters. Imtiyaz wants to get ahead of Agashe in the police heirarchy and feels that one way of doing so is to rack up a higher body count than Agashe. Shared Sharma about his role, 'Imtiyaz was not a traitor. For him "encounter deaths" was a number game. He was trying to increase his count of encounters from forty-two to match Agashe's count of fifty-six, by whatever means necessary. I had to work carefully on the role. It was based on the real-life story of Police Inspector Daya Nayak; Nayak himself was helping us by working for six months on the script with Nana and director Shimit Amin. Many appreciated that role. My punchline was "Suchak sahib (the corrupt Police Commissioner Suchak, played by Jeeva) ka order hai!" as it was all about obeying the superior officer's orders.'

Consumed by lust for success, a few sportsmen and artistes violate the fundamental spirit of healthy competition—and back stab their peer participants. In *Boxer* (1984), boxer Raghu Raj (Sharat Saxena) tries to get the hero Shankar (Mithun) beaten up by thugs. The reason is that, despite losing the bout against Raghu, Shankar's valiant fight wins many hearts—and Raghu cannot digest that. Said Sharat Saxena about his role of Raghu Raj in *Boxer* (which was inspired by the Hollywood hit and Sylvester Stallone-starrer *Rocky*), 'It was a very important venture for Mithun and me. Both of us would train with a boxer (who was a

Maharashtra State Champion) at the terrace of his apartment or at a gym. The training was quite extensive, complete with rope skipping, punching bag, etc. We did not have a medicine ball (that was shown in the film) though.' According to Saxena, the two fights between Mithun and him were shot in a stadium in Hyderabad over a period of ten exhausting days with lenghthy takes.

Jo Jeeta Wohi Sikandar (1992) saw college students going for each other's throats during a cycling competition, breaking all the sporting codes of conduct. Said director Mansoor Khan, 'For the role of the rich brat Shekhar Malhotra, we had screen tested Milind Soman and a few others including Akshay Kumar who had not made his debut, I think. And about 40 per cent of the film had been shot with Milind including the tricky scenes like the bike race. We had selected Milind for his physique, but Deepak Tijori brought out the "attitude" much better. Replacing Milind with Deepak turned out to be a good decision, after all.'

Be it football or hockey, any coach's most dreadful nightmare is rivalry between members of the same team. Both Tony Singh (Boman Irani) in *Dhan Dhana Dhan Goal* (2007) and Kabir Khan (Shah Rukh Khan) in *Chak de! India* (2007) had to dribble through internal politics and acerbic rivalry between players to make them work as a team. In *Dhan Dhana Dhan Goal*, Tony's decision to recruit striker Sunny Bhasin (John Abraham) into Southall United Football Club meets with intense resistance from senior players of the club, especially Shaan (Arshad Warsi) because of some old enmity. Shaan refuses to pass the ball to Sunny during the game and deliberately injures Sunny during a practise session. This is followed by a locker room brawl between the players after they lose a match. In *Chak de! India*, Kabir Khan has a much bigger problem with his women's hockey team. Most members identified themselves with the domestic team they played for, and not the Indian hockey team as a whole. And then there is the conspirator Bindia Naik (Shilpa Shukla) who instigates the team to defy coach Kabir.

Code of ethics getting compromised wasn't merely in the world of sports. In B. Subhash's chartbuster *Disco Dancer* (1982), Sam Oberoi

(Karan Razdan) loses his fame and fan following to a newbie Jimmy (Mithun Chakraborty). Sam's father Oberoi (Om Shivpuri) stoops to trying to electrocute Jimmy to death. In *London Dreams* (2009), an insecure member of a music band, Arjun Joshi (Ajay Devgn), gets jealous of another member Mannu's (Salman Khan) success. Arjun sets about tarnishing Mannu by getting Mannu addicted to drugs and then planting drugs on him and getting him arrested.

Even members of the so-called intellectual class stoop to cheat on their colleagues. In Tapan Sinha's *Ek Doctor ki Maut* (1990), the government hospital employee Dr Dipankar Roy's (Pankaj Kapoor) path-breaking research on a vaccine for leprosy is systematically sabotaged by the Director of Health Dr Khastagir in multiple ways. Firstly, Dr Khastagir falsely accuses Dr Roy of carrying out a private research in government premises. Khastagir also gets Dr Roy transferred to a remote village where the latter would not be able to finalize his research papers. Then Khastagir deliberately withholds from Dr Roy an invitation letter sent by the London based John Anderson foundation inviting Dr Roy to share his leprosy vaccine research papers with the foundation. These delay tactics by Khastagir actually succeed. Before Dr Roy can complete his research papers, two other foreign scientists (and not Dr Roy) are credited with the successful invention of a vaccine for leprosy.

Ek Doctor ki Maut *drew loosely from the real-life story of Dr Subhash Mukhopadhyay, the man behind India's first test-tube baby.*

At the turn of the millennium, software thieves got a sexy new name: 'hackers'. Varun Sanghvi (Dino Morea) in *Pyar Impossible* (2010) steals software in full public view from the IP owner. One wonders how a geek could make the fundamental mistake of leaving his laptop unlocked and his software unencrypted.

Authors and poets needed to be on their guard too. In *Naya Zamana* (1970), Rajan (Pran), pretending to be wanting to help a guileless struggling writer Anoop (Dharmendra), steals Anoop's manuscript,

'Naya Zamana', and publishes it as his own work of peoms. Ironically, the storyline of *Naya Zamana* was itself an outright copy of Bimal Roy's 1944 classic *Udayer Pathe* (remade in Hindi as *Humrahi* in 1945). However, in the credits of *Naya Zamana*, Producer–Director Pramod Chakravorty failed to acknowledge Bimal Roy's name and merely extended a thanks to B.N. Sircar, the producer of *Udayer Pathe*.[26] Jyotirmoy Roy, the original writer of the story, found no mention in the credits or in the acknowledgements of *Naya Zamana* either.

2

Ghar Ghar ki Kahani
The Scheming Relatives

'Our culture has always portrayed the woman as a sati savitri (pious, virtuous) who can never do anything bad. The truth is that there is a vamp in every home. There is either the evil bhabhi, nanad or the mother-in-law—since time began, since God created woman,' noted actor Bindu Zaveri.

From the 1940s onwards, mythology-based films gradually made way for family dramas, christened 'socials' in Bombay cinema. Demons and demonesses now resided inside one's homes. Schisms in joint families leading to the genesis of nuclear families was a given in the Hindi films of the 1960s. And these schisms were often perpetrated by badi bahus (elder daughters-in-law) like Neela (Bindu) of *Do Raaste* (1969) which was based on a novel *Nilambari* by Marathi writer Chandrakant Kakodkar. Incidentally, despite being the biggest draw of the film by miles, the hero Rajesh Khanna was not the sole attraction of *Do Raaste*. Balraj Sahni, Kamini Kaushal and Prem Chopra had roles which defined the story of an undivided middle-class North Indian family—broken up suddenly due to the machinations of the new urbane daughter-in-law Neela who comes from a wealthy family and has studied abroad. When financial difficulties confront her in-laws, Neela deserts her in-laws' home and moves out with her husband Birju (Prem Chopra) to live a luxurious life while her in-laws get swamped in debts. Interestingly, actress Bindu never wanted to play a negative role, naturally aspiring to be the heroine. 'But then, in the original novel, the home-breaker's name was Nilambari, which was also the title of the novel. So, the director Raj Khosla convinced me saying, "Bindu, you are the heroine of the story." So, of the do raaste (two paths) available to me, I took the crooked path,' Bindu recalls, laughing. The role of Neela turned out to be a career-defining role for her.

These badi bahus of joint families often feel insecure upon the arrival of the more nubile younger daughters-in-law. And an educated chhoti bahu like Prabha (Madhu Chakravarty) in Basu Chatterjee's award-winning 1969 film *Sara Akash* is guaranteed to be in trouble at the hands of the insecure badi bahu (essayed superbly by Tarla Mehta). The mother-in-law, played by theatre veteran Dina Pathak, was not too far behind in joining the wagon of thoughtless cruelty. In the film, the two women heap insults on Prabha, treat her like a maid and doubt her fidelity just because she happens to look out of the window. The film was based on the first part of the two-part Hindi novel *Sara Akash* by revered Hindi litterateur Rajendra Yadav. Extrapolated from a real-life story, where the couple (Samar and Prabha) did not speak for ten years (which was shortened to six months in the film), *Sara Akash* was shot at Rajendra Yadav's ancestral home in Agra.

Debutant director Basu Chatterjee played a Hitchcockian cameo of the schoolmaster. 'The actor who was supposed to play the role did not show up and the crew suggested that I should play that myself,' said Chatterjee.

It would not be far-fetched to assume that the notoriety of the two badi bahus Durga and Maya (especially the elder one, Durga, played by

Bela Bose) in *Jai Santoshi Maa* (1975) was the precursor to the swathe of saas-bahu TV serials that were to become huge successes in later decades. Durga's acrid tongue and shocking insensitivity to her brother-in-law Birju (Ashish Kumar, real-life husband of Bela Bose) and his newly-wedded wife Satyavati (Kanan Kaushal) contributed to the film's humongous success. Durga and Maya, taking advantage of Birju's absence from the house (feared dead in a boat capsize), physically and mentally traumatize Satyavati to such an extent that only divine help in the form of Santoshi Maa could help.

Jai Santoshi Maa also remains Bela Bose's career highlight. She could never replicate the success she achieved playing Durga in the film. But her exceptionally brilliant portrayal of Durga may be seen as something of a template for television actors that followed.

These elder daughters-in-law often fired the gun from their confused husband's shoulders. For instance, in *Avtaar* (1983), daughter-in-law Sudha Kishen (Priti Sapru) refuses to let her husband Ramesh (Shashi Puri) part with even INR 500 for her in-laws for a pilgrimage that the old couple wish to take. Worse was to come. And there was the glamourous younger bahu Sapna (Shoma Anand) in *Ghar Ek Mandir* (1984) who violates the sanctity of her in-laws' home by serving liquor to her guests, takes control of the finances and tries to throw her widowed bhabhi (sister-in-law) Laxmi (Moushumi Chatterjee) out; or the pair of villainous daughters-in-law Kamla (Padma Chavan) and Savitri (Sumati Gupte) in *Aadmi Sadak Ka* (1977) who refuse to pay for their sister-in-law's education and their widowed mother-in-law's medication. Maybe there was some semblance of reality in these melodramas, as these domestic fractions met with wholehearted espousal by the junta.

And then there were those bilious mamas, chachas, aunts and chachis. In *Mr and Mrs 55* (1955), the feminist aunt Seeta Devi (Lalita Pawar) hates men and advises her pretty niece Anita (Madhubala) to stay away from men. But since Anita's deceased father's will decrees that Anita would inherit his INR 70 lakh property *only* if Anita were to marry within a month of her turning twenty-one, Seeta Devi coerces Anita to do a chat-shaadi-pat-divorce with a 'husband' hired for this purpose, against Anita's wishes. Lalita Pawar practically patented this screen image of the egotistic, stern woman those days—be it when playing the mother-in-law mad about dowry in V. Shantaram's *Dahej* (1950), the strict guardian in *Professor* (1962) or the detestable mother-in-law Bhavani Devi in *Sau Din Saas Ke* (1980).

Madhura Jasraj, daughter of V. Shantaram, stated that Lalita Pawar's role in Dahej *was her first villain role.*

And then brother-in-law Gajendra in those blue contact lenses held timid Ram (Dilip Kumar) in a circle of everyday fear to get his hands on his wealth in *Ram Aur Shyam* (1967). Gajendra represents all that is evil. He lives off his father-in-law's money, ill-treats the employees of his company, takes undue advantage of Ram's anxiety disorder, often countering Ram's timidity with beastly physical abuse, and lastly plans to get him killed to appropriate his property. It is another matter that his plan goes woefully wrong when Shyam, Ram's twin, takes Ram's place. The character of Gajendra became a stereotype that actors down the decades kept emulating.

In his autobiography, Dilip Kumar shares an anecdote about the scene in which Shyam whips Gajendra: 'For a quick rehearsal I took the whip and gently touched Pran's back with its tip. The camera unit was waiting for Pran to give the shocked expression he was supposed to in that situation. Instead of giving the shocked look, Pran started laughing and running away from me. There was surprise and shock because nobody knew why he was running away. I went after Pran with the whip to find out what was happening, unintentionally pointing the whip towards him, and, to my bewilderment, he was laughing uncontrollably. The entire unit was now laughing. "I have a problem Lalay (as he affectionately addressed me),

> Mujhe gudgudi bahut jaldi hoti hai. *I get tickled very fast." We had to shoot without a rehearsal and, going by the expressions Pran gave as I "lashed" him with the whip, I think he made it one of the most gripping scenes in the film.'*[27]

Five years after *Ram Aur Shyam* came the 'female' avatar of Gajendra—Chachi Kaushalya (Manorama) in the landmark *Seeta Aur Geeta* (1972). Unlike Gajendra, Kaushalya had a comic veneer that suited the rather podgy and squat physical frame of actor Manorama. While her physical characteristics gave her the tag of a comic, there was nothing comical about her attitude. She had no sense of remorse in constantly torturing her meek niece Seeta (Hema Malini), despite the fact that she, her husband and her daughter were surviving on the pension of Seeta's demised father. Seeta's twin Geeta takes Seeta's place and turns the table on Kaushalya with a series of stinging slaps right across her plump face. Next, Geeta picks up a belt and whips Kaushalya's lecherous brother Ranjeet (Roopesh Kumar) who had tried to rape Seeta. As in the case of Ram and Shyam, the switching of Seeta and Geeta is providential. Nothing like fighting fire with fire.

> *Manorama (aka Erin Isaac Daniels) was of part Irish origin, starting her career in 1936 as a child actor under the name of Baby Iris. After being a busy actor in the 1960s and the first half of 1970s, acting opportunities dried up for Manorama and bad times befell her. In her book* Acting Smart, *Tisca Chopra recalls about a visitor at her flat. 'Clad in a nylon sari with rubber chappals and a faint air of desperation stood the old-time actress Manorama....' Tisca further states, 'She just became irrelevant. Out of date. A has-been. She wanted a handout and I did not have the heart to turn her down.'*[28]

The basic storyline of *Seeta aur Geeta* was later recreated in the 1989 *Chaalbaaz* (1989). But the actors, especially the ones playing the villains, needed to bring in something different to their roles. While in *Seeta aur Geeta*, at least the uncle was a kind fellow, in *Chaalbaaz*, the uncle's character—Tribhuvan chachaji (Anupam Kher)—turned into a spectre. Tribhuvan is the younger brother of the father of the twin girls. One of the twins, Manju, gets kidnapped by their nurse. The other twin, Anju (both played by Sridevi), is held prisoner in her own mansion by Tribhuvan and subjected to prolonged, physical and mental torture at the hands of the sadistic Tribhuvan. Tribhuvan is also suspected to have murdered his brother and his wife (the parents of the twin girls) and brought his saali (wife's sister), Amba, to live in the mansion that he had snatched from the deceased parents of the twin girls. He also periodically injects a chemical substance into the scared Anju to keep her under check. Speaking about his role in the film, Anupam Kher shared: 'I wanted to give the character the looks of a fairytale villain. So, we created a plastic nose (it was the pre-prosthetic era). And the bucktooth was not artificially inserted. I pulled my lip inwards just the way that Lawrence Olivier had done for one of his roles. So, automatically the language and the stance changed.'

Rohini Hattangady shared a few insights on her portrayal of the villainous 'aunt' Amba in *Chaalbaaz*: 'I had not seen *Seeta aur Geeta*. Now, my face is not a very particular kind of face … So, how would a modern get-up suit me? The hair was pulled upwards from my forehead—that gave my face a "sharp" look. I made a patch of the curly hair to save time. And I tried out the wine-coloured gaudy dress. I had done all this up at home itself. My body was hefty, so I had to select the clothes accordingly.'

Hattangady also disclosed, 'On the sets, improvisations happened on the spot, e.g., Shakti Kapoor's dance "Nanha sa, pyara sa, chhota sa bacha hoon." There was also this memorable scene in which the replaced twin Manju, as a part of her revenge against Tribuvan and Amba, threatens Amba at knifepoint and forcefully applies grotesque make-up on my face. I was told to "spoil" my make-up myself. So, I "messed" myself up as best I could. Then Director Pankaj Parashar said, "Rohini, do some more."

Sridevi volunteered to help. She got me her oldest wig, touched it up a bit and put it on me, giving me the ghastly look that Parashar wanted. That act of looking at my own face and screaming was an impromptu addition to the script.'

As in the case of back-stabbing employees and partners, identity switch was a trope used by family villains too. Actor Jeevan was the treacherous 'switch master'. In *Dharam Veer* (1977), he plays the rogue mama (uncle) Satpal Singh who switches the infant born to his wife with the infant born to his sister the same day so that his natural child may be crowned prince of the kingdom someday. In *Banarasi Babu* (1973), Jeevan plays Mr Saxena who, denied of a substantial inheritance, switches the scion Sohan with a safe-cracker Mohan (both Dev Anand) so that Mohan may steal the money from a vault and hand it over to Saxena.

There were those uncles who would stop at nothing to serve their perverse pleasures. Amidst the happy confusion and melee in a typical Punjabi *Monsoon Wedding* (2001), it is revealed that Tej Puri (Rajat Kapoor) used to molest a family member, Ria (Shefali Shah), when she was a pre-teen. Just the way in *Highway* (2014), Veera (Alia Bhatt) was abused by an uncle of the family when she was a child, leaving her with lifelong trauma.

———

And then there were a few parents who were convinced that their stance on matters related to their children's choice of life partners was always correct and immutable. The misery they inflict on their children draws from a sense of false pride based on their own economic status, caste, and linguistic and religious backgrounds. Hence, like a few other family members, these parents too are the antagonists of the script.

Right from 1935, *Devdas* has been the victim of caste and social discrimination. In the 1955 version by Bimal Roy, Narayan Mukherjee (Murad) cites the Chakrabortys being of a socially lower status as the reason for not accepting Paro as his daughter-in-law. In the 2002 version of *Devdas* by Sanjay Leela Bhansali, the stately Mukherjees simply cannot accept their England-educated son marrying into a family of once-nautch girls. Paro's mother is humiliated by the Mukherjees when she comes with a marriage proposal for her daughter with Devdas (Shah Rukh Khan). Poor Devdas dies a ruinous alcoholic's death in every edition. One can understand Badshah Akbar (Prithviraj Kapoor) behaving this way during the sixteenth century, as shown in *Mughal-e-Azam* (1960). But even in 1973, the wealthy Mr Nath (Pran) in *Bobby* religiously protected class divide, violently objecting to his son Raj dating a fisherman's daughter.

Danny Denzongpa recalled an incident from early 1984. 'Around that time, Mithun Chakraborty and I were working on another film being shot in Shimla. Somewhere near the beer factory in Solan our cars crossed, and I saw Mithun walking towards me in a long shawl and kurta-pyjama, his head bent. I hugged him and said, "Anything wrong? Did the recently released *Boxer* flop?" He said, "Dan-Dan, you can't imagine. Very few people came to the theatres. I just can't understand what went wrong," We both sat on the parapet, downed beer, looking down into the beautiful valley. I told Mithun, "Look at the beautiful valley, enjoy the fresh air. Forget the failure. Just concentrate on the next film at hand. *Ye picture aisi chalegi tere ko malum nahi.* (You cannot even imagine how well your next film will do.)"'

The film Danny was referring to was *Pyar Jhukta Nahi* (1985). It went on to become a thumping box-office success, in which the girl's parents (played by Danny and Bindu) not only stonewall their daughter Preeti's (Padmini Kolhapure) decision to marry Ajay (Mithun), a photographer, but also lie to Peeti that her baby was dead. In reality they had given the child away to an orphanage. However, a happy ending in which Preeti gets reunited with her child ensures that all's well that ends well.

Not all NRIs are liberal with their children either. Baldev Singh (Amrish Puri) in *Dilwale Dulhania Le Jayenge* (1995) coerces his

Britain-bred daughter Simran to marry the son of Baldev's friend just because Baldev had made a promise to his friend twenty years ago. Baldev is insensitive to the fact that the Britain that Simran grew up in is very different from the Punjab that he grew up in. That is why he is the antagonist of the story, if not an outright black villain. Amrish Puri played a villainous father again in 2001—that of the Pakistani Ashraf Ali in *Gadar: Ek Prem Katha*. With cruelty embedded in his character, Ashraf Ali simply cannot digest the fact that his Pakistani daughter Sakina can have an Indian as a husband. He descends to unthinkable levels of violence and his radicalism almost claims his daughter's life.

The North Indian–South Indian crevasse swallowed Vasu (Kamal Haasan) and Sapna (Rati Agnihotri) in *Ek Duje Ke Liye* (1981). Not only is Mrs Kundanlal (Shubha Khote) fundamentally opposed to the idea of her daughter Sapna marrying the South Indian boy Vasu, she is a party to the murder of Vasu. Despite being strongly alerted of a killing contract out on Vasu, she deliberately witholds the information from Vasu. Both Vasu and Sapna die a tragic death.

A stepmother has most often been the devil's chambermaid. The stepchild is often ill-treated, screamed at, unfed and let go into the streets, as we observe in *Saraswati Chandra* (1968) and *Ganwar* (1970). In *Beta* (1992), the stepmother, Laxmi Verma (Aruna Irani), sets standards of bilious wickedness hitherto unheard of. Laxmi plots to divert her innocent stepson Raju's (Anil Kapoor) share of inheritance to her natural son. As if that weren't enough, Laxmi attempts to poison her step daughter-in-law to death so that a natural heir to Raju may not be born … But Indian film scripts have been kind to the parents. Laxmi Verma learns her lesson when Raju, refusing to believe that his mother could poison his wife, drinks the liquid himself and hovers on the brink of death. Raju survives, Laxmi turns a new leaf, and all is well.

——

Generational rivalry between families has proved to be no less vicious a villain. There is a landmark film which dealt with a generations old bloody feud between two families—that of Dhanraj Singh (Dalip Tahil) and Randhir Singh (Goga Kapoor). Ratan Singh, the son of Randhir Singh, impregnates the unwed sister of Dhanraj Singh and then refuses to marry her. The girl commits suicide and, as revenge, Dhanraj shoots Ratan to death. Many years later, one offspring from each rival family falls in love with the other and they decide to marry. Mansoor Khan shared an anecdote about this landmark film which had the working title *Nafrat ke Waris*. 'The two families were in a *Romeo and Juliet*-type feud. They simply could not reconcile. We had shot two endings—happy and sad. All the elders advised my father against the sad ending. On the other hand, the youngsters in the family and our friends were all for the sad ending. After some confusion, my dad was convinced on going with the sad ending. But then the title had to be changed, as *Nafrat ke Waris* sounded too khatarnak (dangerous)! My father suggested a title that we did not understand the meaning of. But it sounded good.' The title that Nasir Hussain, father of Mansoor Khan, had suggested was of course *Qayamat se Qayamat Tak* (1988).

———

When it comes to wealth, siblings may murder siblings too. In *Laal Kothi* (1978) the family will stipulated that till Tanu's (Tanuja) minor child attained adulthood, Tanu's husband would be responsible for handling the estate, including their red bungalow. But Tanu's husband could choose to assign the ownership of the property to someone else if he wished. This was just the opening Tanu's father's brother, Mr Sen (Utpal Dutt), needed. Mr Sen bumps off his brother and plants two pawns—Ajoy (Ranjit Mullick) as Tanu's husband and Sunam (Danny Denzongpa) as a blackmailer so that Ajoy can smuggle the will from the mansion and assign the ownership to Mr Sen. Utpal Dutt had minimal screen presence in the film, with the blackmailer Sunam being projected as the villain throughout. This decoy that kept the audience guessing as to who the real mastermind was, added to the suspense of the film.

Danny Denzongpa, who played Sunam in *Laal Kothi*, was an alumni of Film and Television Institute of India (FTII). He shared a fun story about how the film came to be made: 'My friend Batra Mohinder (also from FTII) who was going through a lean patch as a director told me that he had been approached by a producer from West Bengal to make a Bengali film. He wanted me to act in it, convincing me that the language would not be a problem. I asked him, "Where is the script?" He said, "It is in your cupboard." The bloke had convinced my servants and flicked the script that I had written for making a Hindi film and had read it! The name Sunam was selected by me as I had written the script. Mohinder had directed the film. But he was facing some litigation so his name could not be given in the official credits … So, we gave Kanak Mukherjee's name as director.'

Perhaps the best ever story based on sibling rivalry is in Veda Vyasa's epic *Mahabharata*. Shyam Benegal's *Kal Yug* (1981), based on the *Mahabharata*, is arguably a close second. Shyam Benegal, one of the founding fathers of Parallel Cinema, did poetic justice to adapting the epic for popular modern cinema. Two organizations, Khubchand & Sons Limited and Puranchand Dharamraj & Bros Engineering Works Limited, run by two different cousins are in head-to-head competition with each other, with Khubchand being run by Dhanraj (Victor Banerjee, the equivalent of Duryodhana in the epic) and his brilliant friend Karan Singh (Shashi Kapoor) whose parentage is unknown. Puranchand is run by Dhanraj's cousin Dharamraj (Raj Babbar) and his brothers, Balraj (Kulbhushan Kharbanda) and Bharatraj (Anantnag, the equivalent of Arjuna). From relatively parliamentary acts like undercutting in a tender, the rivalry between the competing organizations escalates to poaching employees and Karan Singh inciting a rival trade union in Puranchand leading to a lockout in Puranchand factory. Soon, it's sabotage and murder time as Balraj's son is run over by a lorry at the behest of Dhanraj. With finely chiselled characters vulnerable in the face of constant conflicts, Benegal kept *Kal Yug* racing with the velocity of a thriller. All the characters have some flaw, making them real and relatable—just the way they are in the epic. In an interview, Shyam Benegal shared, 'There was no villain in *Kal Yug* (1981). Not even Dhanraj who played Duryodhana is justified in what he was doing as he felt that he had far greater legal rights to the business. After all, it was *his* father who had created it.' And no version of the *Mahabharata* is complete without that one tragic hero—Karna. Said Benegal, 'Karna suffered neglect all his life. In the end, he was killed by trickery.' Karna was pierced down while trying to extricate his chariot wheel that got stuck in slush. Karan Singh, revealed to be an illegitimate child of the Puranchand family, gets run over by Bharat's hitman while replacing a flat tyre of his car.

Kulbhushan Kharbanda played Balraj, the equivalent of Bheema except that Balraj's craving was not exactly for food. Said Kharbanda, 'In the seven to eight day intense discussions ahead of the production, Shyam Benegal had briefed me on Balraj's character who, even after eighteen years of marriage is always horny, much to his wife's embarrassment. I kept thinking for an idea for some signal to my wife to come to the bedroom—something that no one else in the family should be able to make out. A few days later, after the shooting had started, the idea of a whistle as a signal came to my mind. The tune 'Dheere dheere' *from* Kismet *(1943) that I would whistle to Reema Lagoo (who played my wife) to signal her to come to the bedroom, was suggested by Vanraj Bhatia, the composer for the film. I did not know how to whistle. I kept lip syncing.'*

3

Pati, Patni aur Who?
The Intruder

One of the frequently portrayed conflicts in Hindi cinema has been the presence of a third person in a marriage. A nuclear family consisting of the husband and wife is often the stopover for the 'intruder' who creates a deep rift in the relationship and, in many cases, causes it to disintegrate, even if temporarily. Conservative wisdom advises that the intruder needs to be categorized as an antagonist because he/she is guilty of breaking (or at least attempting to) someone's family. Let us explore a film on this subject that made headlines. The intruder is a woman. And in this story, the rift between the husband and wife is permanent.

Arth (1982) is Mahesh Bhatt's most talked about film. In a story bordering around the theme of woman empowerment, the dalliance between ad film-maker Inder Malhotra (Kulbhushan Kharbanda) and actress/model Kavita Sanyal (Smita Patil) necessitates Inder's wife Puja (Shabana Azmi) to try and discover who she truly is outside of the identity of being only 'the wife of'. The transformation of the loyal and loving wife to a woman who values her independence is what gives 'arth' (meaning) to her life. The issue is not a mere personal war between two women over a man. It is far more complex. Firstly, why would Inder, who was apparently happy enough with his loving and considerate wife to gift her a new flat, jump into a relationship with Kavita? What does he miss in Puja? Secondly, does Kavita, an ambitious career person, *not* have a right to seek out the next rung in the career ladder or some emotional stability? But Inder finds Kavita's over-possessiveness coupled with her hysterical mood swings highly stressful to handle. And then, suddenly, and without any solid reason, Kavita breaks up with Inder almost impulsively *after* he has formally divorced Puja and is all set to marry her. Was Kavita consumed by sudden guilt for having destroyed Inder's marriage? In which case, was Mahesh Bhatt guilty of the templated notion that a homemaker is always good and that a home-breaker is bad? Said Kulbhushan Kharbanda in an interview, 'When Mahesh started the film, he told me that it was about three normal people. They are not bad people but they get stuck in this situation. But as the plot developed, we sensed a bias building up in favor of Puja, the wife. We pointed out to Mahesh (Bhatt) that, by and large, *Arth* had got told from the wife's point of view. It was the easy way out as the audience's sympathies lay with her, whereas the loner girlfriend is someone whom society despises. To which his response was that he had no option.'

One particular scene, in which a telephonic conversation between Kavita and Puja takes place and Puja begs Kavita to let go of her husband, became one of the dramatic high points of the film. '*Shabana ne Smita ki chutti kar di* (Shabana has outclassed Smita),' people said, referring to this scene. While the film was intense and the protagonist Puja resolute without being unnecessarily feisty, a few melodramatic elements like these threatened to overshadow the underlying seriousness associated with the issue. *Arth* is actually about exhausting conflicts. Compared to the other genres of villainy, we see more balance in storytelling in the plots involving extramarital ones. The characters have looked truly grey and more real, with the screen uncomfortably mirroring some untold reality within.

Said Kulbhushan Kharbanda of his role in *Arth*, 'Look at it from the man's standpoint. He is in love. He was not a one-night stand sort of a guy. People who are in love go through pain. Only then does a conflict like *Arth* take birth. Caught in conflict he gets vexed sometimes at his girlfriend to a point that he wants to tear his hair out … it is maddening. Love is not easy. It is a full-time job (laughs). And I was doing overtime! *Arth* was so real that a famous film personality (name withheld under request) who I met one morning when he was jogging, asked me "Kulbhushan, you are not even married. But in *Arth*, you displayed this sandwiched feeling between the two women so well. How did you do that yaar? That's exactly what I'm going through in my personal life!" Every character of *Arth* was identifiable with someone.'

In fact, the characters and plot were identifiable with Mahesh Bhatt himself, who admitted in an interview with the author, 'I made *Arth* based on my extramarital affair with Parveen Babi. That suddenly found takers and gave me a new lease of life.'

Amar (Rajesh Khanna) and Mansi's (Sharmila Tagore) marriage in *Aavishkar* (1974) has been strained for the past year. The chemistry and communication have deteriorated to an extent that arguments and flare-ups are now the only 'conversations' between them. Unable to rekindle the love that had brought them together two years ago, Amar finds a vent in his attractive colleague, Rita (Minna Johar). Though Rita appears in only two scenes in the film, it is obvious that Rita (a divorcée herself) and Amar have been seeing each other for quite some time. Would it be fair to bill Rita as the other woman? In any case Amar's case is different from that of Inder. Amar was *not* seeking out another woman. As is reiterated in the dialogues, he was looking for his same old lover in Mansi, the one who would tease him, make him smile and sing with him. Even when Amar is out on a movie date with Rita, his mind is homeward bound. He excuses himself from the movie theatre and picks up flowers for Mansi on the way back home for their anniversary.

Rinki Roy Bhattacharya alludes to similarities between the scenes of Aavishkar *and incidents involving her and Director Basu Bhattacharya whom she was married to then.* 'Aavishkar *was straight out of our personal experience. Scenes were rewritten from actual situations that happened during our courtship. The last scene, for example, between the estranged couple, sitting in the open space behind Mount Mary Church was the location where we secretly met at predawn. It was shot at that precise hour.*[29]

It is very obvious that when an intruder sneaks into a marriage, it is because either party has left a trapdoor open for the intruder to sneak in. It is implied that Vikram (Shashi Kapoor) has an affair with the foreigner Lucia (Jennifer Kendal) in *Bombay Talkie* (1970) because his wife Mala (Aparna Sen) couldn't bear him a child.

To be fair, not all 'other women' are necessarily home-breakers. In fact, very few men are lucky to have a woman like Chitra as a friend in *Abhimaan* (1973) who does *not* take advantage of Subir Kumar's (Amitabh Bachchan) estrangement from his wife Uma (Jaya Bachchan). To an extent that Chitra actually meets Uma and asks her if Uma suspected her of trying to create a rift between the married couple. Bindu said of her role as Chitra, 'The audience carried the perception that whenever this woman comes on screen, she will do some gadbad (mischief). But it turned out that she was a real friend of the hero. Chitra genuinely cared for Subir, professionally and personally.'

But Sapna (Sarika) in *Griha Pravesh* (1979) is definitely the intruder in the married life of Amar and Mansi. The men at Sapna's workplace ogle brazenly at her deep-necked, sleeveless tops so much so that her boss is forced to move her to a secluded cabin—a cabin which she is asked to share with Amar (Sanjeev Kumar). And she deliberately entices her colleague Amar, making knowing passes at him, leading him on and winking at him.

Adultery, when the perpetrator is a woman, has not been very practically dealt with in Hindi cinema. More often than not, especially in the B&W era, the moral compass of the film-makers (and consequently that of the audience) was mostly as the name of the medium suggests— black and white. And usually tilted favourably towards the man. A well-known example of the same was B.R. Chopra's *Gumrah* (1963) in which the wife Meena (Mala Sinha) is mentally tormented and blackmailed by her husband Ashok (Ashok Kumar) to the point of a breakdown and confesses about her relationship with the intruder Rajendra (Sunil Dutt). All the while, the viewer is aware that Meena had married her brother-in-law Ashok from a sense of duty after the accidental death of Kamla (Nirupa Roy), Ashok's first wife and Meena's elder sister. Meena had sacrificed her love for Rajendra for the sake of the widower Ashok and his children. Meena and Rajendra's old love rekindles when they run into each other again. But what is distressing was that Meena failed to get the sympathy of her husband. The film's story makes her out to be a rule-breaker. Married women, her husband reprimands her, have no business meeting men outside their sharply demarcated Lakshman Rekha—the home. And somehow, Rajendra is spared having to face a gruelling trial.

Gumrah, they say, was based on the real-life relationship between Dilip Kumar and Kamini Kaushal, with the latter having to marry her widowed brother-in-law for the sake of his children.[30]

Maybe the lure of an earlier relation ██████ kindles something deep within. Chandni (Rekha) in *Silsila* (1981) also seeks out her past love with Amit (Amitabh Bachchan) despite being in a stable marriage with her doctor husband. In *Silsila*, there are two intruders—Amit and Chandni, each poking into the other's marriage. And the debate will continue forever on whether Chandni and Amit can be classified as antagonists or not. Do they not have a right to seek out relationships of their choice?

In actress Rekha's biography, Yasser Usman mentions the near-palpable tension on the sets of Silsila *between Mrs Jaya Bachchan and Rekha. 'I was always on tenterhooks and scared because it was real life coming into reel life. Jaya is his wife and Rekha is his girlfriend; the same story is going on. Anything could have happened because they are working together,' recalled Yash Chopra in an interview with Sonia Deol on BBC Asia in 2010.*[31]

Divorce was not an option back then. Barring pre-Independence films like *Talaq* (1938), one would struggle to think of a mainstream Hindi film of the 1950s/1960s/early 1970s dealing directly with divorce. A Hindu marriage was labelled as saat janam ka bandhan, no matter what. In *Griha Pravesh*, Amar confesses to his wife Mansi (Sharmila Tagore) of his affair with Sapna, bringing their marriage to the brink of collapse. And then one day, back from work, a weary Amar is taken aback as his dowdy home suddenly looks splendid and his wife Mansi looks dainty and fresh. It becomes a griha pravesh (entry into a new home) for him. Amar and Mansi make a fresh start in their 'new home' while the intruder Sapna, whom Mansi had wanted to meet, moves on. Mansi manages to avert a meltdown.

Telling the story from the other woman's viewpoint is far tougher. In *Fashion* (2008) and *Dil toh Bachha Hai Ji* (2011), Director Madhur Bhandarkar advocated for the other woman's right to her desires and ambitions. Former model Anu Narang (played by Tisca Chopra) in *Dil toh Baccha Hai Ji* is the trophy second wife of a multimillionaire Harsh Narang. Outside her marriage, Anu quietly beds a young playboy Abhay (Emraan Hashmi) in luxurious hotel suites and indulges in expensive gifts for him. Yet, the script is not apologetic and does not label Anu Narang as the stock lady villain. Tisca Chopra said, 'I urged Madhur Bhandarkar to please show *her* heart. Anu, now in her mid-thirties, was also looking for that romance that she was missing in her marriage. Yet, she is not going to break her marriage. But then, what if Abhay had been serious about a long-term relationship with Anu? She might have contemplated leaving Harsh, who knows?' added Tisca, 'Her heartbreak and pain at the break-up with Abhay made the character very real and relatable. You don't see her as a fucking bitch just because she is screwing around. You feel empathy.'

Curiously, Anu was running the risk of breaking her own home, not anyone else's.

While characters like Kavita Sanyal, Rita and Sapna make for good old fireside debates over a drink over on whether they are antagonists or not, there are a few characters who are definitive sinners, guilty of having violated the wife of a close friend, thus betraying his trust. From time immemorial, thy neighbour's wife has been seen as a sweet but forbidden fruit. One of the earliest instances of this was *Bharosa* (1940). Rasik (played by Chandramohan) takes advantage of his friend Gyan's (Mazhar Khan—not to be confused with the actor of the same name in 1980s) lengthy tour to Africa and has an affair with his Gyan's wife Shobha (Sardar Akhtar). Rasik and Shobha have an illegitimate child that her husband Gyan assumes is his.

Stories of bad men who would enter into illicit relationships with their friends' wives abound in Hindi cinema. *Yeh Raste Hain Pyar Ke* (1963) and *Achanak* (1973) are based on the infamous real-life trial of Commander Kawas Manekshaw Nanavati vs State of Maharashtra of 1959 in which Nanavati was accused of shooting his wife's lover, Prem Ahuja, and causing his death.[32] In *Yeh Raste Hain Pyar Ke*, Ashok Srivastava (Rehman) seduces his pilot friend Anil Sahni's (Sunil Dutt) lovely wife Neena (Leela Naidu) when Anil is away for a stretch of four months. Getting Neena into bed is a premeditated plan by Ashok that included coaxing Neena to consume alcohol at a party and then spiking her drink. Ashok is an inveterate infidel with dalliances with multiple women despite being engaged to Asha (Shashikala).

Rustom (2016) too is a fictionalized account of the Nanavati case with Vikram Makhija (Arjun Bajwa) seducing Cynthia Pavri (Ileana D'Cruz), wife of his good friend Rustom Pavri (Akshay Kumar). Another story-track of corruption within the Indian Navy was added in *Rustom*, however. Vikram connives to send the honest Rustom Pavri away to

London for a year on an assignment so that Rustom cannot interfere with the corruption within the Indian Navy that Vikram is party to. And in that one year, the casanova Vikram swoops in like a vulture on his friend's wife in her weaker moments. There are scavengers too waiting to prey on wives with marital problems. One such scavenger was played by Pran in *Ziddi* (1948). Shanta (Kuldip Kaur) is frustrated at her husband Pooran's (Dev Anand) constant aloofness towards her, as their marriage took place without Pooran's consent. Pran sees a furtive opportunity in Shanta's situation. He saves her from suicide but with an ulterior motive of eloping with her. Very soon Shanta figures out his intent. In her struggle to break free from him, both plunge to their death as their getaway vehicle slides off the bridge. However, all three of them—Shanta, Neena and Cynthia—were repentant. It was a one-off occurrence of human fallibility. In each case, it was the husband's friend who is the villain of the piece.

But there is a separate breed altogether in which both the wife and her husband's friend are unified partners in an extramarital affair for a prolonged period of time. For such an on-screen wife it was neither a momentary lapse of fidelity nor did she go on to regret her act. In fact, she enjoyed it.

Pushpa (Lily Chakravarty) in *Achanak* (1973) is Major Ranjeet's (Vinod Khanna) wife, in a consensual physical relationship with Ranjeet's friend Prakash (Ravi Raaj). And their surreptitious relationship is an edifice of deceit built on a foundation of shaky truth. For example, Pushpa doesn't hide from her husband Ranjeet the fact that she has been to meet Prakash at his boathouse. But she claims that she went there for fishing. Likewise, Prakash conversationally mentions to Ranjeet that he had taken Pushpa to the pictures to watch the film *The Dirty Dozen* (1967). For Prakash and Pushpa, their public rendezvous become an alibi for their adulterous relationship. They try to legitimize their relationship with half-truths. But what they do not know is that Ranjeet has caught them in the act. He murders them both.

Mala Sahay (Bindu) in *Dastaan* (1972) takes advantage of her simpleton, trusting husband Vishnu Sahay (Dilip Kumar) while being in an illicit relationship with Vishnu's best friend Rajen (Prem Chopra). Like the Pushpa–Prakash 'pair', the Mala–Rajen one too is an arrangement between them for some extra fun. They seemed to derive a perverse thrill from cheating someone who innately trusted them. When Vishnu Sahay is feared dead, Mala sheds a few proverbial crocodile tears. And soon they get down to carrying on their relationship, now with enhanced freedom. Said Prem Chopra who plays the rogue Rajen, 'In the 1970s Bindu and I made a very curious "pair" that everyone wanted to see often as a zabardast chemistry had built up between us. Distributors would specifically ask whether Prem Chopra and Bindu were there in the crew!'

Dastaan *was B.R. Chopra's remake of his own debut film* Afsana *(1951) with Pran playing the cheating friend of the hero and Kuldip Kaur playing the wife.*

Rohini (Sarika) in *Qatl* (1986) is a shameless woman who finds a willing partner in her husband's (Rakesh, played by Sanjeev Kumar) friend Ranjit (Marc Zuber). She has an affair with both the men, marries Rakesh and continues to sleep with Ranjit. An aspiring actress with a great body but mediocre talent, manipulation is in her genes. And Ranjit has no scruples about bedding his friend's wife. What makes Ranjit's and Rohini's characters even worse is that they are taking advantage of Rakesh's physical handicap: blindness.

And then there is Ranjit Mullick (Prem Chopra) in *Do Anjaane* (1976)—the 'dazzling jewel' among all wife-snatchers. Not only does he entice his old friend's wife Rekha (played by Rekha), but he also pushes his friend Amit Roy (Amitabh Bachchan) to an imminent death …

Rekha's lust for a dancing and acting career in *Do Anjaane* becomes the bone of contention in an otherwise stable, middle-class, domestic life with her husband Amit Roy. Enter the middle-class husband's foreign-returned friend, Ranjit Mullick. Fascinated by her talent and her natural sex appeal, Ranjit dangles the carrot of a career in showbiz in front of Rekha, knowing she will bite. Ranjit organizes a dance programme for Rekha and further stokes her ambition. But there is one roadblock that stands between Rekha and her goal—her husband Amit, who is reluctant about Rekha pursuing a career in acting. Ranjit devises a way to solve this problem. He pushes Amit out of a galloping train.

Six years pass and Amit is determined to avenge what Rekha and Ranjit Mullick had done to him. He returns disguised as a producer, keen to make a film with his once-wife and now actor Sunita Devi and her current manager, Ranjit. Rekha, who had been given the impression by Ranjit that Amit had committed suicide by jumping off the train, comes to know the truth. Ranjit, who subsequently tries to kill Amit, confesses his crime and is handed over to the police.

In an interview with the author, Prem Chopra shared, 'My character had many shades, as a rich man who gets fascinated by the wife of his best friend and tries to promote her career. That woman became his weakness over a period of time. She was ambitious and I had the means. Director Dulal Guha knew the character fully well and his narration was very interesting.'

Ranjit Mullick is the name of a real-life leading Bengali film hero. While there have speculations galore on the choice of the name Ranjit Mullick, the fact is that the name was retained from the story by Dr Nihar Ranjan Gupta on which Do Anjaane *was based.*

Between Ranjit and Rekha, Rekha was the deadlier villain. She swallows the story of her husband committing suicide without making any apparent effort to retrieve Amit's dead body; almost as if the suicide was providence. She then packs her son off to St. Paul's, Darjeeling, rarely visiting him. Her son refers to her not as his mother but by her screen name, 'Sunita Devi'. In fact, having got the stepping stone she wanted, Rekha quietly sidelines Ranjit as well. The manipulator Ranjit becomes the manipulated and ends up like something of a poor clown. Regarding the two very different looks for his character—one while wooing the woman and another after he has won her over, Prem Chopra said, 'I conceived my two different get-ups myself. The first one as the person who had just returned from abroad, was a flamboyant one. And then I revert to my original get-up because, in the process of promoting Rekha, Mullick becomes a pauper and Rekha treats him like dirt.'

The story—'Rater Gari'—which is also the name of the film within the film, written in the 1960s has the hero and the heroine separate at the Bagdogra airport. And that's exactly what was shot, pointed out Partha Guha, son of Dulal Guha, in an interview with National Award-winning author and film expert Anirudha Bhattacharjee in November 2019. Distributor Gulshan Rai, a man of considerable clout in the film business, insisted on an alternative and naturally happy ending. While Dulal Guha went to Tirupati and later to Madras for planning the shoot of Dil ka Heera *(1978), Rai released* Do Anjaane *with the alternative ending. Unfortunately, the happy ending was not exactly the springboard to a great review. Critical reception was mixed.*

Prem Chopra won his only Filmfare Award for this role. He recounts an interesting incident that happened post the release of *Do Anjaane*. 'I was shooting for *The Great Gambler* in Amsterdam. One morning Shakti Samanta suddenly came to my room. Assuming that he had come to ask me why I was so late for shooting, I said, "Sorry yaar, I am just getting ready." He said, "No, I have come with some good news for you. You have won the best supporting actor award for *Do Anjaane*." That was a pleasant surprise and we had a party that evening. Amitabh Bachchan was feeling low as he too had been nominated for the best actor award, but couldn't make it to the ceremony.'

Kabir Bedi was the original choice of the role of Ranjit Mullick. In an interview with film expert Anirudha Bhattacharjee, Partha Guha, son of director Dulal Guha, said, 'We had shot a few scenes with Kabir Bedi at the Oberoi Grand, Calcutta. Somehow, things did not work out as expected. Prem Chopra was a good replacement. He understood the character of the comical angle of villain well and did full justice to the role.'

In *Bemisal* (1982), Dr Sudhir Roy (Amitabh Bachchan) seduces his friend's fiancée Ruby Dutt (Sheetal) for a specific reason. Years ago, Ruby had tried to seduce Sudhir's brother Adhir Roy, who was her teacher. On failing to do so, she frames Adhir as the person that tried to molest her. Ruby's father whips Adhir mercilessly and lets loose a ferocious canine on him. This traumatizes Adhir physically and mentally enough for him to land up in a mental asylum. His brother Sudhir's act of enticing Ruby away from her wealthy fiancé Hiralal (Deven Verma), who is also an old friend of Sudhir's, dumping her when she is ready to elope with him, and then exposing her duplicity to Hiralal thus breaking her engagement with Hiralal, was Sudhir's revenge against Ruby. While Sudhir Roy was not the villain of *Bemisal*, his act in this specific subplot was nuanced.

The *Dastaan* saga was partly recreated in *Jurm* (2005) in which the 'good friend', lawyer Rohit (Milind Soman), uses his professional skills to dispose of his friend Avinash (Bobby Deol) to jail for life so that he could carry on a live-in relationship with Avinash's sultry wife Sanjana (Lara Dutta) in Malaysia. And Bollywood scriptwriters have been kind to husbands who murdered their wives and/or their wives' lovers. The husbands' acts have been justified as being led by a sudden rush of anguish at the discovery of their wives' infidelity. As film historian Kaushik Bhaumik observes, 'Maybe their hurt was too private for them to go to the law!' In *Khoj* (1989), a film inspired by *Chase a Crooked Shadow* (1958), Ravi Kapoor (Rishi Kapoor) murders his wife on seeing her in bed with another man. He is captured by the Kathmandu police but is led away to the police station almost apologetically. Major Ranjit in *Achanak* gets a tearful send-off to the gallows and Rustom Pavri in *Rustom* becomes a cult hero with 'Rustom'-branded merchandise selling at a premium! Rakesh in *Qatl* (1986) winks at the law—he can't be taken to court for the double murder of his wife Rohini and her lover Ranjit because he's blind.

4

Mehndi Rang Layegi
Blood on Her Hands

'*Ye murder hoga Lolita, jaanti ho*? Murder! (This is murder Lolita, do you realize? Murder!)', says Vishal. Lolita replies, '*Mm … hmm* (disagrees). *Zyada se zyada mercy killing hogi. Jab kisi ghode ki taang toot jati hai, to usse shoot nahi kar dete kya? … Kisi ko shaq bhi nahi hoga Vishal* (No, it would not be a murder. At most it would be termed a mercy killing. Don't they shoot a lame horse dead? No one will suspect a thing, Vishal).' These lines are spoken by Lolita (Rashmi) in *Ek Nari Do Roop* (1972), while justifying to her boyfriend Vishal (Shatrughan Sinha) why he should kill her quadriplegic husband. And then she adds that Vishal could make it look like an accident. And why is Lolita hatching this diabolic plan? For one, there is no sex life for Lolita inside her marital life, which is why she got into bed with Vishal in the first place. Secondly, upon her husband's death, Lolita stands to inherit INR 10 lakhs (1 million) from her deceased husband's wealth which she and Vishal can live comfortably off of once they're married.

Desire can take myriad forms. For a few bad married women, an extramarital affair wasn't invigorating enough. There was their husband's money, a bigger lure. On becoming aware of his young wife Chanchal's (Shubha Khote) philandering ways, old man Dayal in *Paying Guest* (1957) signs a legal document expelling her as his inheritor and also lets her go from his estate. To suppress that document before it becomes public, Chanchal gets Dayal killed with the help of an accomplice, the lame, dipsomaniac Prakash (played by Yakub). Chanchal and Prakash push Dayal into a river during a boat ride. But then the wily-as-a-fox Prakash turns a blackmailer and proves to be Chanchal's Frankenstein's monster. A few years later Mrs Rai Bahadur Singh (Kamini Kaushal) in *Anhonee* (1973) gets her wealthy husband liquidated for his wealth and lets the blame fall on her stepdaughter. The curious thing, however, was that nobody in the audience suspected either women until much later in the two films, because both Shubha Khote and Kamini Kaushal had never played the role of a vamp. But the fact that Kamini Singh, the nymphomaniac second wife of the wealthy businessman in *Hawas* (1974), would murder her husband was a foregone conclusion. (It was a role with shades as distinct as those of Mrs Robinson in *The Graduate*, 1967). That was because Kamini was played by Bindu, the Queen Medusa of Bollywood of the 1970s. Bindu sort of monopolized this sort of character, and went on to play a near identical role, that of Rani, a sex-starved young wife of a wheelchair-bound wealthy old man in *Joshila* (1974).

At times, the women would murder out of pure jealousy. In *Caravan* (1971), the gypsy Nisha (Aruna Irani) wants to sabotage and even kill her 'rival' Sunita (Asha Parekh), in her quest for Mohan (Jeetendra). In *Tumhare Liye* (1978), Kalavati (Neelam Mehra) poisons Gauri (Vidya Sinha) to death so that she can marry Gangadhar (Sanjeev Kumar). In their reincarnations, Renuka (Neelam Mehra again) attempts to poison Gauri to death once again! This concept of a bloodstained love triangle spilling over to the next lifetime was replayed in the 2017 *Raabta*, with the murderer Kabir reborn as Zak Merchant, again trying to drown the same person in his second life.

Remember Nadira, the silent menace? With her lips curled slightly downwards and the eyebrows twitching upwards, she famously played the temptress Maya in *Shree 420* (1956) and Kusum, the domineering wife of the good doctor, in *Dil Apna Aur Preet Parayi* (1960). Never did a cigarette held between a woman's fingers look more threatening. If Lalita Pawar glowered and hollered, Nadira's snake-like eyes sniped like a silent cobra. Nadira aged well. And so did her scheming habits. In *Aashiq Hoon Baharon Ka* (1976), she was the old man's second wife, hatching a plot to steal her unsuspecting husband's wealth. (Mercifully, she didn't mean to kill the old man …)

If these ladies were notorious enough, Kamini (Simi Garewal) in *Karz* (1980), has a bank vault where her heart should have been. She teams up with a rogue called Sir Judas (Premnath) who, having lost a legal battle for young Ravi Verma's (Raj Kiran) property, coaxes Kamini to marry Ravi Verma and then murder Ravi to take control over his property in Coonoor. Sir Judas is very much the mastermind of the game. Come to think of it, Kamini was fundamentally not much different from any other honey-trapping moll. But hers was a landmark villain character because it was the first instance of a moll being given the spotlight usually reserved for the lead. In an interview, Simi Garewal analysed, 'In my mind, I don't think this girl had an emotional attachment with her newly-wed husband at all. She just went about doing the job because she wanted a lot of money and the power that came with it.'

Garewal further threw light on how the role came about. 'For almost eighteen months, Mr Subhash Ghai kept offering me this role and I kept saying no because I couldn't bring myself to do a role that is so mean, so horrible. I didn't want people to always remember me for this role as, post this, I would only get offers to play the villain! Mr Ghai kept coming back with newer versions of the script where the role was made more human. Finally, he said that if I didn't do the role, he was not going to make the film. Then I told myself, oh my God, this person has put so much hope on me to do it and maybe I should really consider it. Then I sat and talked to him. A few modifications on, and I finally said, "Okay theek hai, I'll do it." The rest of it was so exciting to do. I've never had a challenging role like this.'

> *There are two different versions of the story behind Simi Garewal's decision to take on the role. Recalled Sachin Bhowmick, the scenarist in* Karz, *'I reasoned out with Simi saying that actors in other countries don't judge a role based on whether it is a negative or positive role. They just look at whether it gives them scope to act. "People would remember you for this role," I said. She said, "Okay, there is a Chinese restaurant called Wang near Sun 'N Sand Hotel. Food is very good there. If I eat there I'll decide." Over the Chinese lunch, I asked her, "So what do we do?" She replied, '"The food is good. The role is good too. I'll take it."'*

Once Simi Garewal was given the role, she wanted to create 'a new person whom, if you met, would never believe she could be so evil. On the outside, she had to be a normal, socially very charming and physically very glamorous upper-class woman. And that is when the contrasting evil within would create a shock which was far, far worse.'

These villainous women were as meticulous as they were evil. In the 1958 British suspense drama *Chase a Crooked Shadow* a rich young heiress Kimberly Prescott is taken aback at a stranger landing up at her place and claiming to be her deceased brother, Ward Prescott. Everything in the house from Ward's picture in a family photograph to Ward's fingerprints has been reconstructed to match that of the stranger. Even close family members identify the stranger as the Ward they always knew. Finally, on the verge of a nervous breakdown, Kimberly confesses that the stranger cannot be her brother because … she had killed him by sabotaging his car brakes. The stranger claiming to be Ward is actually an undercover policeman sent to investigate the death of Ward Prescott. *Chase a Crooked Shadow* inspired Dulal Guha's *Dhuan* (1981), in which the leading lady, Gayatri Saxena, is the murderess. It is a similar story of a cop being planted as the dead brother-in-law of Gayatri. Finally, unable to bear the stress of the fabricated truth, Gayatri confesses to having murdered her brother-in-law in order to get her hands on documents containing national secrets. It had an unusual star cast with Rakhee playing the villain Gayatri Saxena. Film expert Anirudha Bhattacharjee shared another little-known film called *Ikraar* (1979) directed by Kailash Advani with Rameshwari playing the femme fatale who murders her lover. *Ikraar* is based on William Wyler's *The Letter* (1940) which, in turn, is based on Somerset Maugham's play of the same name. Neither *Dhuan* nor *Ikraar* did well commercially, however.

The bad ladies of the new millennium dutifully followed the footsteps of their predecessors. In *Jism* (2003), Mrs Sonia Khanna (Bipasha Basu) brings back the blood-and-sperm thirsting legacy of Bindu of the 1970s. Sonia needs every inch of her muscular lawyer-lover Kabir (John Abraham) to satisfy her raging hormones. She also eggs him to murder her husband Rohit (Gulshan Grover) after altering the will so that she would inherit all of Rohit's wealth. Interestingly *Joshila*, *Ek Nari Do Roop*, *Karz* and *Dhuan* had had a good-girl character in the cast apart from the lady villain. But Sonia Khanna in *Jism* was the lead cast. This was a shift in Bollywood—the lead cast didn't necessarily have to be the good man/woman.

However, Mahesh Bhatt disagrees that *Jism*'s Mrs Sonia Khanna was the villain. 'She uses her body as an asset to get what she wanted—money and her man. If it is okay for a man to use a woman's body for his end, why can't a woman do likewise? And no woman in the world uttered the lines that Bipasha says, "*Yeh jism pyar karna nahi jaanta … yeh jaanta hai sirf bhookh … jism ki bhookh.*" (This body does not know love. It knows only lust.) Unfortunately, this is looked upon culturally as an attribute of a depraved person. By the structure of the film, she is an antagonist, but she does not come in the category of a villain.' True, anyone has a right to use any asset lawfully to get what they want. But do they have a right to murder someone? That is where Sonia Khanna needs to get classified as a pure-black villain as opposed to someone like Pushpa in *Achanak* who breaches the moral norm (and not the law) by being in a physical relationship with her husband's friend. Pushpa is immoral. Sonia Khanna is a criminal.

And while we are talking about murderous wives, why not add some spook masala? In the Ramsays' flagship *Do Gaz Zameen ke Neeche* (1972), Anjili (Shobana) and her boyfriend Anand (Imtiaz Khan) plot to murder her husband Rajvansh for his wealth. Rajvansh is buried (but aren't Hindus cremated?), but rises from his grave and ... you know the rest.

An aged Bollywood actor of the 1970s vintage, a musician cum restauranteur of the R.D. Burman legacy (Franco Vaz), the flashback to the *Karz*-ish black widow with a (driving) license to kill ... Sriram Raghavan rekindled retro-Bollywood nostalgia in his *AndhaDhun* (2018). Upon the discovery of her affair with Manohar (Manav Vij) by her husband Pramod Sinha (Anil Dhawan), Simi Sinha (Tabu) kills her husband. Manohar and Simi proceed to clean up the mess and plan to dispose the body. But then someone discovers their act and the core plot daisy chains into subplots. Raghavan shared, 'Pramod Sinha getting killed was circumstantial. He just happened to be at the right place at the wrong time. His wife Simi Sinha didn't hate him. She would have merely carried on her affair with Manohar on the side as it was not affecting her relationship with her husband. After much debate I decided that I didn't want her to be that *big* villain. And so, it was important that she weeps after killing her husband. But as in *Johnny Gaddar*, once you know that you can commit a murder and get away with it, it emboldens you. A lot of inspiration for *AndhaDhun* came from *Fargo* (1996) by the Coen Brothers which is a humorous film in its own way. I had a fascination for these kinds of people who commit a crime under some stress or circumstance.'

And then killing becomes a habit for Simi Sinha. 'The last scene in which she tries to run down Aakash (Ayushmann Khurrana) was the only reason we chose the screen name "Simi" for Tabu (from Simi Garewal in *Karz* whose preferred style of killing was mowing the victim down by her jeep).'

Sriram Raghavan also shared the story behind the climax scene of *AndhaDhun* ...

Kenneth Douglas Stewart Anderson (1910–1974) was a hunter of British origin who lived in South India. Official records state that he had shot eight man-eating leopards, seven tigers and a few rogue elephants as well. Kenneth Anderson chronicled the stories of his hunting in over half a dozen books, some of which are *Nine Man-eaters and One Rogue* (1954), *Man-Eaters and Jungle Killers* (1957), *Tales from The Indian Jungle* (1970). It was indirectly from one of Kenneth Anderson's books that Sriram Raghavan got the idea of how Simi Sinha would meet her deserved death in *AndhaDhun*.

Shares Sriram Raghavan, 'Initially we were mulling over the various possibilities of Simi's car meeting with an accident, e.g., a tree falling over across the road or something sabotaged about the car that she wasn't aware of, etc. But those were too stereotyped. Then I remembered a story by Kenneth Anderson that my co-writer had narrated to me in some other context. One day Anderson went hunting and couldn't snare anything all day. Then he spotted a big wild hare that kept jumping around. Anderson kept shooting and the animal kept escaping. Anderson kept chasing it and finally after two hours or so, managed to kill it. I suddenly remembered this story and we developed this idea over multiple sessions and finally, while watching the trailer of *Get Out* (2017) in which the deer comes in the way of two people driving, I hit upon the idea of a rabbit hitting the windscreen of Simi's car.'

But there was a bizarre irony to all this. After killing that wild hare that day, Kenneth Anderson walked up to the dead animal and discovered something. The wild hare was blind. Its eyes had been gouged out.

It had been jumping around andhadhun ...

5

Saudagar
The Wife-Exploiters

'*... Shaadi ka paigham laakar mujhse sauda kiya, sauda! Agar mujhse jee bhar gaya tha to saaf saaf keh dete ki "Majubi, ras ka Mausam khatam ho gaya. Gud ban chuka. Ab tumhari zaroorat nahi. Tum jaa sakti ho"... Chal, bol de woh alfaaz jinko zubaan pe lane ke liye tu itna bechain ho raha hai*' ('That marriage proposal to me was a deal. If you had had enough of me, you could have stated plainly that with the jaggery season now over, you didn't need me any more. You could have asked me to leave ... Anyway, go ahead and say those three words that you can't wait to utter'), said Mahjubi (Nutan) to Moti.

In *Saudagar* (1973), Moti (Amitabh Bachchan) has no qualms about marrying a poor village widow, Mahjubi, for her jaggery-brewing skills and then, a year later, discarding her with three simple sentences, '*Mai tumhe talaq deta hoon. Mai tumhe talaq deta hoon. Mai tumhe talaq deta hoon.*'

A few spineless Bollywood husbands have used their wives as meal tickets. When the cherished middle-class dream of owning a house in the big city looks like its falling apart, Sudip (Amol Palekar) in *Gharonda* (1977) coaxes his girlfriend Chhaya (Zarina Wahab) to marry a wealthy but ailing Mr Modi (Dr Shriram Lagoo) so that they can be reunited and rich after Mr Modi's imminent death. It is Sudip's plan for a back-door entry into owning a flat in Bombay. But Mr Modi doesn't die. In fact, his health stabilizes and Chhaya settles into her life as Mrs Modi. Sudip is left out cold. Said Amol Palekar in an interview, 'The audience reaction was, "What is he doing? He is telling his girlfriend to marry someone else, and then we will loot his money together? He is such a third-rate person." I tried to bring the vulnerable and desperate side to a character which made it so humane and realistic.' Sudip was breaking no law. Yet his act was morally and ethically questionable.

> Palekar shared that the the original idea of the story that one sees unfold in Gharonda *was by Dr Shankar Shesh, a Hindi playwright of repute, and a dear friend of Palekar from his theatre days. Director Bhimsain, Shesh and Palekar would sit together and discuss the nuances in the character and that enabled them to bring in all these shades.*

In *Andhi Gali* (1984) Hemanta Roy's stance on his wife pursuing a modelling career is equally narcissistic. Hemanta (Kulbhushan Kharbanda) books a flat in Bombay. But escalating property prices in the city put the price of the flat beyond his reach. He borrows from every available source. And finally, at someone's suggestion, he convinces his wife Jaya (Deepti Naval) to become a model in return for a handsome amount with which Hemanta is able to finally take possession of the flat. But the modelling agency contractually locks Hemanta into a situation where Jaya has no option to turn down any modelling assignment. Jaya is petrified at the thought of telling her husband about having done a shoot in revealing clothes. But to her shock, Hemanta's reaction is, '*Tasveerein hi kheenchi hai na? Kothe pe to nahi bitha diya na tumhe!* (They only took your pictures. They did not put you in a brothel!)' Hemanta's behaviour is worse than that of Sudip's in *Gharonda* because Hemanta is coercing his wife to strip in front of a camera against her will and without her consent, which is illegal. In any case, Hemanta is a spineless coward. His backstory reveals that he had been part of an underground communist movement in Calcutta and had deserted his compatriots to flee to Bombay after betraying his comrade Suranjan's whereabouts to the police.

Says Kulbhushan Kharbanda on his experience at playing Hemant in Andhi Gali, *'I had lived for a few years in Calcutta since 1972 and had been a witness to the Naxalite movement. I used to frequent College Street and Indian Coffee House. I had met a few people who had participated in this movement but had eventually come out of it and joined the mainstream society. I noticed an inner conflict in them—they were unable to get over the trauma of police torture and everything else that they had gone through.'*

Ravindra Bharti (Anil Dhawan) in *Do Raha* (1973) is a nuanced character. He believes that a socially extroverted wife can help him further his career. Ravindra, a struggling author, gets a career breakthrough from Naveen (Roopesh Kumar) who pays Ravindra hefty signing amounts and perks like a car and flat for writing cheap, soft-porn novels. Naveen is a party animal and also a womanizer who makes passes at Ravindra's sexy wife Geeta (Radha Saluja). Ravindra can sense Naveen's intent but, entrapped and obligated by Naveen's largesse, Ravindra nudges Geeta to start drinking and partying with Naveen so as not to offend him. But Ravindra isn't prepared for what happens next—Naveen gets Geeta drunk at a party and seduces her. Ravindra's *'My Fair Lady'* act of modernizing his wife ends up ruining his family life. Will Geeta forgive Ravindra?

Keshav Dalvi (Amol Palekar) in *Bhumika* (1977) is different—he is far worse that Sudip or Hemanta Roy. Keshav Dalvi has no problem in living off his actress-wife Usha's (Smita Patil) earnings and at the same time disdains her success. He is an insecure control freak who acts as Usha's manager, pushes her to take up roles that she does not enjoy doing and still suspects her of having an affair with a co-star. Dalvi is a degenerate in every possible way, right from lusting for Usha when she was a child, to coerceing her family into giving him her hand in marriage despite being twenty years her senior.

Amol Palekar shared a few insights about the role. 'I knew the Marathi novel from which the movie was adapted inside out. Also, Hansa Wadkar, on whom the film was based, was my next-door neighbour at Shivaji Park. I would spend a lot of time at her place with her daughters and Wadkar's co-artistes too. Shyam Benegal offered me the role of the hero, but I told him I would rather play the villain Keshav Dalvi. For a moment, he was taken aback, but then agreed and immediately called for the crew and announced this to them.' Taking up a negative role after three successive silver jubilee hits as a hero—*Rajanigandha* (1974), *Chhoti Si Baat* (1975), and *Chitchor* (1976)—had its obvious risks. Says Palekar, 'Other producers and industry colleagues were aghast at my foolhardiness. But I have never let my life be governed by commercial aspects. I've always been motivated by what I liked and what I wanted to do.'

Characters like Keshav Dalvi exist in every strata of the society. The domestic help played by Rohini Hattangady in *Arth* (1982) (she has no screen name; she is referred to throughout as 'bai') is the constant victim of her wastrel husband's (played by Suhas Bhalekar) verbal and physical abuse. He drinks off her wages and accuses her of seeing another man— whereas it is he who has kept another woman.

Rohini Hattangady had contributed to the script of Arth *too. 'B.R. Ishaara had written the dialogues in a "thet" Mathura-Awadhi dialect with phrases like 'Saat phere'. But in Maharashtra we refer to it as "Saptapadi" with whom we had tied "padrachi gaanth". I pointed this out hesitantly and suggested that I could intersperse a few Marathi phrases and lines into my dialogue. The assistant director (who was also a Maharashtrian) and I wrote down the alternate Marathi phrases.' Hattangady had also researched into the body language and mannerisms. 'How to tuck-up the nine-yard sari while mopping the floor sitting on the haunches—those I had learnt from my servant maid in Pune,' she disclosed.*

The husbands in *Zehreela Insaan* (played by Vijay Kumar, younger brother of Johnny Walker) and *Doosri Sita* (played by Kuljeet) are nothing but pimps, directing their wives to sleep with other men, the wives being a part of the deal between the husbands and the counterparties. Mukesh Mehra (Arjun Rampal) in *Om Shanti Om* (2007) goes to the extent of burying his actress-wife Shantipriya (Deepika Padukone) alive because her pregnancy is about to ruin his chances of marrying the daughter of a key investor who is investing INR 40 lakhs in Mukesh's movie project and offering co-ownership of a film studio as 'dowry'. Shanti and Mukesh's marriage was a secret. Mukesh wanted to keep it that way.

———

A physical disability of some kind often results in an acute sense of insecurity, leading to exceptionally violent behaviour. For instance, in B.R. Chopra's *Dhund* (1973),[33] one sees wheelchair-bound Thakur Ranjit Singh (Danny Denzongpa) needlessly heaping insult upon insult on his wife Rani (Zeenat Aman) for the most trivial reasons, and also shooting cats and dogs with the gun he keeps on him, the gun with which his wife will eventually end up killing him. In a chat, Danny revealed little-known details about *Dhund*. 'Mr B.R. Chopra was my examiner at FTII (Film and Television Institute of India). I scored well and he assured me of a break in Bombay. In *Dhund*, he wanted me to play the role of the Police Inspector whereas I was keen on the role of the disabled husband for which Amitabh Bachchan was originally chosen. Then they signed up Shatrughan Sinha for that role but Shatru annoyed Mr Chopra by not turning up for an appointment. I finally convinced him to put me through a screen test. Pandhari Juker, the make-up man, made me look at least ten years older. After I gave the shot, the entire unit started clapping. Chopra sahib looked at me and said, "You got it.'"

But bagging the role was easier than playing it. Danny was obviously not used to the wheelchair, for one. He learnt to be comfortable in it. He would swivel in it while at the hotel, in the lobby, and also at the dining table in between shoots.

'Then there was this story in the newspapers that my voice had been dubbed by Raza Murad! Mr Chopra called the press and clarified that it was indeed Danny's own voice!' revealed Danny.

Danny had also choreographed his own entry scene. 'Mr Chopra let me suggest my entry shot. I suggested a "50 lens" mid-shot because I was going to turn and throw the plate at the camera. In the shot I just turned and threw the plate—it went straight at the camera, hit the light studs and broke into six pieces. When he saw the shot, Mr B.R. Chopra hugged me and said, "You do not know what you have done." When the film released, every magazine commended Chopra sahib's direction in that particular shot! He called the press conference and had the guts to tell the critics, "This boy has taken the shot. It is not my shot!"'

One may deduce that the subjugation Rani suffers at the hands of Ranjit Singh is symptomatic of the frustration he experiences for not being able to impose himself sexually on his wife.

For a few bad husbands, the wife wasn't the meal ticket—she had to be merely available whenever he needed to be, for sexual gratification. Jaisingh Jadhav (Marc Zuber) in *Kamla* (1984), in a state of drunkenness, drags his wife Sarita (Shabana Azmi) into bed, retorting with 'Bloody bitch!' when she resists. It is marital rape, nothing less.

The violence one inflicts on the wife is not always physical in nature. In *Saheb, Bibi Aur Ghulam* (1962), Chhote Babu (Rehman), the zamindar, could not do without a dose of raas-rang (entertainment by nautch girls) and his drinking with a paid keep every night. It was psychological abuse. But the wife was often fully aware of this arrangement Chhote

Babu had with the nautch girls and the khandaan proudly saw it as a symbol of his virility. Even in the evenings that he spends with his wife Chhoti Bahu (Meena Kumari), he makes her drink with him. Instead of a wife, her role was that of a stand-by mistress. The 'Ghulam' of the pack was an empathizing family servant called Bhootnath who is a symbolic character representing the 'Saheb' that the 'Bibi' longed for. Bhootnath is also Chhoti Bahu's messenger of hope, bringing her the 'Mohini sindoor' which she believes would attract her husband's attention. When that doesn't work, she asks Bhootnath to get alcohol as her husband preferred the company of a woman who could drink with him.

Decades have passed and yet one doesn't see much of a difference between men like Chhote Babu of *Sahib, Bibi Aur Gulam* and Ranjit Kapoor (Kay Kay Menon), the corporate honcho in *Life in a Metro* (2007) who has a sexual relationship with a junior colleague Neha (Kangana Ranaut), and doesn't find it necessary to explain this to his wife Shikha (Shilpa Shetty). Like Chhote Babu, Ranjit is utterly insensitive to his wife and has long since taken his wife for granted as the unpaid homemaker. And there is a 'Bhootnath' in this film too—the stuggling theatre artiste Akash (Shiney Ahuja), who provides succour to Shikha's abused psyche. The relationship between Akash and Shikha is entirely platonic (they come within a centimetre of kissing each other but get interrupted by a knock on the door), just the way it was between Bhootnath and Chhoti Bahu.

Celebrity creative ad designer Sunil Verma (Marc Zuber) in *Yeh Nazdeekiyan* (1982) is another man of that ilk. Sunil is married to the lovely Shobna (Shabana Azmi), and they have a child; but none of this matter to him. He gets into a dalliance with a leading model, Kiran (Parveen Babi). Film star Mahendra Kumar (Suresh Oberoi) in *Ek Baar Phir* (1980) is the human version of a parasite in addition to being a hypocrite. He publicly praises his wife Kalpana (Deepti Naval) for being his pillar of support and, within an hour, he coaxes a young aspiring actress at a party to do a cabaret number and cavorts shamelessly with her in Kalpana's presence. Mahendra is morally bankrupt, unable to keep his hands and eyes off women. Sick of his promiscuity and his exploitation of colleagues and associates, Kalpana parts ways with Mahendra and finds someone else. Mahendra had it coming.

Bollywood seems to suggest the preponderance of these extramarital escapades in men from showbiz. Abhijit Sarin (Arbaaz Khan) in *Fashion* (2008), the creative head of a fashion house, is someone who is used to getting his way with women by using his position and influence. He trades a lucrative modelling contract with aspiring model Meghna Mathur (Priyanka Chopra) for a physical relationship. But unlike Sunil of *Yeh Nazdeekiyan*, and Mahendra of *Ek Baar Phir*, the Abhijit of *Fashion* isn't a philanderer. For Abhijit, his dealings are pure business. And Meghna, propelled by ambition, enters into a consensual relationship with Abhijeet. But both the directors—Vinod Pande of *Yeh Nazdeekiyan* and Madhur Bhandarkar of *Fashion*—do not show either Kiran or Meghna as being of loose character. The two women are single, ambitious and have the right to seek out a stepping stone in their careers. In both the cases, it was the husbands who took their wives for granted that ruined the marriage.

One doesn't know how to categorize Ranjeet Chaddha (Sanjeev Kumar) of *Pati, Patni Aur Woh* (1978). He isn't a wife beater. Nor does he exploit his spouse financially. He never harasses her. In fact, he is a good family man who loves to spend quality time with his son and occasionally pull his wife Sharda's (Vidya Sinha) leg. But Ranjeet needs a woman at the workplace to make him feel good about himself. He lies to his secretary Nirmala (Ranjeeta) that his wife is terminally ill and wins her over. On getting caught by Sharda with incriminating evidence, he makes up stories on the fly. He doesn't mean to leave his wife and walk away with another woman. He simply believes that two is better than one—another woman to spice up his ordinary life. The two women trap him and make him confess. Nirmala leaves her job to save her boss's marriage. Does Ranjeet learn his lesson from this episode? No. The minute a new secretary walks in, he is at it again ...

For all these 'saudagar' husbands, the wife is a means to sexual gratification, sometimes even a meal ticket or an unpaid housekeeper. But when they get into trouble in their dalliances, they come scurrying back to their wives like timid rabbits.

If we've learnt anything, it's that morally bankrupt characters never show remorse.

6

Aabroo
Sexual Domination

'The villain kidnaps the heroine and takes her to his house. She is trembling with fear as she turns her back to face a wall. The villain unsheathes his sword and cuts the string of her choli (upper garment) in one single stroke. The terrified heroine covers her bosom with her arms. The villain rips her saree with his sword and reveals (a part of) her thigh and leg.'[34]

This is a scene from *Khooni Khanjar* (1930), a film by V. Shantaram from the silent era—probably the first rape scene in Hindi films. As Madhua Jasraj reveals in *V. Shantaram*, 'The Censor Board found this scene very risqué. After a series of arguments between the Board and the producers, it was finally agreed to keep the scene after reducing its length by half.' In a discussion with the author, film historian Sanjit Narwekar shared that the rapist villain in *Khooni Khanjar* was Dnyanoba Mane, better known in films as Mane Pahelwan. And the victim was actor Vijaya. This film, along with a picture of this particular shot, was mentioned in Narwekar's book *Marathi Cinema In Retrospect*.

Apart from the hero, nobody had a right to the heroine. In their bias for the hero, scripts would make comedians out of some of the rest of the characters. In *Padosan* (1968), Mahmood plays Masterji—arguably the first comic villain—providing tough competition to the hero in his desire for Bindu (Saira Banu), who is also his favourite music student. Apart from getting into a singing contest with the hero, Bhole (Sunil Dutt) hires some goons to injure him. But finally, conventional storytelling wins. That Masterji would eventually lose his love interest to Bhole was a foregone conclusion.

The heroine is predestined for the hero. Despite being handsome and maybe even eligible, the villain stands no chance. For example, in *Raja Jani* (1972) the villain, Pratap Bahadur (Prem Chopra), is reduced to a farcical character and made to do a comical dance.

Prem Chopra shared a story from when he was shooting for the comical song sequence 'Kitna mazaa aa ra hai' in which the heroine is trying to make the hero jealous. 'During the shot, I started dancing impromptu and everyone started laughing, including choreographer P.L. Raj. The cameraman fell down, clutching his stomach with laughter at my dance. This became the highlight of the film. During the premiere in Delhi everyone enjoyed a good laugh while the song played.'

Rejections led to serious villainy too. In B.R. Chopra's *Naya Daur* (1957), Krisna (Ajit), stung by Rajni's (Vyjayanthimala) rejection, almost sabotages the livelihood of the community of horse-carriage wallahs by damaging the wooden bridge over which Shankar (Dilip Kumar) was to ride his horse carriage in the race against the motor lorry. Shankar's horse carriage losing the race would mean that the passenger lorry would replace horse carriages as the means of transport. Lakha (Yashpal Sharma) in *Lagaan: Once Upon a Time in India* (2001) does something similar. Jealous over Gauri's (Gauri Singh) acceptance of Bhuvan (Aamir Khan) as the love of her life, in the cricket match against the British,

Lakha deliberately drops catches and fields badly so that Bhuvan would get blamed as the captain of the villagers' team for the loss. Said actor Yashpal Sharma about the role, 'When I heard the story, I couldn't believe that I was getting this role. This was the best role, as Lakha was the turning point in the story. This was a negative role but even a negative role remains human, i.e., in shades of grey, neither black nor white. Lakha's character needs to be viewed in the background of the fact that he loves Gauri and wants to win her over. The next day I auditioned for the role. Ashutosh Gowariker sent my rushes over e-mail to Aamir who gave his approval at once.'

In *Manmohan* (1936), a storyline resembling that of *Devdas*, Ashok (Surendra) loves Vimala (Bibbo), but Vimala is engaged to Jagdish (Yakub). Sensing competition, Jagdish tries to get rid of Ashok. A similar desperation could be seen in the battle to win Prabha in *Chhoti si Baat* (1975). Nagesh Shastri (Asrani) fancies his chances of winning the heart of his lady colleague, Prabha (Vidya Sinha), instead of a timid Arun (Amol Palekar). But after undergoing a training course on confidence-building, it is Advantage Arun. That is when Nagesh poisons Prabha's mind with insinuations that Arun will drug her and molest her in his home. 'Yes, Asrani's was a negative character,' agrees the film's director, Basu Chatterjee.

The making of Chhoti si Baat *wasn't a smooth voyage between Basu Chatterjee and Producer B.R. Chopra. Basu Chatterji recalled: 'When the film was completed, B.R. Chopra called me and said, "Basu, what have you done? We will get beaten up. This won't run for a day. I'm sending you a copy of* School for Scoundrels. *Just copy it." And I was left thinking, what is he saying, asking me to reshoot the whole film? But fortunately, around that time B.R. Chopra went away to Dehradun on personal work. His Business Manager C.V.K. Shastry wasn't privy to this exchange between me and Chopra. I took the money from Shastry and completed the film. The film released and became a superhit. B.R. sent me a telegram, "Happy proved Wrong."'*

While we have Sunil (Shah Rukh Khan) in *Kabhi Haan Kabhi Naa* (1994), who is no more than a naughty mischief-monger, we also had Dilnawaz (Aamir Khan, in a jaw-dropping performance) in *1947 Earth* (1999), who turns the personal loss of his love interest Shanta (Nandita Das) to another young man into a communal cataclysm. Burning with jealously on seeing 'his' Shanta making passionate love to Hassan (Rahul Khanna), Dilnawaz reveals Shanta's hiding place to the frenetic mob running amok during the riots of 1947. And then, sitting on his haunches and taking drags of his cigarette, Dilnawaz watches with puffed-up satisfaction Shanta's pitiful screams as she's dragged away by the mob.

———

By the 1970s, the villain had realized that attempts to impress the heroine through dance, music or wealth wouldn't necessarily work. In his desperation to win the woman, the villain began adopting more violent methods. Rape looked like a good option to them. And the rapist had a loathsome on-screen personality with that lewd look in his eyes. He also needed to make the act of rape look frighteningly real. The actor who checked all these boxes was Gopal Bedi—better known as Ranjeet. He became the archetypal rapist villain in *Sharmeelee* (1971) and *Victoria No. 203* (1972), among others.

In an interview, Ranjeet shared, 'On the flight back from Rajasthan, where we were shooting for *Reshma aur Shera*, Rakhee told me that she had signed *Sharmeelee* with Subodh Mukherji and she suggested that I meet him. I did, and he told me that I was to be there in the cast of the film—playing the role of a rapist. It became a superhit and I got the stamp of a new villain—the rapist villain. And rape would become the stock act of villainy for decades to come.' Bollywood had turned an ugly corner.

The actor, however, didn't have it easy at home. During the premiere of *Sharmeelee* in Delhi, Ranjeet's family members left the auditorium midway (in the scene in which he rapes Kamini), their faces morose. They would later accuse Ranjeet of sullying the family name. Even though he was disowned by his family, acceptance would come his way eventually. The role of the rapist in *Sharmeelee* made Ranjeet so popular that 'film distributors would suggest to the director to force fit a scene in which the heroine has a nightmare that she is being raped' just so Ranjeet could make an appearance. As Ranjeet recalls, the heroines, too, would recommend that he be cast in such roles. Ranjeet would also contribute towards choreographing these scenes. 'I would also give them instructions like asking them to dig their fingernails into my face, push me, pull my hair, etc., to make the scenes realistic.' Ranjeet came to be known as the 'compulsory blind', i.e., directors would include a role for him even before the story had been be conceived.

Actor Sharat Saxena shared how in 1972, Ranjeet was shooting for eight films a day and working on dozens of films simultaneously. 'He would sleep in his car. He would shoot all day and then go for dubbing.'

And how comfortable would the ladies be in these rape scenes? Discloses Ranjeet: 'None of the top heroines with whom I had acted in rape scenes used a body double. There was no tension, tantrum or drama between the lady and me. They were very cooperative and comfortable with me, because I never touched them inappropriately.'

About the process of doing such difficult scenes, Ranjeet shares an incident. 'There was this tender new girl, who was horrified at the prospect of the rape scene. After the shot, they asked her if everything was okay. She replied, "I did not feel that he even touched me." So, the shooting of the rape scene is like any other scene.' Incidentally, the 'tender new girl' was Madhuri Dixit.

Even shooting such serious and violent scenes was not without its share of on-set humor. Ranjeet recounts the famous seduction song-sequence *'Thoda sa thehro'* played by Saira Banu in *Victoria No. 203*. Just after the song Ranjeet (Ranjeet) tries to rape Rekha (played by Saira Banu). 'I was acting with Sairaji for the first time. When the rape scene was being shot, the clasp of her bikini broke. I immediately covered her with my arms to protect her modesty. The lights were switched off and a big towel was brought in. I was very worried people would think I had broken her bikini clasp deliberately. I was a newcomer. I could not sleep that night thinking that Dilip Kumar would come and beat me up!'

One of the most controversial Hindi films ever around the subject of rape was *Insaaf ka Tarazu* (1980) with Ramesh Gupta (Raj Babbar), a wealthy businessman, playing the rapist villain. His character outlined another transition in Bollywood villainy. Initially Ramesh Gupta is a Pran-like gentleman—chivalrous and courteous with an intent to court the leading model of her day, Bharti Saxena (Zeenat Aman). But Bharti's constant rejection and her preference for another man turns Ramesh into a lewd, Ranjeet-like rapist. *Insaaf ka Tarazu* also showed how the rapist makes the ugly power of sexual domination a habit. Emboldened at being acquitted by the court on the charges of raping Bharti, in a show of insane megalomania, Ramesh rapes Bharti's sister Neeta (Padmini Kolhapure) too.

Zeenat Aman shared insights about the filming of the rape sequences in Insaaf ka Tarazu. *'B.R. Chopra sahib showed me the shooting rushes of the rape scenes, asked for my suggestions for the final edits and actually implemented those. We had workshops prior to the shoot, which was unheard of. When he made Padmini strip, there was not an inch of vulgarity or sensuousness. It was very collaborative and so well-choreographed and shot.'*

In the section of the book where we discuss 'outlaws', we observed that the rural Indian zamindars (landlords) believed that they owned not only the land, but also the women of the village. This mentality of entitlement has not been limited to rural India.

A social thriller, *Pink* (2016) centred around a victim of sexual molestation—an urban, educated woman who, after filing an FIR against the perpetrator, a politician's nephew, is accused of being of a questionable character—and the ensuing court trial. The riveting drama brought up the issue of consent in a sexual encounter, and also highlighted the speciousness of societal prejudices in India when it comes to women and sexual independence. And there are teenaged perverts like Sameer Deshmukh (Rishabh Chaddha) in *Drishyam* (2015) who blackmail a female classmate Anju for sex after stealthily filming her while she is bathing. Sameer draws his power and a sense of immunity from his parentage—his mother was the Inspector General of Police.

This sense of entitlement extends to women, too. The attractive Ms Sonia Roy (Priyanka Chopra) in *Aitraaz* (2004) (an adaptation of *Disclosure*, 1994) seeks to control Raj Malhotra (Akshay Kumar) sexually. Sonia and Raj had been in a relationship a few years ago but they parted ways since. Sonia is currently perched higher than Raj in the same organization, i.e., she is his boss and hence feels a sense of power over Raj. Her acts are evidently not about sex alone; it is about the power she socially wields. On being thwarted by Raj, Ms Sonia Roy files a case of harassment against him. Ms Sonia Roy is another case study of certain people—male or female—believing that their social superiority over another person gives them a license to sexually dominate the other person. This aspect of villainy was very similar to the one of Meredith Johnson (Demi Moore) in *Disclosure*.

Come to think of it, in Bollywood films, the male colleague expecting sexual favours at the workplace is implicit or explicit—but it is there. The women have been objectivized and taken for granted. Like this playboy in *Yes Boss* (1997) Siddharth Chowdhary (Aditya Pancholi), who molests his female colleague Seema (Juhi Chawla). Movie producer Dayal (Ajit Vachhani) in *Khamosh* (1985) requests and then coerces Soni (Soni Razdan) to come to his hotel room in return for a plum role in his next film. And get slapped in public by her. In *Red Rose* (1980), the employer Anand tells the lady interviewee, '*Hum tumhe rakh rahe hain* (I'll keep you)'—and quickly, in mock correction, adds, 'I mean, as a steno'. Till the 1970s, these junior female employees usually had screen names like Suzy or Maria or Ms Roberts (Shashikala in *Gumrah*, 1963—a role which won her the Filmfare Award) suggesting the preponderance of young ladies from the Christian or the Anglo-Indian community at the workplace. To underscore the point, in *Dastak* (1970), the camera zooms in on the crucifix pendant that the gorgeous office typist Maria (Anju Mahendru) is wearing around her neck. And a few bad employers like Arvind Desai in *Albert Pinto ko Gussa Kyoon Aata Hai* (1980) presumed that hard-working colleagues like Stella (Shabana Azmi) were available for a fling just because they were socially outgoing and fashionably dressed. One evening, while dropping Stella home in his car, he makes an advance at her—and gets slapped. His pride hurt, Desai instantly fires her.

7

Haazir Ho!
The Professionally Corrupt

Outside of family and close friends, lawyers and doctors are among the very few privy to a person's intimate secrets. But are these professionals always worthy of that trust? In practically every courtroom sequence in Bollywood one of the two lawyers are infamous for distorting facts to suit their clients, and even intimidating and humiliating witnesses. In *Kala Pani* (1958), in his hurry to protect the real murderer, Prosecutor Rai Bahadur Jaswant Rai (Kishore Sahu) refuses to entertain key evidences proffered by the police.

But what we see in *Mohan Joshi Hazir Ho!* (1984) is nothing short of medieval entertainment in modern times. Mohan Joshi (Bhisham Sahni), an elderly chawl dweller, approaches his landlord Kundan Kapadia (Amjad Khan) for renovating his house in the old chawl which is in a very poor state of maintenance. But Kapadia is happy to let the chawl crumble so that he can sell the land to two real estate promoters. Mohan Joshi appoints two lawyers, Malkani (Naseeruddin Shah) and Gokhale (Satish Shah), to file a case against Kapadia demanding that Kapadia fix the house. But Malkani and Gokhale, in collusion with the defence lawyers Rani (Rohini Hattangady) and Desai (Deepak Qazir), keep prolonging the case with each camp having its own excuses for this prolongment. This suits Rani and Desai as it gives them a steady revenue from the wealthy Kapadia while Malkani and Gokhale keep milking Mohan Joshi who keeps paying them by digging into his sparse retirement funds. The case drags on for more than three years till Mohan Joshi runs out of money and pawns his wife's jewellery to pay Malkani and Gokhale their fees.

Mohan Joshi Hazir Ho! is enriched with uproarious wit. With their shameless atrocity and adultery, the learned lawyers make you roll on the floor laughing. And tunnelling through this 'Joke of Justice' is Mr and Mrs Mohan Joshi's 'Sound of Silence'. 'Their plight is the real form—the stark reality', said director Saeed Akhtar Mirza in a chat with the author.

Saeed Mirza termed this entire court drama a tamasha. Said he, 'I actually visited lower courts and high courts as a part of my research for the film and I saw that the club of judges, lawyers, clerks, peons, bailiffs, litigants and defendants are all players in an orchestrated pantomime. If you go to a courtroom and if your eyes can see, the faces of the litigants that have come to seek justice will tell you a thousand stories. They are terrorized at the grandiose Sanskrit and Persian legalese and the endless stacks of files. Will they ever get justice here?' In *Mohan Joshi* ... the opposing lawyers are seen having side conversations with each other right in the courtroom by day. And at night the defence and prosecution are in bed together discussing tactics on how to keep prolonging the case.

In the finale, all the characters run all around the chawl like headless chicken—yet, someone seems to be controlling their movements with a string. Saeed Mirza shared the genesis of the climax scene, 'I was inspired by the poem 'Butchered to Make a Roman Holiday' by Lord George Byron which was about a spectacle in a coliseum in which the entire crowd is roaring for that one gladiator to die for the people to celebrate. The gladiator is fatally wounded. With each drop of blood his life is ebbing away. The poem runs thus:

The arena swims around him—he is gone,
Ere ceased the inhuman shout which hail'd the wretch who won.
He heard it, but he heeded not—his eyes
Were with his heart and that was far away;
He reck'd not of the life he lost nor prize,
But where his rude hut by the Danube lay …

The court is Mohan Joshi's last post for justice. But if the judiciary is corroded, where could he go? To the mafia? Or to the political warlords? Did he have the money to go to them? So, what does Mohan Joshi do? He becomes a Samson and pulls the house down, killing himself in the process—just the way the poem ends

… There were his young barbarians all at play
There was their Dacian mother—he, their sire,
Butcher'd to make a Roman holiday.'

Rohini Hattangady has very pleasant memories of Mohan Joshi … 'No elaborate preparation went into my role since Saeed Mirza knew me as an actor. The Do Tanki Chawl was on the road leading away from Bombay Central station. It was the late monsoon period of September. We would take the first shot and the rains would come pouring down. The entire crew (most of us from the theatre world) would be sitting around in make-up in one room in the chawl, chatting away, waiting for the rain to abate. Since my little one would keep waking me up throughout the night, I would often doze off in a small bed in between shots. For nearly seven days we were shooting intermittently amidst bouts of rain. So, we decided to postpone the shoot for a month by which time the rains would have stopped. But … the day we packed up, it was bright sunshine from the next day onwards!'

———

Subhash Kapoor's *Jolly LLB* (2013) and *Jolly LLB 2* (2017) were the two most obvious follow-ups to *Mohan Joshi* ... Both the 'Jolly' films are fearless caricatures of the judicial system, not even sparing the fat, gluttonous slob of a judge. The 'orchestration' that Saeed Mirza spoke of was once again on display in the *Jolly LLB* series with the judge Sunderlal Tripathi (Saurabh Shukla) and the defense lawyers—Tejender Rajpal (Boman Irani) in *Jolly LLB* and Pramod Mathur (Annu Kapoor) in *Jolly LLB 2*—discussing property deals, each other's salary ranges and wedding outfits right during court hour. In *Jolly LLB*, Tejinder Rajpal is Delhi's superstar lawyer who, on alighting from his Mercedes Benz at the portico of the District and Sessions Court, walks through swarming mediapersons without as much as making eye contact, returning a couple of 'good morning's perfunctorily on his brisk walk from the main entrance to the courtroom with two junior counsel and his clients in tow. Rajpal has poise, panache and enjoys dressing expensively. His marble-floored office resembles a presidential suite of a super luxury hotel and is endowed with a minibar stocked with Bombay Sapphire gin and single malts. Rajpal doesn't bother respecting courtroom etiquette, fiddling with his mobile phone even when the judge is speaking to him. He goes to the extent of doctoring the police FIR to save his client's son who is guilty of running his vehicle over pavement dwellers. But this was nothing. Rajpal's behaviour is no different from a criminal, getting the public prosecutor beaten by goons. He is also an egomaniac. When the client pays him less than the agreed professional fees adding, '... Don't be greedy', Rajpal is stung. Actor Saurabh Shukla analysed, 'You see how Rajpal takes this insult. He just smiles and says "okay". When a labourer works hard and the landlord pays them less than what is their right and says, "What I am giving you is more than enough", the labourer can sabotage.' Rajpal rigs a false eyewitness to siphon off INR 2 crores from his own client, claiming that he needed that amount to bribe the 'eyewitness' to remain silent. Having got his fill, Rajpal reclines in his deeply upholstered chair and tells the universe, 'I only demand what I deserve. And nobody calls me greedy.' So much for his trustworthiness.

Pramod Mathur (Annu Kapoor) in *Jolly LLB 2*, Lucknow's heavyweight lawyer, is the defence lawyer for a rogue policeman, Inspector Suryaveer Singh (Kumud Mishra), who kills an innocent Muslim youth in a fake encounter. '*Papsi aur Pramod apna formula batate nahi* (Pepsi and Pramod never disclose their formulas),' he brags. Despite both being corrupt lawyers, Pramod Mathur is crafted very differently from Tejinder Rajpal of *Jolly LLB*. An estimated 30 per cent of Tejpal's dialogues are in lustrous English. Even his Hindi has an urban gloss. But Pramod Mathur in *Jolly LLB 2* has a coarse body language and speaks in Lucknow-styled Hindi almost throughout, with his odd English words suggesting a vernacular-medium education. '*Baaton ka batangar banakar hi Luchnow shehar ka basht um basht vakil bana hoon main* (My talent in playing with words is what has made the decidedly best lawyer in the city of Lucknow),' he claims, pronouncing 'best' as 'basht'. True to his villainy, Mathur layers simple truths under verbose lectures, coerces witnesses, makes unprofessional, personal remarks about Jolly and his family background. Mathur has the audacity to tamper a narco-test video of a murder witness in a fake encounter by Inspector Suryaveer Singh.

And what about the trusted doctors?

By the early 1980s, gangsters started keeping doctors on their payroll. So, they became part of the nexus that included lawyers, politicians and policemen. In *Aakrosh* (1980), the elderly Dr Vasant M. Patil (Arvind Deshpande) performs the post-mortem on the Adivasi woman Nagi (Smita Patil) who has been allegedly murdered by her husband Lahanya Bikhu (Om Puri). It is evident in the cross-examination that the integrity of the post-mortem process has been compromised by Dr Patil. For one, there was no civil surgeon present with Dr Patil during the post-mortem on Nagi's dead body. Secondly, there were scratches in many parts of the dead victim's body including the area between her navel and private parts. Yet, in his post-mortem Dr Patil chose not to examine the cause of those injuries. That is because Dr Patil is an integral part of the card-playing club of the village, one of whom (More, the forest contractor, played by Achyut Potdar) orchestrated the rape of Nagi. No wonder the benevolent looking Dr Patil had been shifty when the defence lawyer Kulkarni (Naseeruddin Shah) had wanted to speak with him.

In *Saaransh* (1984), Dr Bhatt (Vijay Kashyap) tries to kill a foetus in the womb of Sujata (Soni Razdan) under orders from an unscrupulous politician Gajanan Chhitre (Nilu Phule). The unmarried Sujata was pregnant with the child of Vilas, son of Gajanan Chhitre; a fact that would have wrecked Chhitre's prospects in the upcoming municipal elections. In *Aakhree Raasta* (1986), it is the corrupt Dr Varma (Bharat Kapoor) who destroys the evidence of the rape of an innocent housewife Mary (Jaya Prada) at the hands of a criminal politician Neta (played by Sadashiv Amrapurkar). In an interview with the author, Sadashiv Amrapurkar talked about his role of 'Neta' in *Aakhree Raasta*, 'The script was written by K. Bhagyaraj who could speak neither Hindi nor English. He would mime and show us what he wanted, and I would mime back. And he was quite happy at the precision of my miming. In the scene in which I rape Mary, this concept of the captor pre-empting the dialogues of the hostage was a novelty, lending a certain freshness. And that scene became immensely popular.'

In *Pitaah* (2002), a nine-year old village girl Muniya is raped by two perverted sons of the almighty Thakur. The child suffers a skull fracture too and is hallucinating from the trauma. The village doctor (played by Anjan Srivastava) whose medical testimonial would be key, gruffly refuses to sell himself out to the Thakur when approached with a bribe of INR 1 lakh. '*Paanch lakh se ek rupaiya kum nahi loonga* (I will not settle for anything less than five lakhs),' the good doctor adds. And he acquiesces to furnish a report that the two cuplrits were admitted in a hospital the day the nine-year-old was raped. In *Criminal* (1995), the doctors turned cannibals. It was one of the earliest films to depict organ sale in hospitals. And why not? A pair of kidneys of a woman with a rare blood group can fetch up to $1 million, as Dr Swami (Zakir Hussain) states in *AndhaDhun* (2018).

———

Medicine is an investment. Businessmen invest money in building hospitals—and they need to recover that money. Which is why people like Dr Chaturvedi (Vinod Mehra) in *Bemisal* (1982) conduct illegal abortions in their hospital for hefty sums of money. 'Yes, running a hospital is a business', said actor Tisca Chopra in an interview with the author, referring to director Suhail Tatari's classic *Ankur Arora Murder Case* (2013) which was partially inspired by a real-life story. Young Ankur Arora is admitted to Shekhawat General Hospital for an appendicitis surgery. Dr V. Asthana (Kay Kay Menon) of the hospital lies to Ankur Arora's mother, Nandita (Tisca Chopra), that the OT wasn't available until the day after in order to bill the family for an additional night. '*Hospital paison pe chalta, sirf acchai pe nahi* (A hospital runs on money, not just goodwill),' states Dr Asthana. Further, busy discussing over his mobile phone an upcoming black-tie event, Dr Asthana ignores a critical pre-surgery process. As a result of this negligence, Ankur Arora slips into coma. 'I messed up,' admits Dr Asthana within the closed doors of the Operation Theatre. But then immediately follows Asthana's elaborate and systematic hush-up. He threatens the doctors and an intern present in the OT to play along with his false story of a post-operation lung failure. Else, he would derail their careers. Instead of admitting to a professional error, Dr Asthana's reconstructs facts around the pre-operation phase, forges reports, bribes the on-duty nurse and sends her away on a vacation. All this to purportedly protect the hospital's reputation. In fact, the hospital's credibility would have been served better in issuing a sincere apology and a compensation to the unfortunate family.

Said Tisca Chopra who played the distraught mother of Ankur Arora, 'The film wasn't about Dr Asthana being corrupt. The larger case was an evolved subject. Asthana is the top doctor and the face of the hospital. His situation was like that of a CEO's image being managed by the PR because the company's share value is linked to his image. If he fails, the reputation of the hospital fails too.'

In an interview with the author, Kay Kay Menon who played Dr Asthana agreed, 'When I was playing Asthana, I felt that he was running an organization more than a medical profession. He is an expert and therefore overconfident that nothing can go wrong. And when things go wrong, his is unable to accept it. He makes desperate attempts to cover up his mistake. He turns into a criminal.'

III
BAAGHI
The Outlaws

These are the gun-toting 'daku' or 'dacait' who hide in the ravines of North India. Often wearing moustaches (sometimes twirling ones) and tika (vermilion) on their foreheads, they come thundering on their horsebacks and loot the wealthy zamindar and plunder the nearby villages. There are also those Hollywood Westerns-inspired variety of outlaws with sunburnt faces, wearing ponchos and rugged jeans with holsters by the side, who are game for a duel under the sun with an adversary. There is, of course, much more than meets the eye.

1

Do Bigha Zamin
The Zamindars and Moneylenders

'We weren't dacoits. We were baaghis (outlaws),' said former dacoit Malkhan Singh, in an interview with Poulomi Banerjee of *Hindustan Times*, thirty-five years following his surrender. 'Some people in my village wanted to take away the 100 bighas of land that was the property of a village temple. When I protested, they started implicating me in all sorts of false cases. I was harassed and became a *baaghi*.'[35]

And these realities of landlords and moneylenders who exploited illiterate villagers was reflected in the storylines of Bollywood films. These landlords and moneylenders would lend money to the villagers at exorbitant rates, landing the poor man into a debt trap for life. Knowing that the poor man will never be able to repay the loan, the landlord would coerce him to pledge his land as collateral. Sometimes, by sheer dint of muscle power, the landlord would let loose his lathi-wielding goons to forcibly snatch away the poor farmer's land for a pittance—sometimes not even that. Thakur Harnam Singh (Murad) in Bimal Roy's *Do Bigha Zamin* (1953) is the iconic zamindar (landlord) who coerces the illiterate villager Shambhu (Balraj Sahni) to sell his two bighas (approximately 1.25 acre) to the Thakur so he could further sell to a company to build a factory. When Shambhu refuses, the angered Thakur orders Shambhu to repay a loan that Shambhu had taken from the Thakur. It turns out the Thakur had made Shambhu (Balraj Sahni) affix his thumb impression on a doctored loan document that showed an amount of INR 235.50 due against the INR 65 that Shambhu believed he owed. Sukhilala (Kanhaiyalal) of Mehboob Khan's *Mother India* (1957) is another loan shark who had lent INR 500 for Radha's marriage and then, asked the hapless Radha, now a penurious mother of two, to sleep with him when she was unable to repay the loan.

Mother India *was a remake of Mehboob Khan's* Aurat *(1940) which, in turn, drew partially from the film* Good Earth, *based on Pearl S. Buck's novel.*[36] *Incidentally,* Aurat *and* Mother India *were shot at the same locations in Gujarat, with Kanhaiyalal playing the same role of the moneylender.*[37]

Prior to these films was Chetan Anand's *Neecha Nagar* (1946)—a cogent portrayal of the rich–poor class divide with overt socialist overtones. In *Neecha Nagar* (inspired by Maxim Gorky's novel *The Lower Depths*), the wealthy landowner Sarkar denies even water to people dwelling in the valley. Actor Rafi Pir played the antagonistic, smiling menace, Sarkar. He meets his quietus in his own mansion, but not before suffering a mental breakdown.

In Chetan Anand: The Poetics of Film, *Ketan Anand and Uma Anand shared: 'Chetan had the rare ability to make an adverse situation into an asset. Raw-stock on license was not only limited, but often old and cloudy. It could not be replaced. So he used this damaged stock for outdoor twilight scenes. They were shot at dusk; with blazing mashals as the only source of illumination in the extraordinary torch-lit procession of the climax ...' The authors also narrate an anecdote during the shooting, 'Pali Hill in those days had dark groves of twisted mango trees running down to rolling green downs, where there was a nine-hole mini-Golf course. The groves, downs, fairway and hillocks provided the perfect location for the winding torch-lit mass procession, snaking its way to strike at the gates of Sarkar's citadel.*[38]

In rural India, caste rivalries were another reason behind the rise of outlaws. *Kuchhe Dhaage* (1973) is about a generational caste war between caste Brahmins and the belligerent Thakurs. In *Bandit Queen* (1994), it is Jat vs Gujjar, in *Gangs of Wasseypur* (2012) it is Pathans vs Qureshis, and in *Wounded* (2006), it is a face-off between Thakurs, with a Parihar refusing to give his daughter's hand in marriage to the son of a Sengar.

Forget property or caste, even basic justice wasn't forthcoming for the villagers. In *Paan Singh Tomar* (2012), the District Collector, who is supposed to arbitrate a land dispute between two claimants, vacates the scene without heeding Tomar's (Irfan Khan) plea for his family's safety till the dispute is resolved. 'Ye hai Chambal ka hukum, apne aap nipto. (This is the law of Chambal. Resolve the issue yourself),' he says. Gulzar's *Maachis* (1996) brought to the screen a story where the entire ecosystem, in the aftermath of the 1984 anti-Sikh riots, betrays an innocent Punjabi youth. Jassi Randhawa (Raj Zutshi) is a simple villager in Punjab. Unable to trace a suspected militant, the Punjab police detain Jassi and inflict brutal injuries on him. Later, they suspect him again for a murder of ACP Vohra and torture him in police custody, driving him to suicide. The police could not differentiate a peace-loving Sikh from a terrorist. No wonder they turned innocent men like Kirpal (Chandrachur Singh) into revenge-thirsty outlaws.

The wealthy and the powerful, fully aware that the poor would have no recourse to law, would also pick on the women. In *Madhumati* (1958), Raja Ugrasen (Pran) remains in hot pursuit of the village belle, Madhumati. In *Teesri Kasam* (1966), the zamindar Vikram Singh (Iftekhar) would not take a 'no' for an answer from the dancer Hirabai

(Waheeda Rehman), who refuses to be a mehmaan (guest) at the zamindar's mansion. It was the power of Raja Ugrasen and zamindar Vikram Singh speaking.

Shyam Benegal speaks very cogently about this dominance of the zamindars over villagers in a feudal system in *Ankur* (1974) and *Nishant* (1975). In *Ankur*, Surya (Anant Nag), the son of a wealthy landlord, has an affair with the household help, Lakshmi (Shabana Azmi), whose deaf-mute husband, Kishtayya (Sadhu Meher), has been outcast from the village for stealing wine. Later, when rumours are rife about an illegitimate relationship between Lakshmi and Surya, a pregnant Lakshmi is driven out of the house by Surya's wife. *Nishant* is almost a carry-over from *Ankur* with an even cruder villain. Surya of *Ankur* at least carried some semblance of guilt, whereas Anjaiya (Anant Nag) and Prasad (Mohan Agashe), the younger brothers of the landlord (Amrish Puri) in *Nishant*, have no scruples at all in forcibly abducting Sushila (Shabana Azmi), the attractive young wife of the new schoolteacher (played by Girish Karnad). In both these films, the zamindars feel they are entitled to the women of the village. Said Benegal in an interview with the author, 'What Surya (Anant Nag) in *Ankur* went through at school and college was the acceptance of feudal relationships; that he was the boss and others were his slaves. But even in a master–slave relationship, you're responsible for the slave because there is a human relationship as well. But he falls into the pattern and then he cannot take the responsibility. Therefore, willy-nilly, he becomes a villain.'

In Govind Nihalani's 1980 film *Aakrosh*, what chance does the illiterate tribal Lahanya (Om Puri), whose wife Nagi (Smita Patil) has been raped by the feudal lords' henchmen have, to approach the police or the courts? Govind Nihalani shared, 'Observe the anger of the raped and dead victim Nagi's husband Lahanya who is totally disempowered. He is just a tribal. He has been framed for his wife's death, but can't defend himself. He does not even have a lawyer. His anger is more primaeval.

Quite disturbingly, the scenario portrayed on-screen does not seem to have changed for the better since the time the tribal Ghinua's (Mithun Chakraborty) wife in *Mrigayaa* (1976) was abducted by the landowners in British India. Even in the new millennium, the helpless labourer's nine-year-old daughter gets raped by the sons of the Thakur in the heart-rending *Pitaah* (2002).

2

Chambal ki Kasam
The Typical Dacoits

In May 1960, Acharya Vinoba Bhave addressed a group of bandits in the Chambal River Valley to surrender and join the mainstream.[39] It is believed that this event started the trend of dacoit-based films in Hindi cinema with Raj Kapoor's *Jis Desh Mein Ganga Behti Hai* (1960) being the first in the series. True, in *Jis Desh Mein Ganga Behti Hai*, dozens of dacoits lay down their arms and join the mainstream just the way seventeen bandits surrendered their arms to Vinoba Bhave in May 1960. But the *Jis Desh Mein* ... film received its censorship certificate in late 1960. Therefore, for *Jis Desh Mein* ... to be a direct outcome of the Vinoba Bhave rally, the film needed to have been conceived and shot in the three-month period between June and August 1960, which is unlikely.

Moreover, real-life dacoits including the Indian Robin Hood Sultana Daku were already active in the 1920s. So Bhave's reform drive in the Chambal may not have been the direct precursor for film-makers to start making dacoit films. There had been dacoit films earlier, too, like *Daakoo ka Ladka* (1935), *Daakoo ki Ladki* (1933), *Daakoo Mansoor* (1934) and, of course, the seminal *Mother India* (1957) and *Azaad* (1955). Even *Awara* (1951) was about an outlaw: Jagga (K.N. Singh). It could, however, be said that for some reason, before 1960, dacoit films as a genre hadn't arrived.

The one thing, though, that *Jis Desh Mein ...* will be remembered for, is Pran's landmark performance as the bandit Raaka whose men break into homes and make away with their money, ambush a marriage party, kill the groom and loot the jewellery meant for the bride. There is a reward of INR 10,000 on his head for anyone who captures Raaka dead or alive. Though Raaka is a ruthless, murdering dacoit, there are softer shades to his character too; he genuinely loves Kammo (Padmini) and wants to marry her. But in the end, Raaka's love for Kammo prevents him from firing his gun. Now, Raaka's mind is conditioned to using force as the first option. In a severe disagreement with Kammo's father (who is also the good-hearted sardar of the dacoit gang, played by veteran actor S.B. Nayampalli) over who Kammo should marry, Raaka shoots sardar to death. Raaka's subtle transformation in the last half hour of the film underlined this fact, making Pran's performance even more special. So much so that, during the film's premiere in Calcutta, veteran Bengali actor Pahari Sanyal, known for his stiff upper-lip demeanour, walked up to Pran to congratulate him on his performance. In his biography of actor Pran, author Bunny Reuben quotes the actor: "'When Raj Kapoor narrated the story of this film to me and asked me to play the role of the dacoit Raaka, I became extremely eager to do the role. From that moment on, I thought only of my role—and what my 'look', my moustache, wig and costume would be.'"[40] Reuben also quotes Pran on how the actor found the right get-up. "'Eventually, one day an English 'daily' came to my rescue. There was a news item about the capture of a gang of dacoits and they had published a photograph of one of them. If that particular dacoit had not been caught, details about him and his capture would not have been known. It turned out that he was the most cruel dacoit of his gang. When he was killed in the police encounter, his body was riddled with twenty-one bullets! Looking at his picture, I felt: 'This is Raaka!'. I cut out a clipping and showed it to Raj Kapoor who agreed with me.'"[41]

———

But apart from characters like Raaka, the dacoits, like anti-heroes, are usually not pure black villains. Dacoits are the ugly offspring of the exploitation of the poor villager by the rich zamindar or the moneylenders whose behaviour we discussed in the last chapter. Dacoit Birju (Sunil Dutt) in Mehboob Khan's *Mother India* (1957) is a product of exploitation by the moneylender Sukhilala (Kanhaiyalal). Dacoit Gunga Singh in Nitin Bose's *Gunga Jumna* (1961) is again, very similar to Birju—a simple villager, Gunga is forced into the life of an outlaw by the village zamindar who falsely accuses Gunga of a crime.

Interestingly, in both *Mother India* and *Gunga Jumna*, there was this 'conscience voice' manifested in the form of a character, warning Birju and Gunga Singh of the consequences of their outlawed life. They were Birju's mother, Radha (Nargis), and Gunga Singh's brother, Inspector Jumna Singh (Nasir Khan), respectively. Back then, the storytellers were still conventional in their thinking—the 'justifiably correct' cannot dominate the 'lawfully wrong'. Radha shoots to death her son Birju and Police Inspector Jumna Singh shoots his brother Gunga Singh in a police encounter.

In his autobiography, Dilip Kumar spoke about the death scene in *Gunga Jumna*. 'I took the cameraman, V. Babasaheb, into confidence and told him to keep everything ready as there would not be a rehearsal or a second take … What I did was my own idea. I took several rounds of the studio's premises, jogging at first and then running. When I felt breathless and I thought that I would just collapse, I entered the sets where Babasaheb was ready with the camera running to perfection.'[42] The scene was done with no rehearsals or retakes.

Despite strong misgivings expressed by his brother Nasir Khan about playing an outlaw, Dilip Kumar went ahead with his intuition and played the dacoit Gunga Singh in *Gunga Jumna*, asking Nasir Khan to play the policeman Jumna Singh. About his role of Gunga Singh, Kumar said: 'It took me back to my relationship with my elder brother Ayub Sahab who was intellectually ahead of all of us and I always felt he could have become somebody important in the administration had he not been physically debilitated.'[43] So Gunga wasn't unfamiliar to Dilip Kumar as a character. In fact, by Dilip Kumar's own admission, he was offered a role in *Mother India* by Mehboob Khan: 'The role he could offer me was of one of the sons of the heroine Nargis and I pointed out that it would be an incongruous casting after all the romancing she and I had done in earlier films such as *Mela* (1948) and *Babul* (1950).'[44] Four years after *Mother India*, Dilip Kumar gave the story a different flavour and, along with director Nitin Bose, created yet another classic.

Though apparently similar, outlaws are different from anti-heroes. Dictionaries define the word 'outlaw' as someone who has broken the law, especially one who is a fugitive. Outlaws must hide underground, because the police are in their pursuit; these outlaws are hardcore killers, looters, those that vandalize—sometimes all three—and are therefore, wanted by the law. An anti-hero, on the other hand, is, by definition, very much a part of the system, one who walks the town freely as an ordinary man. In fact, in *Deewar*, Vijay purchases an extravagant property in upmarket Bombay by signing legal documents. No outlaw could have done that even if he had the money. The anti-heroes in *Mere Apne* were students, and in many others, they were policemen too. If the anti-heroes were wrongdoers, their offenses ranged from petty crimes to alleged involvement in smuggling. Alleged—because sometimes, the police wouldn't have a speck of evidence against the anti-heroes. For example, they had to ask Vijay to sign a confession to his being a smuggler, without which they had no proof against him. An outlaw's face, on the other hand, would be on the 'Wanted' notice on every other wall in the town.

Because of the fact that these outlaws, like anti-heroes, were intrinsically good young men who were upset with the system, this genre attracted the leading men of the industry to take on these roles, despite the negative traits of the characters. In *Azaad* (1955), Dilip Kumar plays a forbiddingly attractive bandit from the yonder hills while Rajendra Kumar plays the charming titular bandit in the blockbuster *Suraj* (1966). These characters were like Robin Hood, fighters, saviours and protectors, no matter what they had to do to ensure that good was restored in the world.

Who would have thought that the stylish Feroze Khan would be able to discard his leather jackets and bikers' accessories and pull off the role of Daku Shakti Singh in *Mela* (1971), which was a remake of *Gunga Jumna*? And yet, he did. For the urbanite hero of the 1970s, the ravines, horses and dhoti were like a break from the Big City, where a significant percentage of the stories seemed to be based. While Dharmendra's role as dacoit Lakhan Singh in *Samadhi* (1972) was too brief to allow any significant recall, his role as the kind-hearted daku Ranjit Singh in *Patthar Aur Payal* (1974) brought him, as well as the film, great success. Sunil Dutt, who looked his best in tailored suits, slipped easily into the horse-riding, villager-turned-dacoit *Heera* (1973) in which Heera is framed for a murder that he did not commit. Like Dharmendra, Sunil Dutt followed up this dacoit role with another soon after, in *Pran Jaye Par Vachan Na Jaye* (1974), playing the quintessential Robin Hood-like outlaw Raja Thakur who helps the helpless by risking his own life. Box office colossus Amitabh Bachchan played the village yokel-turned-dacoit Jeeva in *Ganga ki Saugandh* (1978). The innocent Jeeva rubs the rogue Thakur Jaswant Singh (Amjad Khan) on the wrong side, and thus, is framed and thrown out of the village. Needless to say, he turns into a dacoit and takes revenge against the Thakur. Rajesh Khanna, after his luckless dabble as a dacoit in *Bhola Bhala* (1978), once again became a bandit in *Dharam Kanta* (1982), with slightly better results. Younger heroes like Sunny Deol and Sanjay Dutt picked up the baton and charged their horses ahead through the 1980s and 1990s in films like *Dacait*

(1987) and *Jai Vikranta* (1995), with very similar storylines of simple young men going underground because they or their families had been wronged by the village-elite. And the police and judiciary could not bring the offenders to book.

———

Not only the men, but even the resolute village women, after being horribly violated, raped or oppressed in myriad ways, had only the gun with which to fight back. Like their male colleagues, the leading heroines too picked up the gun and jumped on to the horses. For example, in *Taaqat* (1982), the illiterate village girl Devi (Rakhee Gulzar) marries into a wealthy Thakur household where she is sexually harassed by her stepbrother-in-law Deepu. Devi kills Deepu in self-defence against a rape assault by him and is denied a fair trial in court as the Thakur household taints her as an immoral woman. Aided by the good-hearted dacoit Bhavani Singh (Pran), Devi escapes police custody and becomes a dacoit to take revenge herself. In *Ramkali* (1985), Hema Malini plays Raksha, whose cop-brother gets killed by the rogue Thakur Shankar Singh and his brothers Thakur Zaalim Singh (Goga Kapoor) and Thakur Bhushan. But the police themselves are helpless against the mighty Thakurs, leaving it to Raksha to avenge her brother's death; she then goes underground and becomes a bandit. Similarly, in *Sherni* (1988), Sridevi plays Durga, the village girl whose mother and sisters are massacared by Thakur Dharampal (Kader Khan); Durga herself faces imprisonment on false charges fabricated by Dharampal in collusion with the corrupt village policeman. She flees and becomes a dacoit. In *Daku Hasina* (1987), Zeenat Aman plays the villager Roopa who is drugged and raped by the wealthy Raja (Raza Murad), who gets her parents killed too. Roopa escapes and, mentored by another dacoit Mangal Singh, becomes a dacoit.

———

'Baat ki baat Hukum, agar aap mujhe Thakur Hanumant Singh kehte to aur accha lagta (As a matter of fact Sir, it would please me more if you addressed me as Thakur Hanumant Singh),' says the policeman Hanumant Singh (Amrish Puri) to his superior officer, DSP Rajender Singh (played by former Pakistani cricketer Mohsin Khan), in *Batwara* (1989). *'Oh? Toh aap Police Officer se jyada Thakur hone me fakr samajhte hain?* (Oh? So, you feel greater pride in being a "Thakur" than a policeman?),' asks DSP Rajender Singh. *'Baat ki baat Thakur sahab, bas aisa hi samajh lijiye* (As a matter of fact Thakur sahab, yes, you may say so),' replies Hanumant Singh, changing his salutation from 'Hukum (sir)' to 'Thakur sahab'.

Caste is a very significant factor in rural North India and it seeps through the police force too. In the example above, Hanumant Singh belongs to the higher caste of Thakurs and nonchalantly kills a lower-caste farmer in police custody and justifies it by saying, '*Keede makode to marte hi rehte hain* (Insects keep dying all the time).' Singh keeps referring to people he considers inferior as 'chhote log'. The caste factor also bound people on opposite sides of the law, weakening the police; for example, in the same film, rogue policeman Sumer Singh (Dharmendra) joins hands with his erstwhile rival Kalla Daku because they both belong to the same caste. More recently, Anubhav Sinha brought out the historical significance of the caste aspect of rural India ever so lucidly in *Article 15* (2019). A policeman's identity is subordinate to his identity as a Dalit, a Chamar, a Brahmin, etc. It is not the count of stars on an epaulette that is the decider. It is his caste.

Adding to the caste factor that inhibited their effectiveness in dealing with dacoits, the police in rural India were unbelievably corrupt. In *Dacait* (1987), the jailor Vishnu Pandey (Paresh Rawal) shoots two innocent labourers and reports to the superintendent that he has successfully eliminated two dacoits in an encounter. Yes, the police in mofussil towns is a law unto itself, far as it is from the glare of news media and aided by weak supervision by their superiors. This enabled policemen like Vishnu

Pandey to run an extortion racket in the same village for years without getting transferred.

——

There have been many on-screen dacoits whose motivation to become the terrifying villains they were did not draw from any past trauma or injustices meted out to them, their family or community. It simply suited them to be the fiends they were.

In addition to Raaka (*Jis Desh Mein Ganga Behati Hai*) and Jagga (*Awara*), there were Chandan Singh aka Nawab Sikander aka Dharma (Pran) in *Dharma* (1973), Mangal (Narendra Nath) in *Jwala Daku* (1981)[45] and Hiralal in *Paraya Dhan* (1971) who killed and looted for money just like Raaka did, with no backstory of any injustice to justify their behaviour. Unlike the good-hearted, Robin Hood-ian dacoits, the ones in *Dharma*, *Jwala Daku* and *Paraya Dhan* lacked rectitude. In *Dharma* (1973), Bhairav Singh (Rajan Haskar) tries to rape his sardar Dharam Singh's wife and in *Mera Vachan Geeta ki Kasam* (1977) Mangal (Ajit) rapes the village lass Champa (Saira Banu).

When it came to the actors who played these dacoit-villains in the 1960s and early 1970s, apart from Pran and K.N. Singh, the larder for the pure black dacoit-villain was empty. In the pre-1975 era, however, there emerged a new face that came as a breath of fresh air on the silver screen. In *Mera Gaon Mera Desh* (1971), the dreaded Daku Jabbar Singh points the barrel towards a six-year-old boy and, with lesser hesitation than that of a jungle beast gorging on a rabbit, pulls the trigger. The boy's father has already been gunned down by Jabbar Singh moments earlier, despite pitiful pleas for mercy from the victim and his wife. Who was this dreaded monster? It was none other than Vinod Khanna, arguably the handsomest villain Bollywood had seen. Suspending the hero-dominance legacy, the audience began applauding for Daku Jabbar Singh more than the hero. Vinod Khanna, the new star-villain, had arrived. Unlike his contemporaries, Vinod Khanna almost legitimized the villain that he played. He got to play the bad dacoit Sarju once again in *Patthar aur Payal* (1974). The film was about interpersonal rivalries within a group of dacoits, first triggered when a dacoit named Mahavir (Ram Mohan) surrenders himself to the police. A traitor has no place in the team, and he is soon gunned down by Sardar (Ajit) and his men, something which aggravates Mahavir's brother and second in lead Sarju (Vinod Khanna). Sardar's brother Chhote Thakur falling in love with a village girl Sapna (Hema Malini)—whom Sarju had tried to rape—furthers the rift.

Khanna's run as a villain was, however, short-lived.

Not all these black dacoits lacked a moral compass. For instance, if any gang member were to torment the weak, the sardar would be quick to chastise him. In both *Paan Singh Tomar* (2012) and *Bandit Queen* (1994), the outlaws promise the safety of women and children during raids in villages. In *Mera Saaya* (1966), Daku Suryavar Singh (Prem Chopra), reunites Geeta (Sadhana) with her husband Thakur Rakesh Singh (Sunil Dutt), even as life ebbs out of him. The dacoits did indulge in watching nautch girls dance, but that was because they wanted entertainment; unlike the zamindars, they never raped women. Not even Gabbar. In the sequence in which Gabbar forces Basanti to dance, he does not touch Basanti inappropriately. In *Sonchiriya* (2019), hardened baaghis (rebels, outlaws) furiously debate amongst themselves and eventually decide to help a young villager woman take her wounded twelve-year-old sister to Dhaulpur hospital. They know the risk but they are also chivalrous in their own rustic way.

An incident occurred during the shooting of the song 'Jab tak hai jaan'. 'In the heat of the performance, Amjad gripped Hema's arm a little too tightly. It hurt .... By the evening, Hema's arm was sore and the bruises showed. At the dinner table, Dharmendra could barely control his anger.'[46]

Not all dacoit films were based in the ravines of Chambal valley, or even in India for that matter. A few were spin-offs from the *Arabian Nights*, such as the Indo–Russian ventures *Alibaba aur 40 Chor* (1980) and *Ajooba* (1991) or *Baghdad ka Chor* (1977) in which the plunderers charging on horseback from behind the sand dunes, were straight out of the bedtime tales we tell children—and therefore, pure fun to watch. However, as these films were not very well made, these raiders vanished like mirages, leaving little scope of public recall.

Sanjay Khan's *Abdullah* (1980), however, was an imaginative adaptation of the story of Lord Krishna's birth. In the film, the ferocious Arabian raider, Khaleel (Danny Denzongpa)—the equivalent of the mythological rogue King Kamsa—loots hamlets in the desert regularly upon the advice of the sorcerer (Bob Christo), his sidekick. On being told by the sorcerer that he would be killed by Krishna, a child born to the late Yashoda (Farida Jalal), Khaleel embarks on a mission of killing the child. Between him and his mission stands one man—Abdullah (Raj Kapoor).

Danny's on-screen chemistry with Abdullah (Raj Kapoor), in fact, made a huge impact, even overshadowing the hero Sanjay Khan. The actor had had a very unique experience that he shared: 'Abdullah was the second film directed by Sanjay (Khan). Here is where I had a direct confrontation with Raj Kapoor. I was an established villain by then. We were all clad in exotic costumes and riding horses in Rajasthan where we were shooting. I love horses, by the way. After shooting for a week Rajji arrived. I had a very important sequence with him in which I had to abuse him, shake him up, call him "buddhe" (old hag). I was feeling very uncomfortable and nervous. Now I had met Rajji when I was in FTII. He would throw parties for us, sing songs with us. But I had never acted with him. I told Abbas bhai (Sanjay) that I was feeling very nervous and requested him for some lighter scenes with Rajji to start with. But Abbas said, "No yaar, *is jagah pe yahi* sequence *hoga*. (No yaar, there can only be this particular sequence at this point.)" So, I remember waiting for Rajji, even as the costume man was trying to fix a turban on my head. And then Rajji arrives in his jeep, seated on the front seat, amidst a cloud of dust. I got my pugree removed and bowed down to touch his feet. Guess what? He pulled his feet away, gave me a dirty look and walked away. I went back to my seat tying my turban and feeling very hurt wondering how such a great man, whom I appreciated so much, could behave with a newcomer this way. Slowly the hurt turned into burning anger. The shot was ready. During the shot, I grabbed him, shoved him on the ground, picked him up, crucified him and abused him. There was so much anger in me that the shot was okayed in the first take. And then ... Raj Kapoor comes to me, smiles at me and says, "I helped you, right?" He had acted in a cold manner with me deliberately to create that anger and hatred inside me, so that I could do that scene realistically! I bent to touch his feet and this time, he did not move his feet away. "I know how to coax the actor," he said. After that we became very close.

'Abbas bhai later told me that he and Raj Kapoor had planned that act all along!'

3

Robin, Phoolan, Veerappan
The Biopics

In Indian crime folklore, three dacoits have carved out a cult status for themselves: Sultana Daku (the Indian Robin Hood), Phoolan Devi and Veerappan, and their lives have been the subject of biographies that have been turned into films.

The story of Mohammad Hussain's *Sultana Daku* (1972), with his favourite hero Dara Singh in the title role, was very similar to the true-life Sultana Daku, but the film *Sultana Daku* succumbed to poor production values. However, Anurag Kashyap's highly acclaimed *Gangs of Wasseypur* (2012) showed Sultana Daku (played by Pramod Pathak) to be alive even in 1941 when, officially, he was known to have been sent to the gallows by the British government in 1924.

The real-life Sultana Daku had abducted a nautch girl named Putli Bai, who later became his wife. There were two films with the title *Putlibai*, one each in 1972 (released in a staggered manner across the country, reaching theatres in eastern India in 1977) and 1999. Though not official biopics, the storylines in both ran close to the truth that Putlibai (played by Jaya Mala and Shivangi, respectively) was a nachnewali (dancing girl) who gets abducted by a dacoit Sultan Singh (played by Sujit Kumar and Hitesh, respectively). 'The name Sultana Daku may have been changed to Sultan Singh in the 1972 film to avoid any censorship objections around the glorification of the real-life dacoit,' opined Kaushik Bhaumik. The 1999 version of Putli Bai was consistent with Putli Bai taking over the dacoit gang as its head, following Sultan Singh's death, just the way that the real-life Putlibai had taken over the mantle from the real-life Sultana Daku.

Shekhar Kapur's *Bandit Queen* (1996) is an official biopic of popular Chambal dacoit Phoolan Devi. According to *The Guardian*, the events in the film are based on the prison diaries of Phoolan Devi herself, as narrated to Mala Sen.[47] These diaries were compiled and published as *India's Bandit Queen: The True Story of Phoolan Devi* (The Harvill Press, 1991). A victim of poverty, child marriage and repeated sexual abuse and violation, Phoolan went on to head a gang of bandits and later became a Member of Parliament. An eleven-year-old Phoolan gets raped by her husband, groped by the village headman's son, gets thrown out of the village and is raped by the police. Her life story was a window through which one witnesses the oppression and caste-related discrimination that exist in society.

Actor Saurabh Shukla (who played the role of Kailash in *Bandit Queen*) said in an interview with the author, 'Seema Biswas was my colleague in the National School of Drama Repertory in Delhi. Director Shekhar Kapur had heard of her and he contacted her for the role of Phoolan Devi. Seema wasn't sure whether to do this film or not because people could have called that film anything, even a porn film, because of the nudity it depicted. But we had full faith in the film and in Shekhar.' The faith did not go unanswered. Among the numerous awards it won, *Bandit Queen* also received the National Film Awards for Best Feature Film in Hindi and Best Actress in 1996. In fact, in response to a tweet from director Ram Gopal Verma about *Bandit Queen*, Shekhar Kapur said: 'I think it's my best film because it was shot completely intuitively.'[48]

Paan Singh Tomar was a soldier in the Indian Army and a seven-time gold-medal winner of the 3000-metre Steeplechase at the National Games, and a national record holder in this category. He also represented India at the 1958 Asian Games. But Paan Singh Tomar got into a land dispute with his cousin Babbu Singh Tomar, his nephew and a rogue landowner leading Paan Singh to gun down Babbu, thus forcing Paan Singh to turn into a baaghi. Paan Singh Tomar was ultimately shot to death on 1 October 1981 in a police encounter in Bhind, Madhya Pradesh. The 2012 Tigmanshu Dhulia film *Paan Singh Tomar* is based on Tomar's life, with Irrfan Khan in the lead role. It was a huge commercial success and also won several awards including two National Awards in 2013.

Veerappan, the sandalwood dacoit who had eluded law for twenty years in the jungles of Mysore and Tamil Nadu, too, was 'honoured' with a biopic in the form of *Veerappan* (2016) by Ram Gopal Verma in which Sandeep Bhardwaj played the title role.

There were other notorious dacoits, too, like Daaku Maan Singh on whose life *Mujhe Jeene Do* (1963) was based. This Moni Bhattacharjee film, starring Sunil Dutt as Dacoit Jarnail Singh and Waheeda Rehman as Chameli, was shot in the Bhind-Morena ravines of Chambal valley. Jarnail Singh was a heartless and unscrupulous monster. In the first couple of scenes he commits two murders; one of the victims has a wife with a baby in her arms, but even her pleas for mercy don't faze Jarnail. Complex in its composition, the film touched upon various angles relevant then and even now, like a Hindu, Jarnail Singh, marrying a Muslim, Chameli, the conundrum associated when an outlaw aspires to a normal, healthy life, and most importantly, how difficult the assimilation back into society can be. In as much, the story surely was a part template for dacoit-based films like *Pathar aur Payal* (1974) and *Samadhi* (1972).

Sunil Dutt, who till then was cast mostly as a soft, romantic lead (with exceptions like *Mother India*), essayed the role of a hardened criminal who has a change of heart commendably.

'Sunil Dutt's intention was to show the reality of dacoits, and that was the interesting thing about the film—eighty-five per cent of the story was based on real-life incidents, including those involving the notorious "daaku" Maan Singh,' stated Waheeda Rehman of *Mujhe Jeene Do*.[49] As Madhavi Pothukuchi wrote in an *India Today* article, *Mujhe Jeene Do* has been considered to be 'one of the most accurate portrayals of dacoits on the silver screen'.[50]

Wounded—The Bandit Queen (2007) is a biopic of the infamous dacoit Seema Parihar, who was born into a Thakur family in Uttar Pradesh. Seema was kidnapped from her home at the age of thirteen and became a dacoit a few years later. She married another dacoit Nirbhay Singh Gujjar. The film *Wounded* was a rare instance of the real-life character, Parihar, being played by the character herself.

Surprisingly, one does not come across any film on the dreaded dacoits Baagi Nirbhay Singh Gujjar, Shiv Kumar Patel (Dadua), Sarla Jatav (part of Nirbhay Singh Gujjars gang and partly responsible for the destruction of the gang), Malkhan Singh (who surrendered to the police in 1982 when Arjun Singh was the Chief Minister of Madhya Pradesh), Rambabu and Dayaram Garadiya.

There was a living, breathing dacoit whose fictionalized version became so larger than life that people forgot that there was indeed a real person of the same name—Gabbar Singh.

The real Gabbar Singh (also known as Gabra) was born in 1926 in the Bhind district of Madhya Pradesh and he was active between 1955 and early 1960s. He had chopped off the noses of over a hundred people, reportedly upon the advice of a tantric. In the late 1960s, writer Salim Khan's father, who had been a Deputy Inspector General of Police at Indore, narrated the terror tales of dacoit Gabbar Singh in the 1950s to Salim. And that is how Gabbar Singh became a part of the script of *Sholay*.

Danny Denzongpa was the original choice for the role of Gabbar. But he did not accept it given his commitment to his friend Feroze Khan for Dharmatma. *In an interview with the author in 2010, actor Ranjeet made a revelation. 'I was shooting in Bangalore for a film with S. Ramanathan when they approached me for the Gabbar role. Ethically I did not sign the film because Danny is a good friend of mine. I told them that I would sign it if they got me a no-objection certificate from Danny.' Other names which had come up for the role were Premnath and Amitabh Bachchan himself (once he read the script). Ironically, Bachchan's desire was to come true many years later. He played the dacoit-villain Babban Singh in Ram Gopal Verma's* Aag *(2007)—an acknowledged remake of Sholay. It was an immeasurably big flop.*

Curiously, Ramgarh was the dacoit's haunt in Patthar aur Payal *(1973),* Sholay *(1975) and* Aakhri Daku *(1977). INR 50,000 was the police reward in all the three films with no adjustment for inflation despite the fact that there was a two-year gap between all the three films.*

It was a rather queer audition that Ramesh Sippy conducted of his prospective Gabbar. As Anupama Chopra narrates in her book on the making of *Sholay*: 'Amjad Khan filled the doorway. He was not a particularly large man, but his lumbering gait, thickset face and curly hair gave him the appearance of one. Ramesh was lying on the diwan with his back to the door. He craned his neck right and up for a look. From the low angle, Amjad loomed larger. Something clicked. "He had an interesting face," says Ramesh.

"I felt very positive."'[51]

He was going to be proved right.

4

The Good, The Bad, The Gabbar
The Curry Westerns

Meanwhile, in the early 1960s, something was happening in Hollywood. The rugged cowboy heroes of the 'Western' genre had emerged as one of the most popular heroes in the West. John Sturges's *The Magnificent 7* (1960) was an outstanding film of that genre. And then Italian–American Sergio Leone's 'Spaghetti Western' movies (the prefix 'spaghetti' owed its origin to Leone's Italian descent) took the Westerns to a new high. Made between 1964 and 1966, Leone's 'Dollars' trilogy', which included *A Fistful of Dollars*, *For a Few Dollars More* and *The Good, The Bad and The Ugly* immortalized lead actor Clint Eastwood's 'cool guy' image. In 1968, Sergio Leone made *Once Upon a Time in The West* with Henry Fonda as the ruthless villain who guns down an entire family.

Far away, Bombay watched. The cowboys on their horses with their rifles, their sun-tanned faces encased under Stetson-made hats, the trademark boots and buckskins, the chewed cigar hanging from the lips, their Hara-Kiri missions, the dusty towns and their terrified inhabitants, the macho pubs with their saloon-style swinging doors—all lent themselves to the desi dacoity flavour. Moreover, the Western genre, starting with the silent movie *The Great Train Robbery* (1903), too, was about revenge or about protecting territories from ranch owners (the Western equivalent of zamindars). Bollywood dacoits were now about to change the way they looked, and the bandits were to act the cowboy way.

As Danny Denzongpa said, 'Those days, during the 1970s, the cowboy films were the craze ... and our Indian film-makers were influenced by these.'

Thus arrived Narendra Bedi's *Khote Sikkay* (1974), its storyline based evidently on *The Magnificent 7*. Further, Bedi borrowed heavily from the Spaghetti Western cult: whether it was the swagger, the cape or the street-corner shootouts. Certain scenes, too, seemed to have been lifted from the English original. The opening scene with Feroze Khan as the lonely horse rider, with the sun in the background, resembles the silhouetted horse rider in the opening credit roll of *A Fistful of Dollars*. As Danny Denzongpa said, 'This was something absolutely typical of Feroze bhai playing the cowboy in that cameo role of the "Man with no name".'

While the theme score was a lift from that of *For a Few Dollars More*, the extremely popular melody from *The Good, The Bad and The Ugly* was also used in some of the sequences.

And, yet, the Western clothes in *Khote Sikkay* were an honestly refreshing change from the standard attire and vermilion-smeared foreheads. The glares were replaced by a beer-cool attitude and there was plenty of raucous comedy that were used as fillers. *Khote Sikkay* is the story of five small-time crooks—Danny (Danny), Jaggu (Narendranath), Salim (Ranjeet), Bhaggu (Sudhir) and Jeet (Kumarajit)—and one village bumpkin—Ramu (Paintal)—being guided by a man with no name (Feroze Khan), in saving a village from the bandit Janga (Ajit) and his henchmen. Janga is the quintessential bad dacoit, who kills the judge (Satyen Kappu) who had sentenced him to lifetime imprisonment. It is revealed much later in the film that the nameless Clintesque hero is the son of the judge who Janga had killed, and while he creates a team to protect the village from Janga, he too has a personal axe to grind with Janga. While Janga always carries a gun, it is his machete he uses to kill people. The film has a softer side too, and ventures into territories like widow remarriage (Madhu Chanda plays Madhu, a widow who falls in love with Jaggu). An inspiration for *Sholay* perhaps?

But the core plot hardly shifts from the violence laden ambience. No wonder, the first dialogue of the film was '*Kamine kutte*', spoken by Janga, setting the expectations rather directly. And to the point.

Danny shared a few anecdotes from the time the film was being shot. 'We had a terrific time shooting at Udaipur. In a fight scene between Ajit sahib and Feroze Khan, Feroze Khan kicked Ajit sahib in the face. But Ajit sahib did not react in time, and the shoe caught Ajit sahib on the eye, causing an injury. The shooting was cancelled. We packed up and came back to Bombay. A month later, we were back in Udaipur. Guess what? The same shot was taken and Ajit sahib got hit again! Luckily, this time Feroze Khan was cautious and had swung his boot much slower. So, the damage wasn't serious. Ajit sahib was sent to the hospital; he stayed there for four–five days. There was more off-screen drama. Then, at the time of editing the film, we noticed a continuity glitch. In one of the shots, Ajit sahib had forgotten to take off the goggles! And for that particular shot we had to go back to Udaipur again for a day, arrange crowd, action, horses all over again.'

Khote Sikkay was not the only film that was inspired by the Western genre or the Spaghetti Western genre of Hollywood movies. In fact, *The Magnificent 7* was not an original itself. Elucidated Danny, '*The Magnificent 7* was based on Akira Kurosawa's *Seven Samurai* (1954). So, in quite a few Bollywood films like *China Gate*, *Sholay*, *Chor Machaye Shor*, etc., the basic themes were all taken from *Seven Samurai*.'

And then, a year later, in 1975, came *Sholay* …. And Gabbar …

Gabbar Singh was, as Javed Akhtar defined him (in multiple interviews)—pure evil. There is not an iota of virtue about him. He terrorizes people, loots villagers, kills colleagues in cavalier fashion, dramatizing the moments with sarcasm, and has fun wiping out an entire family including women and children without any remorse. He dresses in army fatigues, keeps a week-long stubble, has probably never combed his hair and chews tobacco. There had been evil dacoits before him but the manner in which Gabbar goes about doing things is very different. He is gruesome and rustic but does not raise his voice unnecessarily. But when he does, it is fatal. He has a sense of great pride in himself and walks the ground as if he owned the earth. His men are bound to him by sheer fear, as failure usually resulted in death. Succession planning was a term absent in his office. The deputy he loved most was possibly the weakest person in the team, who echoed exactly what his boss wanted to hear.

Within days of its release, *Filmfare*'s Bikram Singh damned *Sholay* as '... The film remains imitation Western—neither here nor there'.[52] They were right. Traditionally, dacoits on-screen have mostly been Hindus from Rajasthan, Madhya Pradesh or Uttar Pradesh. Refreshingly, *Sholay*'s Gabbar Singh did not hail from anywhere in particular, although his speech carried an Awadhi flavour. His army fatigues and threatening demeanour too, were very Hollywoodish. As Anupama Chopra quotes Javed Akhtar: 'He belonged to a place, "somewhere between Mexico and Uttar Pradesh".'[53]

It wasn't easy at all for Amjad Khan. It took a humongous effort on his part to essay the role of Gabbar. 'His army fatigues, picked up from Mumbai's Chor Bazaar, had the right weathered look. His teeth were blackened.' But Amjad struggled. 'He was nervous and it showed; his hands were stiff, his movements seemed rehearsed and his dialogue delivery was shaky. There was nothing natural about his performance; Gabbar was a stranger to Amjad .... For the rest of the schedule Amjad lived in the fatigues, trying to become Gabbar.'[54]

Such sincerity to get into the skin of the character was seen also in Joginder Shelly, who had made a sincere attempt earlier to look different as Ranga Daku in both *Ranga Khush* (1975) and in *Bindiya aur Bandook* (1972). In both the films, he tries to infuse a comedic nuance into Ranga

Daku by emitting a war cry that is midway between a canine yelp and
a horse-like neigh. Later, Joginder went on to file a legal case against
Ramesh Sippy, alleging that Sippy's Gabbar had copied Ranga Daku's
style of dialogue delivery. The truth is that dressing the dacoits including
Gabbar Singh in police/army fatigues and a week-old stubble was
derived from renowned journalist and writer Taroon Coomar Bhaduri's
works on the dacoits of Chambal. Bhaduri had worked in that area for
decades and had published many articles and books such as *Abhisapta
Chambal* and *Behad Bagi Bonduk*. However, the writer-duo for *Sholay*
never acknowledged their debt to Bhaduri's work as the source material.
In an interview with *The Indian Express* in Jan 2015, Bhaduri's daughter,
Jaya Bachchan (née Bhaduri) said that no film-maker that made dacoit
films had ever given credit to her father.[55]

And Bollywood film-makers saw no point in denying the Hollywood
Western inspiration either. Raj Kumar Santoshi's *China Gate* (1998)
opens with '*Our humble tribute to Late Akira Kurosawa.*' Jageera Singh, the
dacoit, was played by debutant Mukesh Tiwari who put up an impressive
performance intoning an Awadhi accent in a musical cadence.

> *Danny, who plays Major Gurung, shared his experience of acting in
> China Gate, 'The item song "Chamma Chamma" (pictured on Urmila
> Matondkar) was picturized when I was away in Mexico shooting for
> another Rajkumar Santoshi film* Pukar *(2000) The ending of* "Chamma
> Chamma" *was in Pahadi tune and that was to be aptly picturized on
> Gurung (me). But I could not come back from Mexico on time. Raaj
> Kumar came back for the song, however. The Pahadi piece in the coda was
> picturized on Amrish Puri.'*

Pramod Chakravarty too got bitten by the cowboy bug and made *Jagir*
(1984) with three hipsters—a superannuated Dharmendra, the evergreen
Danny and the then box-office darling, Mithun Chakraborty. Their
treasure hunt often culminated in discovering chests buried a few yards

under the ground. The contents of the chests were mostly mint-fresh currency notes. Good research has rarely been Bollywood's forte. And in the 1980s, anything could get palmed, too, to the audience. In *Wanted: Dead or Alive* (1984), it was hard to explain why passengers in a suburban Indian railway station would sport cowboy hats and boots—or for that matter, why rural Indian farmers would be in Western clothes! Or why everybody smoked cigars instead of cigarettes. As Kaushik Bhaumik summed it up, 'These (the imitation Western characters) are strange characters belonging nowhere ...' From the pub brawls to card games, Mithun's cape to the scarred faces in shaggy beards, to the background score, *Wanted* was very unwanted by the metro audience.

But a new term was coined for this genre—'Curry Western', a term given by the British press post 1975, according to lyricist and poet Amit Khanna. 'Curry Western', or an Indian adaptation of a Western, became a very popular term in film circles.

In the pre-*Khote Sikkay* era, one didn't see much creativity in the characterization and costumes of the screen-dacoits. But outlaw Vikram (Amjad Khan) in *Mr Natwarlal* (1979) speaks good English and had designed a techno-savvy hideout. And his men look rather handsome in trendy white jerseys with an elaborate 'V' on their jersey front, black trousers and a black sash around their waists. Even the notorious Daku Mangal Singh's (Vinod Khanna) team in *Aakhri Daku* (1978) look very chic in their jackets and corduroys.

There have been urban versions of these outlaws too. *36 Ghante* was a rip-off from the Humphrey Bogart starrer *The Desperate Hours* (1955), with a few ideas borrowed from the James Hadley Chase novel *One Bright Summer Morning*. Three burglars, Himmat (Sunil Dutt), Dilawar (Danny Denzongpa) and Ajit (Ranjeet) get arrested by the police for a daring bank burglary. But the outlaws manage to escape and hide in the residence of a journalist, Ashok Rai (Raaj Kumar), and hold his family hostage. The hold-up lasts thirty-six hours before they are all killed by the police. Danny reminisced, 'It was wonderful working with Dutt sahib

(Sunil Dutt) and Goli (Ranjeet). The shooting was during summer at Famous Studios. Now, I never used to shoot during summer time in Bombay as I used to run away to Sikkim. So I requested the director if they could turn the temperature at the studio down. There was a problem with the AC, but they fixed it soon and we completed the shoot in one and a half months in one single schedule. It was totally an indoor shoot.'

But then, what happened to this dacoit/curry Western genre of villains? Where are they?

5

Aa Ab Laut Chalen
The End of Dacoits

Dacoity was never a long-term prospect for personal and economic reasons.

For one, life must have been boring for dacoits. They could not pamper themselves as they were always crawling on their elbows and knees, and their backsides must have gotten sore from riding on horseback. Even when they ventured out into the villages, they had to keep their faces half-covered with smelly shawls to hide their identities. The dacoits were hermetic, almost ascetic, condemned to a Crusoe-like lifestyle. For security reasons, apart from the odd barbeque dinners, nautch girl entertainment or a eunuch show they could not provide themselves with any entertainment. Or the odd occasions like *Patthar aur Payal*, where their sardar would 'sponsor' their visit to a local village to enjoy the mela. They would be forced to meet their family members under cover, infrequently and fleetingly. They were deprived of even basics, like electricity. Their caves were lit only by fire-torches, adding to the subterfuge. As Daku Mangal Singh (Vinod Khanna) himself admits to his gang members in *Aakhri Daku*, '*Is zindagi me rakha hi kya hai? Itni sari daulat hone ke bawajood, humare paas na koi ghar hai na thikana* (What life is this? Despite having so much wealth, we have home or place that we can call our own).' A smuggler could become a businessman and a politician could become a real-estate promoter. A rogue sahukar could float a cooperative bank or a chit fund company. While the mafia ran scalable financial rackets, could a dacoit even have a bank account? They were that vulnerable as their loot could not be in circulation. It was a life of slealth despite wealth, of camouflage and forced frugality.

The dacoits had one quality though, which nobody could match— they all must have been born with laser vision. Despite no electricity in their hideouts, rarely has any dacoit been seen wearing glasses.

The dacoits haughtily lorded over the uneducated village hicks. 'They lived in the delusion that they were sovereign over a small patch of land,' as Kaushik Bhaumik puts it. But even for Gabbar Singh, the mightiest dacoit in the history of Bollywood, his writ ran no more than 50 kos (151 kilometres). Anywhere outside their circle of influence, they were totally powerless. When they ventured into the big city they would be referred to as doodhwallah bhaiyyas or junglee dehati (as Madan Puri and Premnath call the dacoits who come visiting the city in *Pran Jaaye Par Vachan Na Jaaye (1974)*). In *Bandit Queen* (1994), a paan-chewing quack in Kanpur town easily blackmails the two powerful dacoits Vikram and Phoolan of six thousand rupees.

And with feudal revenge as the only motive for the dacoits, the 'what after that?' question begged an answer. Often, it was death in police crossfire or captivity or separation from family, or reform. With the coming of helicopters, loitering in the open was like offering target practice. In the landscape of the ravines they could not occupy high positions for fear of being spotted. And the urbanization of rural India, coupled with technology like Google maps, mobile signal detection and other technology have smoked out the dacoits even from inside the jungles. Veerappan was liquidated in 2004. Seema Parihar surrendered in 2006. These were among the last of the dinosaurs.[56]

Invariably, all the good dacoits (and a few of the bad ones as well) demonstrated a propensity to shun their ways and join the mainstream society after all. All it took, it seemed, was a good scolding by the leading lady. In *Samadhi, Mujhe Jeene Do, Patthar Aur Payal* and *Khalnaayak*, when the leading lady held in captivity by the dacoit chastises them over their evil ways or display an equivalent valour, they reform, agree to marry the lady and even surrender to the police! In *Pran Jaaye Par Vachan Na Jaaye*, the nautch girl Janiya (Rekha) crushes the bandit leader's braggadocio calling him unworthy of being able to feed a beggar, winning instant respect from the dacoit who had addressed her as a 'randi' (prostitute) a minute ago. In *Sonchiriya* (2019), a story set in 1975, a few dacoits of Man Singh's (Manoj Bajpayee) gang contemplate surrendering to the police who had promised them amnesty. Prison seems safer to them. There is also the promise of regular food. Clearly, they have had enough of the life of covertness and constant fear. Further, they are also haunted by their past karma of having done to death a small girl child, albeit unwillingly. As they repent their act, they have the premonition that their karma may chase them down before the police do.

In an interview with the author, Saurabh Shukla shared an incident about the last sequence in *Bandit Queen*, before Phoolan Devi surrenders to the police. She asks Kailash (Saurabh Shukla) if he has any guns: he replies that he has water. 'Shekhar Kapur had suggested that we have a constant smile on our faces while we spoke their dialogues. Kapur had explained: "She is in a distress situation. And she needs help. The only man she can count on is Kailash. And she knows that Kailash was and is in love with her. So, when she smiles it is almost a reminder that you remember the smile of the girl. The smile was to bring back the memories." Shekhar said, "Saurabh, you will smile as if to say, 'I do remember you and your smile but nothing is going to work'".'

A few of them were lucky enough to leave the dacoity legacy behind and move on. In *Mujhe Jeene Do* (1963), the grandson of Dacoit Zalim Singh transforms into a zamindar two generations later. But some of the dacoits couldn't erase their past. In *Hatyara* (1977), the son of the reformed dacoit is ostracized by society for a past that he was not responsible for.

The famous North-Indian festival of Raksha Bandhan often proved to be a Waterloo for the dacoits, as in *Hatyara* and *Putlibai* (1999). The police would figure out that the siblings, unable to resist the urge to celebrate the brother–sister festival would end up at their sibling's place. In *Chambal ki Kasam* (1980), the two brothers on opposite sides of the law do meet at their sister's place, but strangely, decide not to confront each other on the auspicious occasion.

Their time ran out. The dacoit genre faded. What survived were the spoofs and parodies. With the exception of Raaka and Birju, all the filmi dacoits have ebbed from public memory. Of course, Gabbar Singh is immortal, and continues to be part of popular culture.

Gabbar was the most prominent fictional character to be featured, using the same set and the actors, in advertisements in India. An ad, conceptualized by Lintas was shot when *Sholay* was on its way to become *the* cult film of India. The ad was screened during the interval of the film. The product was Britannia Glucose D biscuits—*Gabbar ki asli pasand*. 'Kids couldn't get enough of Gabbar or Glucose. Sales doubled,' writes Anupama Chopra.[57] Subsequently, mime artistes have made their livelihoods by aping Amjad Khan's portrayal of the role. Amjad Khan acted in his own spoof *Ramgarh ke Sholay* (1992)—and played Gabbar Singh, who had been released from prison. This was one of his last films before his untimely death.

But Gabbar continues to inspire the characterization of villains in Hindi cinema. In Sanjay Gupta's *Shootout at Wadala* (2013), one can find a variant of the Glucose D ad hanging from the wall at Sunny Leone's kotha ....

IV

PAGLA KAHIN KA
The Mentally Ill

Could it be that the bad men that we spoke of in earlier chapters suffered from some mental condition that evinced in this form of antagonistic behaviour? *Sholay*'s Gabbar Singh's uncontrollable laughter at three misfired bullets is perhaps as irrational as that of Arthur Fleck's (Joaquin Phoenix) repeated fits of laughter in *Joker* (2019). In the latter, Fleck's documented medical records show that his condition was due to childhood trauma and abuse. But Gabbar's backstory showed no stated mental sickness (implicit or otherwise). The script chose to focus only on his antagonistic behaviour. Also, in a majority of Bollywood films, a person is either totally mad or perfectly sane. The scriptwriters could not discern the nuances. The 'paagal' person has been the stereotypical asylum inmate who tears clothes, laughs like a hyena, suddenly starts weeping, often wears a shaggy beard, and barks at the moon. There were a few exceptions, though, that made for very interesting dark characters with a mental condition.

1

K ... K ... K ... Kiran
The Psychotics

In the 1940 film *Pagal*, Dr Vasant (Prithviraj Kapoor) plays a doctor in charge of a mental asylum. Dr Vasant had been deceived into marrying Chhaya (Khatun) instead of her prettier sister Parvati (Madhuri). When he looks at his wife, he is reminded of her sister—the one whom Dr Vasant really loves. In his obsession for Parvati he loses his sense of rationality and professional ethics. Dr Vasant injects a drug into Parvati that makes her insane and, with her in that state of madness, he makes love to her. He himself goes insane later and ends up murdering his wife Chhaya.[58] The story peg is not so much about Dr Vasant's villainous acts as his mental instability that was the *root cause* of his antagonistic behaviour. *Pagal* is arguably India's first film around the subject of psychosis. Prithviraj Kapoor's performance as the psychotic doctor was hailed even by a critic of the stature of Baburao Patel in the August 1940 edition of *FilmIndia*. 'The development of the theme was psychological and within natural limits of intellectual understanding ...' he wrote.[59]

143

Of the many attributes of those suffering from psychosis, irrationality is perhaps one of the most obvious ones, i.e., the motives of those suffering from psychosis appear irrational in the world inhabited by those who are labelled 'normal'. In *Agni Pareeksha* (1980) Alok (Amol Palekar), traumatized in childhood from his father's suicide, becomes mentally sick. As a grown-up, even post extensive psychiatric treatment, he demonstrates wild mood swings, an irrational possessiveness about people and needs constant emotional support and the companionship of his friend Sidharth (Parikshit Sahni). But when Alok discovers that both he and Sidharth have a common love interest, Meeta (Rameshwari), his psychotic traits surface in acts like the attempted murder of Sidharth and the cold murder of Sidharth's pet dog. Finally, Alok kills himself and makes it look like murder to get Sidharth implicated.

Remember Kunwar Saheb (Premnath) in *Teesri Manzil* (1966)? He commits three murders. Kunwar Saheb's wife catches him red-handed in bed with another woman. In the ensuing tussle, the gun goes off, killing Kunwar Saheb's wife. But there happen to be two 'accidental' witnesses to the crime and Kunwar saheb has to kill them too. Amol (Amol Palekar) in *Khamosh* (1985) too commits four murders. Soni (Soni Razdan) gets pregnant with Amol's child and she threatens to expose him, an eventuality that could ruin Amol's chances at the election that he is planning to contest. Amol kills Soni and is in a similar bind as he has to now dispose off three more witnesses. Both Kunwar Saheb and Amol are killing for pragmatic reasons. So, what is the difference between Kunwar Saheb and Amol? Kunwar Sahab demonstrates a sincere sense of remorse. He admits that his crimes have bought him a ticket to the gallows—and he prefers to atone for his sins by leaping to his death. Whereas in Amol's case, he progressively develops an insensitivity and, in the climax, actually admits, '*Ab to mujhe ye sab karne me mazaa bhi aane laga tha* (By now I had started enjoying killing),' he admits. In other words, he's become a psychopath.

Amol Palekar recounted a little-known fact about the climax scene in the film (the one in which Shabana discovers that Amol was the killer and Amol captures her), that illustrates the mental condition of the character Amol, 'The original climax scene was set on a golf course. And then, while going through the script at Vidhu's place with editor Renu Saluja and Sudhir Mishra, I said, "Vinod, I have an idea. Now, instead of the standard loud announcement of 'I am going to kill you!', what if, in a whispered tone, I give a very factual, step-by-step cold description to Shabana of how I was going to kill her? Would the effect be more threatening and more blood chilling?" Vinod and Renu got very excited and asked Sudhir to rewrite the final climax scene basis my idea. And Sudhir went into another room and started rewriting the scene. All this was a very collective effort. Also, director Vidhu Vinod wanted this cold menace.' This coldness made the difference. '*Daro mat Shabana. Shabana, mere paas aao* (Don't be scared, Shabana. Come to me, Shabana),' Amol calls out to her in a whisper, smiling when she tries to hide and slither away from him. His left eye twitches, and eyeballs bulge. '*Mai majboor hoon. Ab to mujhe tumhari jaan leni hi padegi na? Tum samajhti kyon nahi? Huh?* (I'm in a fix. I have to end your life now. Why don't you understand?)' he explains in a silky soft voice the way a caring parent would explain to a child why it needed to be admonished. It showed an inner medical condition as opposed to a common villainy. And Amol Palekar was a middle-of-the-road hero who preferred to play unconventional roles like these. Said Palekar in a chat with the author in Pune, 'I was not interested in becoming one of those "larger-than-life" Angry Young Men, macho or romantic heroes. I defined myself as a man who, whatever he did, was believable. And thus, in my roles, I tried to bring out the vulnerability of a person and that made the characters identifiable and even likeable. People could look at me and think, "Yes, I have a friend who behaves just like this guy on screen".'

By the mid-1980s the established mainstream Bollywood heroes were ageing. But they refused to compromise on their conventional hero images that had made them the stars they were. Even the next generation of heroes that took over the baton between 1982 and 1990—Sunny Deol, Kumar Gaurav, Sanjay Dutt, Anil Kapoor, Aamir Khan, Salman Khan, Jackie Shroff—continued playing predictable macho/romantic heroes, almost as if they were worried about diluting their fan base if they did anything else.

It took an outsider to break the norm; a non-Bombayite.

'Want to become a Hindi film hero? You've got to be mad,' parents often tell their children. A Delhi-born actor, who began his career with roles in television serials, did exactly that. He almost became the face of the disturbed, reclusive young man, obsessed with cold revenge or love.

His name was Shah Rukh Khan.

There is only one ambition that consumes Ajay (aka Vicky) in Abbas-Mustan's *Baazigar* (1993): avenging his father Vishwanath Sharma (Ananth Mahadevan) for the betrayal he receives in return for the faith he bestows in his trusted employee, Madan Chopra (Dalip Tahil). A betrayal that leads to the eventual, tragic death of his father, the death of his younger sister and causes his mother to lose her mental equilibrium. Hatred devours Ajay, and he plots to rip apart the Chopra family through deceit and murder. So why does Ajay, who pursues a good motive of avenging his parents' death and humiliation albeit through illegal means, not feature in the anti-hero chapter that comes later in this book? The reason is—the anti-heroes, like the Vijays of *Deewar*, *Zanjeer* and *Trishul* and Shankar of *Yaadon ki Baaraat*, have the morality to ensure that the innocent ones in the enemy camp did not get hurt.

But Ajay in *Baazigar* targets the innocent. First up is Madan Chopra's elder daughter Seema (Shilpa Shetty), whom Ajay kills with great relish. And then two more classmates of Seema are sent to their death in a grisly manner because they are possible witnesses to Ajay's crime. Ajay's preoccupation with wanting to inflict pain on the Chopras makes him psychologically imbalanced, to the extent that he's labelled a psychopath: one who knows he is doing something wrong but nevertheless does it.

And we do see some freaky traits in him that adhere to such a notion; for instance, he *eats* the photograph (instead of burning it), that could link him to Seema's murder.

Doubtless, like all bad men who have committed evil deeds, death visits Ajay in the end. He breathes his last in his mother's lap. But not before killing Madan Chopra. A just punishment, one would say. And yet, it is for Ajay that the audience feels the most in the end. The role won Shah Rukh Khan his first Filmfare Award for Best Actor.

What is interesting is that, initially, the story of Ajay's parents was not part of the larger plot. As Ananth Mahadevan said, 'On completing the film, Abbas–Mustan realized that the hero was actually a villain who was killing people with no motive. That was when they added the track of Ajay's parents and brought in the angle of his mother getting humiliated to justify Ajay's acts and to get him some iota of audience sympathy.'

Shah Rukh Khan followed up *Baazigar* with two definitive roles of the mentally sick OYM (Obsessed Young Man)—Rahul Mehra in Yash Chopra's *Darr* (1993) and Vijay Agnihotri in *Anjaam* (1994). Unlike *Baazigar*, neither of these was a revenge saga. These characters had problems of unalloyed obsessions—plain and simple. Rahul of *Darr* suffers from multiple disorders, in the doctor's own analysis. Rahul has always been a loner with hardly any friends. The one person he 'speaks' with frequently over the 'phone' is his mother—but she died in an automobile accident eighteen years ago. It is hinted that Rahul holds his father responsible for his mother's death since his father was the one at the steering wheel of the ill-fated car. Rahul is definitely delusional. Apart from believing that his mother is still alive, he is also deluded by his belief that Kiran (Juhi Chawla) loves him. He is the crazed lover, who stalks her, wants to be close to her, refusing to surrender to the fact that Kiran loves Sunil (Sunny Deol). Rahul's hysterical laughter, his famous stutter 'K … k … k ….k … Kiran', his suicidal self-destructiveness like walking on a high parapet, engraving '*KIRAN*' on his chest with a dagger, his homicidal tendencies like making multiple attempts at Sunil's life and murdering a drug-addicted friend all point to mental instability. So much so that, in the face of the terror caused by Rahul's persistent stalking, Kiran almost loses *her* mind. Curiously, at some level, the audience sympathizes with Rahul, especially in the penultimate scene in which he pleads with Sunil to forgive him. After all, Rahul is a motherless, lonely, sick boy who needed a bit of care and affection. But since Rahul has blood on his hands, he has to die.

Vijay Agnihotri in *Anjaam* is far worse. Unlike Rahul who becomes a recluse after his mother's death, Vijay has a mental condition that was congenital. He himself admits that, right from childhood, he believed that he had a right to ruin anything that his persuasion couldn't acquire. He starts off with trying to woo Shivani (Madhuri Dixit) in the good old way of serenading her. But Shivani's rejection aggravates his condition and he attempts to kill himself by slashing his wrists. It also turns him into a sadist and he starts killing animals for fun. On being repeatedly rebuffed by her, he murders her husband (yes, Shivani had married someone else) and later, Vijay frames Shivani in an attempted murder case and lands her in prison. Quite aptly, Shyam Benegal describes *Anjaam* as a vastly sadistic and a gratuitously manipulative film. Unlike Rahul of *Darr*, Vijay of *Anjaam* enjoys no audience sympathy. They couldn't wait to see him die. This was Shah Rukh Khan's darkest role and he never played such a black character ever again. But with these three roles, Khan shattered the paradigm that a lead actor's public image would be disadvantaged if they played mentally unsound characters.

SRK also passed on this confidence of going against the grain to his female colleagues. Isha (Kajol) in *Gupt* (1997) is insanely in love with Sahil (Bobby Deol); when they were young, she killed a pet dog that bit Sahil. Dr Gandhi's (Kulbhushan Kharbanda) diagnosis is that Isha has been mentally unstable since childhood, and also has anger management issues. Unable to accept the loss of Sahil to another woman, the familiar irrationality and dangerous symptoms of people with mental disturbance surface in Isha and she murders Sahil's father when he refuses to accept Isha as his daughter-in-law. '*Sahil ko paane ke liye mai sau khoon bhi kar sakti hoon* (To win over Sahil I am willing to commit a hundred murders),' she avers. She kills two persons and almost murders another. Kajol's gamble in accepting the antagonist's role in *Gupt* paid off as she won the Filmfare Award for Best Villain. *Gupt* was also the first time that a woman had been nominated for this category—another big leap forward for Bollywood in breaking stereotypes. We call it Kajol's gamble because prior to *Gupt*, these types of roles were reserved for the supporting cast like Simi Garewal in *Chalte Chalte* (1976) or non-mainstream heroines like Smita Patil in the psychological thriller *Haadsaa* (1983) as the leading ladies perceived these types of roles as being too risky for their public image. Simi Garewal in *Chalte Chalte* (1976) played Geeta, a psychiatric patient suffering from the trauma of having witnessed her husband's murder on their wedding night. Later, when she meets Ravi Kapoor (Vishal Anand), a lookalike of her dead husband, her unsound mind simply cannot accept that Ravi is *not* her husband. Geeta stalks Ravi, invades his private life and, finally, escapes from the mental hospital and attempts to murder Ravi's fiancée Asha (Nazneen) whom Geeta perceives as the culprit, separating her from her 'husband'. In *Haadsaa* (1983), Asha Chakravarty (Smita Patil) too is acutely delusional. She believes the car mechanic Jai (Akbar Khan) is her long-lost childhood friend Guddu. Asha stalks Jai desperately and attempts to murder Jai's girlfriend so that she can have her 'Guddu' for herself. Asha's mental condition is due an unfulfilled marriage with a wealthy husband (played by Amrish Puri) who treats Asha like a lifeless artefact. This loveless life, coming on the back of a traumatic childhood in which she had murdered her stepmother, turns Asha into a sadistic control freak who even cuts the feathers of her pet parrot so that the bird can't escape. In Asha's lifelong desert of pain and abuse, Guddu is the only island of happiness and she must have him at any cost. *Haadsaa* was partly inspired by Clint Eastwood's *Play Misty for Me* (1971) and took around five years to complete.

The stalkers' parade continued through the 1990s with Nana Patekar playing Vishwanath in *Agni Sakshi* (1996). Coming as a follow-up to the pyrophobic Anna in *Parinda* (1990), this role of the abnormally possessive husband Vishwanath fit Nana like a glove. Vishwanath keeps his wife Madhu (Manisha Koirala) under a virtual house arrest and has also banned anyone from coming home. Even when Madhu does step out, he demands a detailed account of every minute. Vishwanath's perverted and erratic behaviour, like whipping her with a belt and making love to her soon after, and his suicidal tendencies, including walking on a parapet and asking an untrained Madhu to shoot at an apple perched on his head, horrifies her. Vishwanath discloses to Madhu that he owed this condition to a bad childhood in which his parents had separated and abandoned him as a child. Madhu manages to break free from this madman and starts a new life with the new identity of Shubhangi—and marries Suraj. All appears well until she runs into Vishwanath once again and he starts stalking her. Her nightmare ends only when Vishwanath shoots himself at the end.

Of the couple of Hindi films that were inspired by the psychological thriller *Sleeping with the Enemy* (1991), *Agni Sakshi* was the one that fared well at the box office. But this genre of mentally disturbed, delusional, destructive men and women in the lead cast was clearly working with the audience in the 1990s.

All the mentally deranged characters discussed so far were consigned to death at the end, albeit with a sprinkling of sympathy at their mental malady. Their inevitable death emphasized that these people could not be rehabilitated and had to go for good at the end of the film. The serialization of these characters hadn't started happening yet. But that too changed in 2001 with Rakeysh Omprakash Mehra's *Aks* (2001), a film which bore resemblances to Hollywood's *Face/Off* (1997) in which the cop and the killer swap faces. Raghavan is a psychotic contract killer who infiltrates the security cordon of the Indian Defence Minister by wearing a face mask of the cop Manu Verma (Amitabh Bachchan) and assassinates the Defence Minister. The face mask is a metaphor for Raghavan's philosophy, '*Chehron me kya rakha hai?* (What is in a face?)', suggesting that there is a 'Raghavan (a bad man)' in every 'Manu Verma (a good man)'. Raghavan is captured but is killed in a shootout. His spirit enters Manu Verma who now turns evil, thus proving Raghavan's dark metaphysics. Said Manoj Bajpayee who played the demented villain Raghavan, 'The subject of *Aks* germinated from the conflict of good vs evil and it was Hindi filmdom's first psychological villain-based film. Mehra was trying to show the impact of what would happen if evil were to be separated from the good. Manu Verma and Raghavan were chemically one and the "same" person, according to the script. He had to become "me".' Another unique attribute that was added to Raghavan's characteristics was his reciting a line from the Bhagavad Gita after committing a murder, to justify his act. As Bajpayee explained, 'Except for the screeching laughter, Raghavan's mannerisms were meant to look like Lord Krishna, including his long, askance look.'

Aks wasn't a commercial success, but there was no denying the impression left by the villain. 'Maybe the people mistook it for a ghost movie,' added Manoj Bajpayee. But his effort to essay something new is worthy of mention. 'I worked hard on the character Raghavan for three to four months. I tried to introduce a physicality in Raghavan's gait by the cocking of the head. And the line from the Gita—that was my idea,' he disclosed.

Said Bajpayee about the scene in Aks *in which he and Bachchan jump off a waterfall, 'Amitji and I actually jumped from the 100 feet waterfall. We prepared for it for four days by taking into account the wind speed, the force of the falling water. Also, we had to be careful to keep a distance from the surface of the waterfall—getting too close meant we would have gotten sucked into it. I suffer from vertigo—fear of heights. But when I saw such a senior actor like Mr Bachchan taking up the challenge, I said to myself, "I'll do it".'*

The final frame of *Aks* leaves behind a chill of fear similar to that in *Omen* (1976) as we discover that the evil spirit of Raghavan has left the body of Manu Verma but has now entered the body of ACP Arjun Shrivastava (Abhimanyu Shekhar Singh). Just as there had been sequels to *Omen*, so there could be another *Aks*. This prospect of seriality was a novelty.

Amitabh Bachchan followed up *Aks* with the role of Vijay Singh Rajput, General Manager of Vilasrao Jefferson Bank Ltd., in *Aankhen* (2002). Vijay is a genius with a mental condition. '*Woh paagal hai* (He is mad)', says Mr Bhandari (Ajit Vachchani), one of the board members of the bank, referring to Rajput's known condition of schizophrenia. In addition to that, Rajput has a problem with anger management and had beaten up people severely in the past. The bank's top brass decides that it is dangerous to keep him on the payroll any longer. Peeved at getting fired, Rajput decides to get even with his employers and hatches an ingenious plan of robbing the bank with the help of three blind men. As the plot unfolds, Rajput toys around with those three blind men, seemingly deriving pleasure at their blindness, bringing into prominence his sadistic streak. Based on a Gujarati play, there are two versions of *Aankhen* with two different endings; one of them being that Rajput evades arrest and starts shadowing the two surviving blind men to extract the loot. 'A dangerous game is about to begin,' Rajput says, breaking into demented laughter. That same seriality again.

Another memorable psychologically unhinged antagonist was the character of Dr Aarti Mahajan (Tisca Chopra) in *Rahasya* (2014) who figures out that her daughter, Ayesha, is actually the child of the domestic help Remy fathered by Sachin (Ashish Vidyarthi), Aarti's husband. As Aarti sees Ayesha growing up and notices Ayesha's resemblance to Remy, Aarti feels a searing hatred for Ayesha.

In an interview with the author, Tisca Chopra helped with understanding the psyche of the killer: 'Something about not being able to conceive a child had taken something away from her anyway in the first place. And then this discovery that her teenaged adopted daughter turned out to be the illegitimate child of her husband with another woman, made it worse. She had reached a point when she was losing control in her head. And that is when that animalistic guttural sense comes out …. Dr Aarti Mahajan gives vent to an inner rage. And being an orthopedic surgeon, she is looking for an opportunity that is equal to the precision employed by a surgeon.' Dr Aarti Mahajan slits open the throats of the three with a scalpel—first Ayesha, followed by another servant who happened to be witness to Ayesha's murder and, later, Sachin. In the final frame, the murderess looks back over her shoulder and laughs menacingly, unfazed by the death sentence that lies ahead, a shot that came out perfectly in the very first take, shared Tisca.

Like Raghavan in *Aks*, there is an implication that Aarti could come back to cause more harm. Again, that seriality.

2

Daaaarling
The Serial Killers

And now to those who kill repeatedly without remorse. Sometimes, these killers have a specific modus operandi, and a specific type of victim; at other times, the type of victim may vary. Serial killers may be said to fall on the extreme end of psychopathic behaviour. According to Professor of Criminology Dr Scott A. Bonn, PhD, most serial killers do *not* suffer from any debilitating mental illness. Referring to case studies of psychopathic serial killers like Ted Bundy, John Wayne Gacy and Denis Rader he says, '… psychopaths such as Bundy, Gacy and Rader have an overwhelming desire and compulsion to kill that causes them to ignore the criminal law with impunity.'[60]

As the serial rapist and killer Gokul (Ashutosh Rana) admits in *Dushman* (1998), '*Ladkiyaan meri bhookh hain. Meri tujhse na teri parivar se koi zyati dushmani nahi hai.* (Women are my hunger. I have no personal enmity against you or your family).' Gokul is a sex-crazed psychopath who salivates at the thought of women and would simply murder anyone that obstructed him from quenching his thirst. He is shown as devoid of any feeling—good or bad. He kills his fiancée too by subjecting her to snakebite. He is a human form of an animal that has tasted blood. But Gokul wasn't the first character of this kind. Arguably, the first-ever hormone-crazed serial rapist was seen in *Shaitaan* (1974). From his childhood, Ashok (Shatrughan Sinha) is a sadist who ends the lives of innocent pigeons by wringing their delicate necks. This pattern grows on him and he grows up to become a demon who gets hyper-excited at the sight of women and cruelly rapes and murders them one after the other. His mother herself discloses that Ashok was born heartless and Ashok's twin brother Anand (a good cop and the protagonist of the film) too refers to him as a 'paagal khooni' (insane murderer). Ashok's condition is congenital.

Around the same time the serial killer arrived in Bollywood with *Khoon Khoon* (1973), an Indianized version of *Dirty Harry*, with Danny playing the serial killing Raghav, the counterpart to Scorpio in the original Hollywood film.

> *Interestingly,* Shaitaan *was initially conceived with just one Shatrughan Sinha in a 'Jekyll and Hyde' role. The script was redone to make it a double role.*

That was only the beginning.

Anand (Rajesh Khanna) in *Red Rose* (1980) outwardly appears to be a normal wealthy businessman but there is something furtive about his private life. There are obvious hints of Anand being sexually active, but he is neither married nor in a relationship. Anand is philanthropic enough to send his boy-servant back to school and fund his education. What is later revealed is that Anand suffered from a mental condition resulting from childhood trauma caused by repeated abuse and deceit at the hands of the women in his early life. He develops a prejudiced hatred for women and starts seeing every woman as an object of revenge. Anand becomes a psychopathic misogynist who murders young women after having sex with them and buries them in the rose garden of his bungalow. It was unusual for an actor like Rajesh Khanna to play a serial killer but he may have accepted the role in the hope of replicating the commercial success of the Tamil original *Sivappu Rojakkal* (1978) in which Kamal Haasan had played the serial-killing psychopath. The medical histories of the mental malfunctions of these serial killers were not always spelt out in the screenplays. Maybe because their behaviour made it too obvious anyway. For example, home alone on a rainy evening, a pretty young lady is scared and telephones her mother urging her to return home soon. Perfectly normal behaviour for a pretty young lady, one might say. With one small difference, though. She is a motiveless, psychopathic serial killer for whom killing is an act of fun. She plunges the knife into her victim's body and giggles, claps and hop-skips on her feet with childlike glee at the sight of the sharp metal instrument entering a human body and tearing the innards out. The egress of blood from a living person and his pitiful scream from unbearable pain excites her. The bone-chilling *Kaun?* *(1999)* with a stunning performance by Urmila Matondkar showed just how innocent and 'normal' a psychopathic serial killer can appear to the world. True, *Kaun?* resembled Roman Polanski's *Repulsion* (1965), but Ram Gopal Verma made it his own act.

The opening frame of another film *Paanch* (2001) says, '*Evil is perhaps a child. It will play any game.*' It is so true for Matondkar's character in *Kaun?* as well.

By the way, Anurag Kashyap's *Paanch* is another compelling example of a young man, Luke Morisson (Kay Kay Menon), with a severely flawed mental state. It was based on the true story of Rajendra Jakkal, a college student in Pune. Between January 1976 and March 1977, Jakkal, along with his three college mates, committed a series of gruesome murders starting with that of Achyut Joshi (a householder from Vijaynagar Colony, Pune) and ending with that of the family of the eighty-eight-year-old Sanskrit scholar, Kashinath Shastri Abhyankar.[61]

The killers were captured and hanged for what came to be known as the Joshi–Abhyankar serial murders. *Paanch* (2001) was based on this incident. What starts as a typical money issue for a bunch of college dropouts who loaf around doing drugs and jamming quickly deteriorates into outbursts over drug deals and scuffles over ticketless travel. Their leader, Luke Morrison, impulsive by nature, turns barbarous, engineering a series of grisly murders—all for money.

Actor Kay Key Menon who plays Luke Morrison said about his role in *Paanch*, 'When I read the script and got inputs about Luke Morrison, I went about living Luke in every scene and getting surprised at myself at the continual change in Luke's character. And out came the things that I didn't know existed within me. I had to be genuinely evil. I was not play-acting.'

But *Paanch* (2001) failed to ever get released in the theatres—maybe predictably, given its extremeties. And months later, when the censors did clear it, there were no buyers. But Kay Kay has no regrets. 'Since there was no yardstick of success or failure here, all the industry said was "Kay Kay Menon is a terrific actor". Period.'

Serial killers are in no hurry. Time stretches on as they keep murdering people. As Dr Scott A. Bonn states: 'Contrary to mythology, It is not high intelligence that makes serial killers successful. Instead, it is obsession, meticulous planning and a cold-blooded, often psychopathic personality that enable serial killers to operate over long periods of time without detection.'[62]

Susanna Anna-Marie Johannes (Priyanka Chopra) hands out 'punishments' to six erring husbands over a period of forty-five years in the black comedy thriller *7 Khoon Maaf* (2011), based on Ruskin Bond's story 'Susanna's Seven Husbands'. In a discussion in 2018, the author shared with us that he'd actually heard of a lady called Susanna who married seven times and each time her husband had vanished mysteriously. Bond based his short story on this real-life character. Said

Bond, 'She was something of a vigilante who had taken it upon herself to punish those men.' It was not about the count of murders that made Susanna a serial killer. It was the sense of enjoyment that she seemed to derive from her acts and how quickly she moved on from being a widowhood to being a bride. She looked so detached from each murder that, apart from the debauched policeman Keemat Lal (Annu Kapoor), none of the other men had a clue that they had married an assassin.

In an interview with the author, Kolkata-based writer Urvashi Mukherjee traced the background of the film. '7 *Khoon Maaf* was a contra of Charles Perrault's grisly 1697 novel *Bluebeard* in which the titular character marries several women and murders them on their wedding night. In a tribute to *Bluebeard*, a copy of the book is seen in one of the scenes in *7 Khoon Maaf*,' said Mukherjee.

> *In the film Susanna ages from twenty-one to sixty-five. In an interview with Bollywood Hungama, Priyanka Chopra shared that the prosthetic make-up for the older age shoots used to take five hours, necessitating her to wake up at 1.30 a.m. And removing the make-up would take a further two hours.*[63]

Raman Raghav, the real-life paranoid schizophrenic serial killer in the 1960s who remained undetected for many years, is a case in point.[64] Director Sriram Raghavan had made a docudrama on Raman Raghav sometime in the 1980s. Inspired by Sriram's docudrama, Anurag Kashyap made *Raman Raghav 2.0* (2016) with Nawazuddin Siddiqui playing the deranged serial killer Ramanna who, apart from committing the murders, also engages in a 'game' with the drug-addicted cop Raghavan Singh (Vicky Kaushal). Ramanna had witnessed Raghavan bludgeoning a drug dealer's neighbour to death and turning up at the crime scene the next morning in his police uniform. Raghavan's two-faced behaviour makes Ramanna believe that Raghavan is not only his alter ego but that Raghavan could be a worthy successor to his habitual killing. In his depraved happiness of having found someone like himself, Ramanna offers to own up to another murder that Raghavan commits. And one more psychopathic killer is born. The hunter becomes the game. Raghavan 'becomes' Ramanna.

The rather dunce-looking, bespectacled Insurance Agent Bob Biswas (Saswata Chatterjee) rings the bell and smilingly greets the elderly Agnes D'Mello with a 'Namoshkar (namaste)' when she answers the doorbell, in a way that any Bengali bhadralok (gentleman) would. Agnes returns his greeting with an equally warm 'Namoshkar'. 'Agnes D'Mello?', the chubby visitor asks. 'Yes', Agnes confirms. '*Ek minute* (One minute)', says Bob, pulls out his revolver from his office bag and shoots her twice on the spot with equal courtesy. Before walking away, Bob thinks to himself, why did Agnes look different from the picture of her that he had been given? 'Oh! Wig tha (it was a wig),' Bob surmises, smiling smugly. He is a contract killer, but it is evident that money is not his motivation. He enjoys killing people. In an interview with the author, Director Sujoy Ghosh spoke about the character Bob Biswas in *Kahaani* (2012), 'There is a saying in Bengali *"Binoyer dada Bhupati"*, which was the basis of Bob—a person humbler than the humblest person. Saswata was always the choice for the role of Bob Biswas because his face is very humble. Also, I always wanted to work with him.' Bob looks like any one of the thousands of commuters on Kolkata's metro railway. Till he gently pushes Vidya Bagchi (Vidya Balan) off the edge of platform in the face of an approaching train .... And then pulls her back in the nick of time. Bob proceeds to offers a mortified Vidya advice in a professorial tone that she should leave Kolkata. Bob Biswas not only kills but has fun tantalizing death. And the other creepy fact in that sequence is that the other commuters do not even appear to notice Bob pushing Vidya off the edge and pulling her back. They only see a portly, smiling, friendly man who looks like he would volunteer to help aged people cross the road. Only a psychopath could look so inconspicuously normal. As Sujoy Ghosh said, 'Bob was created as an average person—and that is scary because there is no way to spot him. So, anyone around you is Bob. The idea was to create fear inside the head than on screen. Nothing runs wilder than imagination especially if something is unknown.'

———

Cult, religion, black magic seems to be typical drivers of serial killing. In *Amrit Manthan* (1934) a Rajguru (high priest) has a fanatical obsession for human and animal sacrifices. In the end, Rajguru offers his own head to the goddess in sacrifice. In *Sunghursh* (1968), priest Bhavani Prasad (played by Jayant) of Kashi, under the excuse of trying to please Goddess Kali, keeps murdering the guests at his inn. The confidence and calm with which he denies murdering his own son is terrifying. He is another pathological liar who has no sense of right and wrong—typical psychopathic behaviour. *Darinda* (1977), too, is about a Shaivite cult and black magic in which the serial Yogi (Sunil Dutt, in an unusual role) hypnotizes seven young girls in front of Lord Shiva and makes them jump off a cliff to their deaths. Like Bhavani Prashad, Yogi, too, was indifferent about his crimes. *Sangharsh* (1999), based on the Oscar-winning *Silence of the Lambs*, is another example about a serial killer Lajja Shankar Pandey (Ashutosh Rana) murdering children during a solar eclipse in the name of sacrifice to Goddess Kali because he believed that this human sacrifice would make him immortal.

Sunghursh *(1968) was based on Mahasweta Devi's novel,* Layli Aasmaner Ayna, *about the thugee cult of Varanasi in the nineteenth century that committed professional robberies and murders.*

The occult was once again behind the serial killings in *The Stoneman Murders* (2009), a film based on true events. The murderer bludgeons eight pavement dwellers in the name of a tantric-prescribed nar-bali (human sacrifice) that he believes will cure his impotency. Shared Kay Kay Menon who played sub-inspector Sanjay Shellar, 'The film consisted almost entirely of night shoots with no blue filters or anything. In fact, 70 per cent of my film career consists of night shoots. Most of the time I am shooting at night.'

The ridiculousness of occult beliefs can go to any extent. To cure his uncontrollable sexual urge, Dheeraj Pandey in *Murder 2* (2011) undergoes a bizarre 'surgery'. Said actor Prashant Narayanan who essayed the eunuch, cross-dressing, psychopathic serial killer, 'This sex-crazed guy is a sort of vigilante who has a problem with prostitutes. So, as advised by a "cult goddess", he chops off his penis so that he wouldn't be distracted from his mission to kill bad women!' Dheeraj's sexual energy now gets channeled into another outlet—that of torturing and dismembering call girls.

'I built the role on the fact that people would have sympathy for the person, deep within,' says Prashant.

3

Many Idiots
The Megalomaniacs, Bigots and Zealots

Some people feel superior to others purely by virtue of their economic or social status. They are the victims of the proverbial 'power went to his head' malaise, and they demonstrate behaviour that is not too dissimilar from the mentally unstable characters we read about in the earlier section.

In Bollywood films, how often have we seen domestic servants, peons, drivers and helpers being snubbed, berated, scolded, verbally abused and even physically kicked or slapped?

Educational institutions too carried these sadists in the guise of teachers. Like the obese schoolteacher often played by the actor Asit Sen who would cane the boys at the slightest mistakes or harmless mischief. And then these morphed into the likes of Viru Sahasrabudhe or Virus (Boman Irani) in *3 Idiots* (2009). A college is believed to be a place for learning, but Virus converts that into a well of death in which only the top rankers can survive. He makes the rest of the boys feel decidedly inferior, subjecting them to public humiliation in the classroom or telling their parents that their child is worthless. One may argue that he's simply instilling a competitive spirit among students, but he does not realize that his attitude has claimed two lives already—that of his student, Joy, who hanged himself to death, and the other his own son. Blackmailed by Virus to testify against another student Rancho, a third student Raju (Sharman Joshi) nearly leaps to his death. In a way, Virus too is a stalker just like Rahul of *Darr*, his very name striking an alarm.

In an interview, Boman Irani shared some insights, 'I was not keen on playing Virus because it was similar to Asthana (in *Munna Bhai M.B.B.S.*). Then Raju Hirani said, "Do it so differently that the audience will forget about Asthana." We went out of town, rented a bungalow and a cook. We would get up in the morning and start discussing ideas. I started improvising. I started talking in this lisp and I needed to do it so matter-of-factly. It should be a part of characterization. It is like wearing a cap or a scarf rather than shove the lisp in their faces. I sourced the wig and the white shirt from different people, wearing the pants high in the manner of old-fashioned people. Teachers and actors are the most imitated people in the world. They have their own "ada", or style. They do the same gestures day in and day out for years together and that becomes their peculiarity.'

Talking of the hilarious 'balatkar' scene, Boman revealed, 'Omi Vaidya (who played the comic Chatur Ramalingam) is from Los Angeles and knows no Hindi. And everybody on the set was told not to teach him any Hindi. I saw his video test; I fell of the chair laughing. I said, "Where did you find this guy?" He was using his fingers to translate the Hindi and it was all wrong. I controlled my laughter while the shot was being taken.'

Boman shared an interesting anecdote about the climax confrontation scene in *3 Idiots*, 'Aamir Khan kept saying, "Boman, to make it look realistic, you've got to hit me. They've put thermocol inside the umbrella to soften the spokes. It's an umbrella, how hard can it hurt me?" During practice I swung the umbrella three or four times on him, and it did not hurt him. However, when we went outside for the take, they put the rain machine on, and the umbrella got wet and it became heavy. So, when I swung it at Aamir during the actual take, his hand became blue after the take. And he was smiling. I really did not know what to say to Aamir.'

Disclosed Boman: 'A friend of mine did not call me to congratulate me for three years. Because his principal had ruined his life. After three years he called me to congratulate me and said that he did not have the guts to call me earlier as Virus reminded him of his own Virus.'

Another character similar to Virus was the hostel warden Arnie Campbell (Tom Alter) in *Aashiqui* (1990). What right he had to interfere in one of the boarders Anu's (Anu Agarwal) choice of men was not clear. But there he was standing in her way like an apparition, monitoring and questioning her every move. People like Campbell mistook their role of the warden to that of a phantom. Shared Director Mahesh Bhatt, 'The character played by Tom Alter was inspired by my memory of the dean of the Bombay Scottish Orphanage where my first wife stayed. It was run by foreigners of Scottish origin who were very strict with the boarders. Now, a few in the audience interpreted that Arnie did not have very clean intentions towards Anu. That was not intended but if it came through that was because my wife often complained that the male teachers in the school looked at the boarders through a sexual prism. So that was something which stayed in my mind.' The degradation in morality among so-called teachers is shocking. From mere caning and classroom punishment, the *Haraamkhor* (2015) mofussil schoolteacher Shyam (Nawazuddin Siddiqui) seduces his fourteen-year-old student Sandhya (Shweta Tripathi) and cruelly thrashes a young male student to death.

———

When bigots and megalomaniacs hold responsible positions in the armed forces and police, they can be as dangerous as mutating cancer cells, especially in conflict areas where they tend to function with impunity. Brigadier Rudra Pratap Singh (Kay Kay Menon) in *Shaurya* (2009) is an Islamophobe. There are complaints of human rights violations against him, but he has somehow managed to retain a clean reputation. Many years ago, his eight-year-old daughter had been raped and murdered by their domestic help; the same man also killed his wife and aged mother. The domestic help's name was Jameel. So, Brigadier Rudra Pratap sees a Jameel in every person of that community—young or old. He becomes so prejudiced that he vows to wipe out that community from the country. He therefore lets loose a like-minded subordinate Major Rathore to shoot-at-sight at people of that community. Brigadier Pratap believed that by doing this, he was protecting the nation, referring to democracy as 'bloody democracy'. Kay Kay Menon talked about his exceptional portrayal of the bigoted Brigadier Rudra Pratap Singh in *Shaurya*, 'The comparison of my role in *Shaurya* with that of Colonel Nathan Jessup (Jack Nicholson) in *A Few Good Men* (1992) often comes up. For Colonel Jessup, it was his ego. Whereas in the case of Brig. Singh, his acts are driven by his bigoted beliefs, not ego. Ego can be smashed. But belief is like terrorism which is very difficult to curb. Brig. Singh was also a megalomaniac and narcissist—he believes that God and Brigadier are one and the same. Deep down he (and I playing that role) knows he has done something wrong. So, the Brigadier presents himself publicly as being so big and so powerful that he dares anyone to come within 100 yards of his fence. That power drunkenness was a foil over his ingrained belief and a cover for his guilt as a man in uniform as well. It was a very complex role.'

Equally cancerous are those religious fanatics like Subodhbhai (Ashutosh Rana) in Mahesh Bhatt's *Zakhm* (1998) for whom the communal riots in the aftermath of the Bombay bomb blast of 1993 presented a ripe opportunity for 'hate business'. *Zakhm* was an autobiographical film, admitted Mahesh Bhatt, 'It was about the trauma of my own childhood. My mother was a Muslim—a fact I discovered much later. She wanted to be buried, not cremated. And then the '93 riots brought the identity issue of "Who am I?" A Hindu? A Muslim? Is this country going to be run as a Hindu nation in which the Muslim is the "other"? People said I must be out of my mind to make a film like this where I would lock swords with the rising right-wing forces. For three months post completion, I had to fence with the Home Ministry to get the film cleared because they wanted to paint the saffron band which the goons wore in the last scene into grey colour because the saffron identifies with one political party. And the joke is, having done that they later gave me a National Award for the best film on national integration which I did not go to receive. It was my bravest film.'

Similar to Brigadier Rudra Pratap Singh of *Shaurya* are bigots like Sanjay (Paresh Rawal) in *Firaaq* (2009) and Bittu Joshi (Manav Kaul) in *Kai Po Che!* (2013). Both films are based on the aftermath of the 2002 communal riots in Gujarat. The entire city is under siege from enemies within—they all look like one another which makes it impossible to tell friend from foe. Even the names of individuals do not reveal which camp they belong to. In an interview, Tisca Chopra who played Anuradha Desai in *Firaaq* said, 'My screen husband's name is Sameer Arshad Sheikh. But he is so scared of the mob during the riots that he adopts his wife's last name "Desai". *Firaaq* is about the loss of identity and about becoming a refugee in your own space. His name Sameer Arshad Sheikh wasn't going to change. But his mind did. That he decides to stay back in Gujarat after all, is the evolution.'

It is heart-wrenching but true that a few good film-makers had given up hope on 6 December 1992. Said film-maker Saeed Akhtar Mirza in an interview, 'Our Constitution is so poetic. My country with all its diversities is a celebration of life. An incredible country like ours born out of slaughter, caste-riddled, community-riddled, feudal ... and yet has the courage to see the future. But, by 1990, the optimism as a thinker had ebbed out of me at the things happening around me—the

Indira Gandhi assassination, the anti-Sikh riots, the Assam massacres, the Mandal Commission …. These were portends of a future. And then finally the Ram Janmabhumi build up to the Babri Masjid demolition. On 6 Dec 1992 when the Masjid was demolished, my Constitution had gone out of the window. It was smashed in front of my eyes. Now, this is the new reality. And that is when I made *Naseem* (1995) which is about the build-up in communal tension in late 1992 ahead of the Babri Masjid demolition. *Naseem* was the epitaph of a nation which has become a communal world. It will become muscular, incredibly harsh and it is not going to tolerate any dissent. The poet (played by Kaifi Azmi) dying on 6 Dec 1992 in *Naseem* is symbolic of the end of the poetry—poetry that is nothing but my country.'

Saeed Mirza is visibly heartbroken. But history says that despite everything, there will be a new naseem (which means 'the morning breeze'). The poetry will start rhyming again. The waves of tanpura will wash away hatred. As we see in the last scene of *Firaaq*, the music sessions will recommence and bridge us over to a new morrow.

V

DON KO PAKADNA MUSHKIL HAI ...

The Gangsters and the Mafia

These are criminals who operate in groups of various sizes with a hierarchy starting with a goonda at the bottom to the chief at the top. Their crimes are 'organized' and include black marketing, smuggling, racketeering, trafficking in narcotics, illegal betting and paid assassinations. The gangsters and mafia form covert networks with the political system and the police to escape the law.

We also know them as the 'underworld'.

1

Ye Hamara Ilaka Hai
The Neighbour Hoods of the 1950s

The terms 'mafia' and 'gangster' are often used interchangeably although they're not synonymous. In an interview with the author, crime journalist and writer Hussain Zaidi explained the difference. 'Mafia and gangsters are not one and the same. The definition of mafia is a crime syndicate which manages to commit a crime and get away with it without getting caught. Every time Arun Gawli committed a crime like murder or extortion (he was never into smuggling, by the way), he would get caught and jailed. Today he has been convicted and thrown behind bars for life. So, Arun Gawli was not mafia. He was just a gangster. Likewise, Abu Salem and Bashu Dada were all captured and tamed. They can't be termed mafia either.'

'Whereas Dawood Ibrahim, Chhota Shakeel and Chhota Rajan were mafia because they could get away to Dubai, Karachi, Bali and other places. And they commanded enough clout in high places to not get extradited back to India. Just the way that Al Capone in *Untouchables* could not get convicted because there was not a single evidence against him. Ultimately, they could charge Al Capone only with income tax evasion,' said Zaidi.

Where did gangsterism begin in Bollywood? From the 1950s onwards, as one cruises through Bollywood films, we come across small-sized gangs that sprouted spread across the big city. This was the earliest avatar of the gangsters which took birth in the early 1950s. Each gang eked out its small territory, conducting its small 'business' like theft, pickpocketing, petty crimes, black-marketing of cinema tickets or hoarding of foodgrains within those territories. In *Footpath* (1953), Noshu (Dilip Kumar) enters into a partnership with the black marketeer Ram Babu (Anwar Husain), who apparently runs a restaurant business but hoards foodgrains and sells those in the black market at higher rates to the rich, thus depriving the poor of their ration. Says Ram Babu, '*5-10 roz me jaise jaise log zyada bhookon marte jayenge, waise waise maal ka daam badhta jayega* (In 5 to 10 days, as more and more people die of starvation, the prices of food will keep rising).' Later, at the outbreak of an epidemic in the city, these black marketeers hoard medicines so that the prices may spiral up. In *Kala Bazar* (1960) Raghu (Dev Anand) and Kalu (Rashid Khan) make a lucrative living out of selling cinema tickets in black. These gangs operating in the metropolis's underground were running something of a separate economy of their own. And hence, the term underworld.

There would be those verbally agreed boundaries and un-inked treaties between the rival gangs with each gang fiercely protective of its precinct. Said Hussain Zaidi, 'When Nehru was hoisting the flag atop Red Fort in 1947, in Bombay there were several gangs but they were not named after their leader. These gangs were named after the territory they came from—Kanpuri, Jaunpuri, Allahabadi, Bengali ...'

The aspirations for these small gangs in the 1950s were still territorial and 'street-corner-ish' (as the very title *Footpath* suggests), hoarding only foodgrains—a minimum necessity for man. Their greed hadn't scaled up yet. And thus, for a mix of reasons, these small-time gangs remained small-time for whom their boss's wish was the proverbial command. And each gang had small teams of no more than eight to ten goondas (toughies) working for them with knives and choppers, added Zaidi.

The 1950s saw the arrival of an important villain actor K.N. Singh, who successfully essayed the role of the slick and swarthy urban don— someone who, with his stature and education, could not only lead a group of goondas, but also command respect from them. *Marine Drive* (1955) was a case in point in which K.N. Singh plays Khanna, an opium dealer and a gold smuggler. Khanna borrows monies from various creditors and defaults in his repayments because his smuggled goods get captured by the Bombay police. Khanna also shoots to death a rebelling gang member, thus conveying a clear message to the rest that they dare not jump the ship even if the waters are choppy. In *Howrah Bridge* (1958), K.N. Singh plays Pyarelal, the suave supplier of cocaine and opium to his Chinese partner-in-crime Mr John Chang (Madan Puri), using the hotel Café Shanghai in Calcutta as a front. Pyarelal is also a partner to Mr John Chang's crime of murdering a man from Rangoon and stealing his priceless Chinese dragon shaped jewel. One had to admit that, for all his nefarious activities, few men looked more sophisticated in a dinner jacket than Pyarelal.

Of course, the mafia syndicate and the gangsters needed foot soldiers to carry out various activities like black marketing, smuggling, extortion, kidnapping and contract killing. These foot soldiers, also known as goondas, have perpetually formed the bottom-most rung of the mafia hierarchy. Incapable of finding proper work, they are lackeys to their leader and must succeed in the tasks assigned to them; betrayal is not tolerated. Tugging at the handkerchiefs that rest around their necks and dragging on their cigarettes through the circle formed by their thumb and index finger, they are available as bouncers to intimidate the weak, as hafta collectors, as hitmen to politicians or as henchmen to landlords hired to evict stubborn tenants, e.g., goondaas like Munna (Sanjay Dutt) and Circuit (Arshad Warsi) in *Lage Raho Munna Bhai* (2006) who work for the landlord Lucky Singh (Boman Irani), or as hitmen for vicious politicians.

The Jaggu, Joe, Mac, Jack, Peter, Dilawar, Zebisko, Braganza and, of course, Shetty played by actors like Manmohan, Sudhir, Bhagwan Sinha, Hiralal, Anwar Hussain, Mohan Sherry, Bharat Gopi, Bob Christo, Yusuf, Dan Dhanoa and Shetty were the stock faces of these goondas who floated through life happily earning that day's bottle of liquor and getting the occasional woman. They would make those near-customary appearances in no more than two to three scenes, to the sound of the audience cheering and whistling, such was their effect.

Not all of them were necessarily *strong* men, physically. There were those emaciated ones like Pedro in *Baazi* (played by Rashid Khan) who were still important in the gang's scheme of things. Dressed in a sharp, grey suit with a cane, confidently sauntering into a gambling den, Pedro was the cunning middleman, the dealmaker. These goondas (sometimes called 'dadas') usually did not have the leadership skills to become a Don themselves. As the new recruit in *House No. 44* (1955) is advised by the bosses, '*Kaan aur aankh khule, muh bandh* …. (Keep your eyes and ears open and your mouth shut).'

With the passage of time these petty goondas started getting paid more. But that also meant that there was an increased risk to their lives. A day job as a black marketeer or a bouncer would have, at most, fetched a jail term of a few months if they were to get captured. But to signal with a torch at the coast in the dead of the night or play the gunman or the informer meant risking getting bumped off by the police or a rival gang. Or sometimes by their own gang. Their big bosses treated them like disposable tissues, either garrotting them to death or silencing them with a bullet or burning them alive when they were no longer needed. What trust? What loyalty?

In his autobiography, Bob Christo discloses an incident about the one-on-one fight sequence with the cop Amjad Khan in Qurbani *(1980), in which Khan overpowers Bob and interrogates him. 'He handcuffs me to the sugarcane press and asks me some more questions. After we finished the shot, nobody could locate the key for removing the handcuffs from my wrists … I was in a very uncomfortable position, half-standing, half-sitting and bent to one side. I kept shouting for them to get me out of the inconvenient tight spot. Nevertheless, I had to wait for two hours until they brought a locksmith who was successful in releasing me eventually'.*[65]

These goondas led sad lives and died tragic deaths. Ironically, even actors like Shetty, MacMohan, Bob Christo, Yusuf, Dan Dhanoa and Salim Ghouse never got to play the kingpin villain. They kept playing the 'Yes-boss, okay-boss' sidekick villain throughout their careers.

———

Meanwhile, by the 1960s, the street corners got cluttered with newer entrants. Moreover, with the cost of survival spiralling high, the appetite for these small gangs would not be whetted by hoarding foodgrains or selling movie tickets in black alone. They had to graduate to the big league. Coincidentally, sometime in the early 1960s, the Arabs smelt the opportunity to smuggle gold from various parts of the Arab world including Saudi Arabia into India. The 'ilaka' (territory) had to expand. And thus, was born the first significant line of business for organized crime syndicates—gold smuggling.

Cinematography changed too. The earlier black-and-white medium was suitable for capturing close-up shots of emotions like conflict and romance, indoor scenes and those of the muhalla (locality) but not of landscapes and panoramic action shots. That is when Eastmancolor arrived to add more intensity to the action scenes involving gangsters and the mafia.

2

Ek Tha Jewel Thief
The Smugglers

Despite having come chronologically rather early, the villains Seth Dhaniram (Manmohan Krishna) and Mohini (Pushpa Hans) in V. Shantaram's *Apna Desh* (1949) were arguably the first big-ticket smugglers. Seth Dhaniram (Manmohan Krishna) and other businessmen like him saw India's newly acquired independence as a license to do what they pleased. *'Ab kya hai? Apna raaj. Sarkari bhaav ka control khatm kara denge!* (Now what? Well we run the show now. We will end government control over prices!)' Rai Saheb Bansidhar hides fresh garments in his godowns and sells them to Mohini (Pushpa Hans) who in turn smuggles them overseas via the sea route. In addition to stashing black money by creating shell companies to avoid paying income tax, Seth Dhaniram strikes a deal with Mohini to supply a thousand guns stolen from a government depot in return for gold bars. And then, Mohini arranges to smuggle this stolen weaponry to a neighbouring country via train in return for gold bars for Dhaniram. While *Footpath*'s Ram Babu's activities were limited to black marketeering within the city, Dhaniram and Mohini are clearly playing a bigger game 'exporting' their stolen goods abroad. But smuggler films were few and far between in the 1950s and 1960s as these decades were largely characterized by family dramas and romantic musicals.

> *According to Shantaram's daughter, Madhura Jasraj, as shared in a chat with the author, Shantaram showed* Apna Desh *(1949) to the then Home Minister of Bombay Morarji Desai who not only approved the film without any cuts but also asked the then Police Commissioner of Bombay to share with Shantaram some of the inside stories about the notorious trade of smuggling to make the script more authentic.*

Another example of this exception was *Smuggler* (1966) which is about a gang headed by Deendayal (Hiralal), running a racket of counterfeit currency inside the Venus Soap Factory. Vijay 'Goldie' Anand's *Jewel Thief* (1967) could be considered to have marked a turning point in films that featured smugglers. A jewel thief commits heist after jewel heist across cities. He is a big fish in the international market, buying and selling diamonds and jewels worth hundreds of thousands of rupees. The police are baffled as no one knows what the jewel thief looks like. By reconstructing seemingly unconnected events, the jewel thief's gang ingeniously misleads the police and public to believe that the jewel thief is a handsome young man called Prince Amar who is a spitting image of Vinay (Dev Anand), the son of the Police Commissioner. And then the gang captures Vinay and brainwashes him using electric shocks to make Vinay believe that he was actually the non-existent Prince Amar, the jewel thief. The rest is easy for the villain—try and get Vinay bumped off, thus 'killing' the jewel thief and closing the mystery of the unknown jewel thief Amar as far as the police was concerned. And then the real jewel thief could comfortably hide in broad daylight. This was a Hitchcockian concept called MacGuffin by Director Vijay Anand (who was a fan of Alfred Hitchcock)—creating a character in the story that doesn't exist at all. Despite its thumping success, *Jewel Thief* did not quite spark off a flood of smuggler films immediately. But its arrival was inevitable because…

'… After the (British) Raj it was the License raj…' Keshub Mahindra, former Chairman of the Mahindra Group of companies, said in an article in the *Economic Times*, referring to the period 1961 to 1970.[66] License Raj meant that procurement and distribution of goods were controlled. There weren't enough snazzy goods to buy within the country and the import tariffs were double that of other countries. Endorsed Govind Nihalani in an interview with the author, 'Spurious liquor and foreign liquor added to the shopping list of the smugglers along with gold and watches.' And therein lay the opportunity for the smugglers. As Hussain Zaidi analysed in a chat with the author, 'By the end of the 1960s there were a number of gold smugglers like Bashu dada and Haji Mastan. They were proper dons of the gold mafia who operated within organized syndicates. These flourished in the 1970s and saw new entrants like Yusuf Patel, Dawood Ibrahim and Pathan.'

Bollywood picked on these reality cues, and the smuggling engine in Bollywood revved up between 1970 and 1972. From merely lording over eight to ten strongmen at muhallas the mafia, in its new avatar, would now lead whole organizations. The smuggler villain in Bollywood was thus the first urban, 'corporatized' villain. And with the emergence of the mafia, the focus was back on the city, too. Men were now ready for action at every turn. Women would be less delicate. There would be romance and music but entwined with action. A couple of notable 'change-agent' films were *Johny Mera Naam* and *Victoria No. 203*.

Johny Mera Naam (1970) is about a gang headed by a smuggler called Ranjit Singh (Premnath) masquerading as Rai Sahab Bhupendra Singh. Ranjit's gang smuggles stolen diamonds from India to Nepal and sells these to 'clients' from Western countries with the payments being remitted in pounds, dollars or rupees. Ranjit has on his team two 'able' deputies—Moti (Pran) and Heeralal (Jeevan). Ranjit's smuggling gang also exports charas, ganja, opium and hashish hidden inside cargoes containing musical instruments like tabla and sitar to America via Calcutta. This was in addition to stealing idols from temples and selling those to overseas buyers. '*Johnson naam ka ek European milega. Woh in cheezon ke badle me tumhe 5 laakh rupees dega ....* (A European named Johnson will pay you INR 500,000 for these ....)', Moti tells Johnny, referring to those stolen idols. Foreign currencies and the humongous profitability that lay in the smuggling business had entered the Bollywood lexicon. '*Yehi patthar Johnson America le jaakar 5 laakh ke bajay 15 laakh dollar kamayega* (Johnson will take these stone idols to America and make USD 1.5 million from this INR 500,000)', adds Moti. The transnational flavour was here and now. '*Agley Somvar ke din, duniya ke bade se bade smuggler duniya ke kone kone se aakar yahan jama honge—America se Al Capone, England se Robert King ....* (Next Monday, all the big smugglers from various corners of the world will land up here ....)', Ranjit brags about the invitees to his private auction of his fabulous collection of stolen jewels and other valuables.

Curiously, *Johny Mera Naam* looked like an extended arm of *Jewel Thief.* In both the films, the villain took someone else's identity.

Both the films were shot in two neighbouring Himalayan nations—*Jewel Thief* in Sikkim (which was an independent country then) and *Johny Mera Naam* in Nepal.

In *Victoria No. 203* (1972), Seth Durgadas (Anwar Husain) and his gang plan to steal the priceless Golcunda diamonds worth INR 3 crores from a museum in Bombay with the obvious intent of selling them to some party abroad. As the hero, Kumar (Navin Nishchal), who stakes his life to prevent this from happening, asserts, '*Ye heere tumhe kabhi, kabhi nahi mil sakte. Ye desh ki amaanat hai aur desh ke paas wapas jayenge!* (You will never ever get these diamonds. They belong to the nation and will go back to the nation)'. Unfortunately, despite a competent performance from Anwar Husain who plays the diamond smuggler Durgadas, the film didn't earn him much mileage. The reason—the comic pair of Raja and Rana (Ashok Kumar and Pran) dominated the show with their spontaneous wit. Nevertheless, the Indianized version of James Hadley Chase's novel *There's a Hippie on the Highway* was a monumental hit of its time.

In 2002, Brij Sadanah's son Kamal drafted in film-maker Ananth Mahadevan to remake his father's biggest hit, but it came with mixed box-office results. In an interview with the author, Ananth recalled, 'The problem with a remake is a catch-22 one. If you make a frame-by-frame remake it fails because the formula of the 1970s does not work today. If you don't do a faithful remake, then people say, "*Ye picture toh Victoria No. 203 hai hi nahi* (This version doesn't resemble the original Victoria No. 203 at all)." It was a learning process for me not to attempt remakes of hit films.'

Kamal Sadanah was the survivor of a tragedy in 1990 in which his father Brij Sadanah, in a fit of rage, shot dead his family members and then, himself.[67]

But then, there was hardly anything new about these Bollywood smugglers. They merely seemed to be engaged in a new profession, but their appearance wasn't any different. There was much that was wanting in their characterization, too. What was perhaps required was new scriptwriters, even a fresh face. Maybe both.

———

There was an actor who, despite talent, had been floating in Bollywood for three decades, playing supporting roles like Pervez in the costume drama *Halaku* (1956), the jealous young friend Krishna in *Naya Daur* (1957) and a stern father in *Andaz* (1970). He was a bit of everything but lacked a distinct identity. He was born Hamid Ali Khan. His screen name was Ajit.

In an interview with Keith D' Costa in *CINEPLOT*, Ajit matched his on-screen wit while talking about his arrival to Bombay circa 1943, 'When I came down to Bombay, I expected all the popular directors like Kardar*saab*, Mehboob*saab* and Shantaram*ji* to meet me with open arms at VT Station! I had this silly feeling that I was the only person to have thought about joining films.'[68] After three decades of mixed fortunes for him, in 1973, two roles came the actor's way. They were both of smugglers and would catapult him to becoming one of the most iconic villains of Bollywood. Both roles were scripted by the duo Salim–Javed. They were Teja in *Zanjeer* and Shakaal in *Yaadon ki Baaraat* and were very different from anything witnessed before.

Both the screen names Teja and Shakaal were adopted from men who existed in real life—interestingly, one was a crook, whereas the other was a good man.

In 1960, a shipping magnate called Jayant Dharma Teja took loans worth INR 220 lakhs to establish the Jayanti Shipping Company. On being discovered that he was actually siphoning off money to his own account, Teja promptly fled the country. (A very flamboyant liquor baron did likewise many years later.)[69] This Teja was Salim–Javed's inspiration for Ajit's character in *Zanjeer*.

The real-life Mr Shakhaal, his full name being G.P. Shakhaal, was a respectable gentleman. He was the publicity-in-charge at Nasir Husain Films. Who would have thought the real name of humble publicist would spell menace when used as the screen name for Ajit in *Yaadon ki Baaraat*? Shakaal pumps bullets into a household couple and separates the brothers. Fifteen filmic years later he is back in a revamped format with well-groomed grey hair and beard.

The name 'Shakaal' sounds similar to the French word 'ChaCal' which means 'jackal', the code name of the man who attempted to assassinate the French President Charles de Gaulle in Frederick Forsyth's thriller novel The Day of The Jackal *published in 1971. Coincidence?*

Shakaal in *Yaadon ki Baaraat* steals precious artefacts and jewels worth hundreds of thousands of rupees from across the country and sells them to buyers like Robert abroad. This includes the invaluable Nataraja statue and Irani jewellery. Shakaal also owns a hotel which doubles up as the rendezvous spot for his gang members.

Teja from *Zanjeer* makes and sells spurious liquor that contains ammonium chloride. People who consume it either lose their lives or lose their eyesight. The police is clueless on who owns this network and how this spurious liquor gets distributed. Both Shakaal and Teja carry a certain assuredness, are rarely hassled and behave like the ringleaders they are. They have a repository of back-up plans and incisive forethought. Shakaal is the 'sutradhar' (as film historian Kaushik Bhaumik puts it)— the narrator. He leaves the job of execution to his men while he is in bed with a woman who certainly is not his wife. His starched, full-sleeved shirts throughout *Yaadon ki Baaraat* were symbolic—Shakaal never dirtied his hands.

With the song sequence '*Lekar hum diwana dil*' playing in the background a grand theft of a valuable Nataraj idol from a museum takes place. This act of a hotelier stealing the Nataraj murti and selling it to someone abroad was probably inspired by a notorious real-life theft of six metal antiques idols including that of a Nataraja belonging to the tenth-century Chola period from Sivapuram temple in Tamil Nadu's Thanjavur district. The originals were replaced by fake idols and the originals changed various hands before ending up with one Manohar Lal (Manu) Narang in Bombay. Narang sold the Nataraja idol for a few lakhs of rupees to New York based art dealer Ben Heller who smuggled the artefact out of India from New Delhi by Japan Airlines. Of course, Manu Narang and his brother Ram Lal Narang were later tried in the court of law. In a discussion with the author, film-maker Chandra Barot shared that Manu had purchased Hotel Ambassador in Bombay. And, that completed the profile of Shakaal, the hotelier-smuggler. Manu

Narang produced a multi-starrer film *Paanch Dushman* (1973), with Narang himself playing the lead.[70]

In a chat, actor Tariq Khan (who played Rattan/Monto in the film) shared an insight about the climax fight sequence of Yaadon ki Baaraat *which takes place at an airstrip. 'The airstrip, an old one made by the British during World War II, is outside Thane in Kalyan. British Air Force planes carrying tanks and war equipment for war against the Japanese would land there. That place was government property but nobody was using it. That airstrip looked as if it was far away from the city in some uninhabited place. But it was in the heart of Bombay. We would shoot there and return home every day. I don't know how Nasir sahib found that place but it needed permissions and police clearance.'*

The 'twin smuggler' characters of Teja and Shakaal went on to establish Ajit as the quintessential smuggler for a long time. Teja and Shakaal were the first author-backed smugglers and were similar in many ways.

It is not very clear how Ajit was chosen for the two roles of Shakaal and Teja given that Premnath, Anwar Hussain and Pran had already played smugglers. But then, Salim–Javed, who were the uncrowned kingmakers in those days, must have had something to do with selecting Ajit for these two roles. Curiously, in Sidharth Malhotra's show *Ek Villain Ek Dastaan - Ajit*, it was disclosed that Ajit was reluctant to take up the role of Teja, but later did so under Salim Khan's insistence as Salim Khan was known to be a good friend of Ajit.[71]

With smugglers came urban glamour and ill-gotten wealth. Hindi films of yore preached that becoming rich through honest means was almost impossible. So, if a young man was already rich, questions around the source of his wealth were raised. And conspicuous consumerism raised red flags too, since it is more often than not the outcome of excess money. Kaushik Bhaumik adds, 'There used to be this prevalent guilt about consumerism. Frugality and austerity were virtues. In other words, the hero, ideally, had to be poor.' Conversely, the bad men were rich because of the lack of those very virtues.

Thus, smugglers were the unashamed faces of consumerism because their wealth could buy them expensive phones, ornate beds (often with half-naked women in them), plush offices, imported liquor, high-street apparel, left-hand-drive cars, fine dining. On celluloid, these props added to the nasty allure of the villain. In an interview with the author, actor Pavan Malhotra seconded the thought saying that in the 1970s, whatever the means, everybody wanted to befriend smugglers. One can check for Page 3 parties in Bollywood in the early 1970s. In most cases, the hosts were producers, distributors or smugglers investing in cinema.

Barring exceptions like Sahuji (Utpal Dutt), who lived in a hill-town in *Barsaat ki Ek Raat* (1981), rarely has any smuggler been seen in a dhoti-kurta. They were always in expensive suits. And for the younger scoundrels played by Prem Chopra, Sudhir, Ranjeet, Roopesh Kumar, Imtiaz Khan, Kiran Kumar and Danny, their turtleneck sweaters, broad belts, bell-bottom trousers, long sideburns, scarves, butterfly shirt collars, collarless full-sleeved V-neck jerseys and chunky lockets dangling from their necks accessorized the characters in such a way that the attire became almost part of the character. If you have the money, you can go places. To hotels and nightclubs, for instance. Historically, there has always been something implicitly contraband about a hotel because it has often been used as a front for smuggling activities, e.g., K.D. Narang (Kulbhushan Kharbanda) in *Shakti* (1983) and Ranjit (Dharmendra) and his boss 'uncle' in *Loafer* (1974). The hotel business gave their illegal activities a quasi-legitimacy, as the smuggler could hide behind the respectable occupation of being a 'businessman'. This gave them an advantage over other category of villains. The dacoits, for instance, could not call themselves anything else.

Apropos to the discussion on consumerism, the embedded action in smuggler films of the 1970s provided the opportunity for a brand parade of sorts. As screeching cars chased each other on the Bombay roads, as police jeeps took sharp turns (with the cop frantically waving the traffic aside), as fruit-carts overturned at the impact of these vehicles and shady briefcases got exchanged at Flora Fountain in Fort Bombay, logos of brands like Bombay Dyeing, Wills, Coca-Cola, Esso, Khatau, Leonard refrigerators, Lambretta scooters, Royal Enfield bikes, Paragon textiles, etc., fleeted past in the background.

'A film has to be visually appealing,' pointed out writer Sanjit Narwekar in an interview with the author. 'A smuggler running like hell ... and suddenly the attaché case snaps open and gold biscuits fall out. Isn't that exciting? But if someone is running away with a pen drive which has national secrets, how exciting can a pen drive be?' he mused.

———

Teja and Shakaal brought forth similar characters. For instance, in *Videsh* (1977), a London-based hotelier running a smuggling racket also doubles up as a yogi. In *Amar Akbar Anthony* (1977), Robert (Jeevan) runs a racket of smuggling in gold biscuits.

> Amar Akbar Anthony *resulted in a permanent fallout between Ranjeet and Manmohan Desai. Disclosed Ranjeet, 'Manji told me to act in a guest role in* AAA. *He said it would take five to six days. But the title song sequence in the climax scene went on for ten to fifteen days. I told him that it was inappropriate to extend my shooting schedules and then make me stand in a corner during the song sequence. But anyway, no tension. But I did not work with Manji much after that.'*

Till the early 1970s, Bollywood still hadn't had a chance to watch a mafioso running an organized and diversified businesses involving drugs, rent extortion, prostitution and gambling, keeping the law enforcement and the political system on their payroll. But it would not be a long wait.

If various kinds of masalas add spice and flavour to Indian food, what would fresh basil leaves, Mozzarella di Bufala cheese and marinara sauce supply?

Hint: These three toppings form the colours of the Italian flag.

3

From Italy, with Love
The Don

In 1972, a young American film-maker by the name of Francis Ford Coppola made *The Godfather* (1972)—a film that would prove to be a turning point in world cinema.

Bollywood, too, sat up and took notes. Production for two significant Hindi films commenced soon after—Feroze Khan's *Dharmatma*, released in 1975 and Chandra Barot's *Don*, which released in 1978. In an interview, director Chandra Barot shared, 'In 1973, Jaya Bachchan, Amitabh Bachchan and I went to London (this was Amitabh's first trip abroad) and watched *The Godfather* there. That day we became aware of the fact that the mafia boss is called "Don".'

The term 'Don' was indeed a new addition to the Bombay dictionary. Revealed Chandra Barot, 'Manoj Kumar called to and asked me why I had named my film "Down". I clarified to him that it was not "Down" but "Don". He said, "Bewaqoof (idiot), nobody will know what it means. Please rename it as 'Mr Don'." I referred him to the dictionary which said that "'Don" meant a Spanish gentleman. So, the "Mr" is already there. We laughed together heartily.'

In *Dharmatma*, Premnath played the role of Dharamdas, the head of the mafia, the mild breathlessness caused by his obesity giving his dialogue delivery a tone similar to that of Brando's raspy mutterings in *The Godfather*.

People may accuse Feroze Khan of plagiarism, but then, he had to retain the core elements of *The Godfather* in his adaptation in order to make it look like an authentic mafia film. In fact, *Dharmatma* should be regarded as arguably India's realistic mafia film for many reasons. Firstly, it was not about smuggling alone. It showed Dharamdas in diverse businesses like gambling, matka (betting and lottery) in a big scale (with betting volumes as high as INR 3.6 crores on certain days), offering protection to anti-social elements and criminals and influencing trade unions. Secondly, family is at the core of Don Dharamdas's life (similar to Vito Corleone's): the film portrayed a villain, who, outside of his professional misdemeanours is a loving father, a devoted husband and a devout Hindu. Like Vito Corleone, Dharamdas makes friends with the establishment; he has enough clout over the Governor to grant a reprieve to a man sentenced to the gallows. Dharamdas is also a philanthropist—partly to launder his black money and partly to garner public goodwill with a view to become part of the establishment by turning into a politician. Both Vito Corleone and Dharamdas stayed away from the drugs business because it would have alienated the establishment and would have ruined the next generation. So, somewhere they still had a streak of morality intact.

Maybe given the year in which Dharmatma *was released, Feroze Khan (who played Dharamdas' son Ranbir) had to bend over backwards to please the then Indian Government by speaking in favour of the Maintenance of Internal Security Act (MISA) which gave the Indian law enforcement agencies broad powers for preventive detention of individuals. In one of his dialogues in the film, Khan tells the two smugglers Anokhelal (Jeevan) and Biradar (Satyen Kappu), 'Yeh MISA ka kanoon tum jaise gundon aur smuggleron ke liye banaya gaya hai Anokhelal, jo jurm karte hue bhi kannon ki zapt se bahir hai* (The MISA is for thugs and smugglers like you who, despite carrying on with their crime manage to evade the Law).'

An important change in the post-*Dharmatma* world was that in the mafia films, the don's family came into view prominently. This had to be the influence of *The Godfather*. Take the example of the Mizya group run by Don Sobhraj (Dilip Kumar) in Subhash Ghai's *Vidhaata* (1982). Behind the veneer of legal businesses like shipping, automobiles, sugar and rubber, the Mizya group is an underworld organization involved in smuggling and other illegal activities. But Don Sobhraj (Dilip Kumar) values his grandson Kunal more than anything else in the world. In a particular scene, Sobhraj begs the other members of the Mizya group to spare his dear grandson Kunal's (Sanjay Dutt) life just the way Vito Corleone enters into a truce with the other Sicilian families over Michael Corleone's safe return to America.

As compared to *Dharmatma*, the 1978 *Don* was a very different film altogether. The nefarious gang that Don belonged to carried out smuggling of gold, silver and drugs in several countries, invoking the Interpol's attention. Recently, they had shifted their base to Bombay and the one person on the Interpol's lookout was Don himself.

While *Dharmatma*'s Dharamdas was the unquestioned big boss of his conglomerate, Don in *Don* appeared to be lower down in his gang's hierarchy, carrying out activities like exchanging smuggled goods for cash at rendezvous spots. These were the sort of errands that flunkeys like Mac (Mac Mohan) would be expected to run. Rather, it was the middle-aged Narang (Kamal Kapoor) who, despite being a peer, appears to be the senior member of the gang guiding Don's activities. In a particular scene, when the other party confirms the time and venue of the cash-for-goods exchange, Narang tells them, '*Don wahan maujood hoga* (Don will be there)'—almost as if Narang was the one directing Don. The gang members address Don as 'tum' whereas they would address Narang as 'Narang sahib'. Of course, the gang leaned on young Don for his incredible charm, his daring, his ability to deliver results and his 'X-ray' ability to spot and eliminate police informers who infiltrated the gang. The gang also benefits from Don's proverbial nine lives of a cat, giving the police the slip every time in the face of imminent arrest. As Don brags cockily, '*Don ka intezar to gyarah mulkon ki police kar rahi hai. Lekin Sonia, ek baat samajh lo. Don ko pakadna mushkil hi nahi, namumkin hai* (Don is wanted by the police force of eleven countries. But Sonia, may you be aware that it is impossible to capture Don).'

Author Diptakirti Chaudhuri added in a chat with the author, 'Don was like a young Turk who had fast-tracked his way up the hierarchy to become a peer of the senior pro Narang. But Narang realizes that sometime soon, Don could overtake him and hence tries to show Don who the boss was.' In fact, despite Don getting killed within the first forty minutes of the film, life goes on as usual for the gang, making it obvious that while Don was a hotshot, an important member, he was not its leader. As the story unfolds, it transpires that not even Narang was the Big Dog of the mafia. It was actually Vardaan (Om Shivpuri), posing as the Interpol cop Malik.

Unlike *Dharmatma*'s Dharamdas, who never had the customary moll, Don always has a woman at his elbow. He is a ruthless lover, astonishingly confident and seems to derive immense pleasure from the crimes he committed nonchalantly. Don did not need to don any of the facial contortions typical of villains. After all, he had on his side actor Amitabh Bachchan's glazed elegance. In a chat with the author, Director Chandra Barot disclosed, 'Producer Nariman Irani's wife was Waheeda Rehman's personal hairdresser. And Waheeda and Salim Khan were good friends. At Waheeda's behest, Salim gave us a story called *Don Wali Kahaani* which had been rejected by Jeetendra, Dev, Dharmendra as they felt this was too Westernized a villain.' But then they got Amitabh Bachchan to agree to play the role, making him the first lead actor to play a full-fledged smuggler. Referring to his trip to London along the newly wed couple Amitabh and Jaya, Barot shared another piece of trivia, 'There is a boutique called Cecil Gee (in London) where we decided to shop for international costumes for Don. We got the green banian, white jacket and the shirt for the Helen's scene (just before the song *'Ye mera dil yaar ka diwana'*) from London. Amitabh was fond of classy watches, a few of which he purchased there and we used in the film.'

Unlike Dharamdas, Don has no family, no last name and no past. Don's first name suggests that he may be a Christian, but there was no concrete proof of this except for the fact that his burial took place at a Christian cemetery—but that, too, was hastily organized by the DSP de Silva, who perhaps assumed that Don was a Christian.

Did Don *also owe its storyline to Shakti Samanta's* China Town *(1959)? In* China Town, *too, there was a smuggler hero and his lookalike. They switch places so that the good chap can infiltrate the gang. 'Yes, absolutely.* Don *was a remake of* China Town,' *confirmed Shammi Kapoor in an interview with the author in January 2010.*

But what took *Don* four and a half years years to release? Chandra Barot shared: '*Hum sab kadke they* (We were all broke)! On the sets of *Roti, Kapada aur Makaan,* Amitabh, Zeenat and I—all of us had decided to get together to help out cameraman Nariman Irani, who had fallen into a debt of INR 12 lakh after his *Zindagi Zindagi* (1973) flopped. The expense for the first shooting schedule was INR 40,000 and I borrowed a cheque for the amount from my sister Kamal Barot. It paid for the studio and the shooting. But we had to keep making the film in pieces—and that's what took four and a half years.'

Given that *Don* was made under such severe financial tight-belting, it needed the largesse and accommodation of a quite a few industry seniors and well-wishers. This included getting Salim Khan to write a story for a negligible fee.

The film's crew also had to 'piggyback' on movie sets where other films were being shot. Barot said: 'The scene in which the DSP shows video clips of Don to Vijay was shot at Waheeda Rehman's residence at Pali Hill. The sauna scene and the hospital scenes were shot on the sets of *Immaan Dharam* at Mehboob Studios, with producer Premji's permission. We agreed to pay for the rent for two days.'

Shared Barot, 'The green lungi in the song "Yeh hai Bambai nagariya" was procured from Hill Road near the Mehboob Studios. And the red shirt was Amitabh's own. The scene in which DSP D'Silva meets the villager Vijay (Bachchan) to convince him to masquerade as Don, was shot at night in the canteen of Mehboob Studios. For that scene, I made Amitabh eat thirty-five paans to give his character that authenticity. It gave the desired effect, but his lips parched the next day and he started swearing at me. Then we decided not to put any chuna (limestone powder) in the paan—only kattha (red sauce).'

Farhan Akhtar remade *Don* in 2006 as *Don: The Chase Begins Again* with Shah Rukh Khan in the lead. *Don* (2006) is about a drugs mafia that was owned by a person called Boris who sources illicit drugs from Afghanistan, Pakistan and India and distributes those in Europe. Boris has two able deputies—Singhania and Vardhaan. Singhania (Rajesh Khattar) murders Boris and takes over the drugs business himself. The other deputy Vardhaan goes missing. Don, the most dangerous and cunning member of Singhania's mafia, runs Singhania's drugs business in Malaysia. But over time, Don's successes makes him arrogant, leading to run-ins with another senior member of the gang, Narang (Pavan Malhotra). Don resents that Narang was a mere figurehead while Don did all the hard work. Said Pavan Malhotra in an interview, 'It's important to understand that Narang was Don's boss. The top boss Singhania gives instructions to Narang who passes those down to others, including Don. But Don, as a sign of dissent, stops taking instructions from Narang and Narang knew that he needed to address that quickly. Otherwise, if Don could have it his way, he would get rid of Narang.'

Also, in the 2006 version, it is not the Interpol Officer Malik but DCP de Silva (Boman Irani) himself who turns out to be the missing Vardhaan, Singhania's once-buddy-now-rival. The 1978 version saw killing by loud bullets and comedy-tinged fight sequences with lathis (sticks). Whereas the assassinations in *Don* (2006) are cold and surgical— Ramesh (Diwaker Pundir) gets injected to death with poison by Don. The police informer Kumar meets instant death as Don hits a golf ball straight at Kumar's nose. Singhania's drink at the party is mixed with deadly poison by Vardhaan. Confronted by imminent death, Singhania (almost gratefully) swallows another glass of the poisoned drink served to him by Vardhaan—who was, after all, taking every effort to make an old buddy's death as painless as possible.

This power-struggle within the gang, focus on drugs, the innovative assassinations and the far-East backdrop gave the 2006 version a more mafia-like feel rather than a mere gangster-feel. The characters of *Don* (2006) were much darker than those in the 1978 version. In a chat with the author, Boman Irani said, 'In the first viewing, de Silva looks like the original de Silva. It is only in the second viewing that de Silva looks like the criminal Vardhaan.'

Boman Irani also shared an anecdote. 'In the climax fight sequence between Shah Rukh and myself on the deck, there was a miscommunication between us and the cameraman in the helicopter above. For this sequence, Shah Rukh wanted to do five takes in a row. Now, since we could not have heard the sound of "Cut!" above the din of the hovering helicopter, the choreographer said he would wave a red flag to indicate the "Cut". But if we had looked up towards the camera in the helicopter, it would have been a "no-good" take. Shah Rukh said, "Don't look up, keep shooting, keep hitting me!" and I kept hitting till we finally we hugged each other and collapsed, exhausted, while the guys in the helicopter wondered what the hell we were doing since they had already cut the camera! I was so tired I could not raise my hand to put the food inside my mouth.' Much as he wished for a hot bath and massage, that was not to be since Boman had to catch a flight to Goa to shoot for Honeymoon Travels Pvt. Ltd.

The drug mafia threatened to destroy generations to come. William Friedkin's *The French Connection* (1971), the American action thriller with the drug mafia at its centre, was all the rage in America upon its release. Coincidentally, *Hare Rama Hare Krishna* (1971), the Bollywood film about ganja-addicted Hippies that released the same year, witnessed stupendous success at the box office. In the film there is a villain called Dronacharya (Prem Chopra), who steals priceless artefacts from temples in Kathmandu to sell abroad—just like many other smugglers. But Dronacharya was constructed as a semi-comical character who turns out to be a pompous laughing stock. The bigger villain of *HRHK* was really the invisible but pernicious drug mafia that claimed victims like young Jasbir/Janice (Zeenat Aman) and her friends.

Shared Prem Chopra in an interview about how the role of Dronacharya came about, 'I was shooting for Manoj Kumar at Filmistan when I was told that Dev sahib wanted to meet me. I met him at his office. He was very active and full of life. "Arre yaar, you have come. Sit down, sit down. I am making a film called Hare Rama Hare Krishna. *You are the king of Kathmandu. Kathmandu belongs to you. Take the role. That is your character. I've got to leave for a meeting. Amit Khanna will come and explain the rest." I had come prepared for a two-hour meeting and it lasted for barely a few minutes!'*

More destruction followed .... Both Reena (Nanda) in *Naya Nasha* (1973) and Roshi (Jyoti Bakshi) in *Bullet* (1976) get addicted to LSD, while Nimmu (Aruna Irani) in *Charas* (1976), dancing staggeringly in a Malta nightclub, has been force-addicted to charas. A rallying against this mafia was urgently needed by all. That precisely was the central theme of Ramanand Sagar's *Charas* (1976). In the opening credits of the film Sagar says, '*This movie is dedicated to those brave people who are risking their lives in the great battle against the Smuggling of Narcotic Drugs—a battle to save human race*'. With his trademark elegant, soft-spoken attitude, Ajit was back again as the unruffled, uber-cool Kalicharan, the smuggler who 'graduates' from smuggling gold to illegal cross-border trade of charas. He agrees to supply charas worth INR 5 crores to Sheikh Abdul Sattar (Sujit Kumar) who almost jumps out of his seat in excitement saying, '*Charas ka market to bahut tez hai Kalicharan! 5 crore ka 50 crore ban sakta hai* (The market for charas is hot. A 5 crore investment can yield a 50 crore return)!' And, to escape the police dragnet, Kalicharan coerces a young dancer Sudha (Hema Malini) to transport the charas by hiding the stuff inside her luggage and delivering the consignment to him in Europe. Innocent Sudha becomes a mule to Kalicharan who also runs a sleazy nightclub in Malta where young girls are forced to do drugs and are used to entertain clients.

Charas *also referenced the true story of the exodus of Indians from Uganda during the Idi Amin regime.*

As we see in *The French Connection*, the big money in drugs lay in the overseas market. Thus Bollywood, too, went international. In *Barood* (1976), a consignment of charas is delivered to Ratan (Sujit Kumar) in Las Vegas from a supplier based in New York. Ratan is part of a four-member international smuggling gang who had fled India fourteen years ago after murdering Police Inspector D.P. Saxena. And Malta in Europe is the destination of the dreaded narcotics in *Charas* (1976), while *Hare Rama Hare Krishna* (1970) and *Mahaan* (1983) in which villains smuggled narcotics hidden inside idols, were set in Kathmandu.

This internationalization of the smugglers, especially the ones dealing in prohibited drugs, continued into the 1980s, with Jethiya Seth (Anupam Kher) in *Kala Dhanda Goray Log* (1986) exporting the end product of opium grown in Shangri La to global destinations.

———

With the discovery of oil in Dubai in 1966 and the birth of the United Arab Emirates (UAE) in 1971, Dubai quickly became a prominent business and tourism hub. An expatriate-friendly environment, zero tax on personal and corporate income and low import duties made Dubai a dream destination for youngsters. The problem was there were a few like the character of Vicky Kapoor (played by Sanjay Dutt) in *Naam* (1986) who assumed Dubai to be Ali Baba's cave with money available for easy picking. But like the fool Qasim in the fable, they got trapped inside.

Continuing with his winning streak with hits like *Arth*, *Saaransh* and *Janam*, Mahesh Bhatt's *Naam* (1986) focussed on the immigration racket by touts dangling the Dubai bait—and into the dragnet of drug mafia. As Bhatt revealed of Vicky Kapoor's character in a chat with the author, 'Because of family pressure, Vicky (Sunjay Dutt) looks for a job in Dubai. And you become vulnerable abroad and become a sucker in the hands of the bigger drug mafia. Vicky was the "grey" in the family who does not mind selling drugs and for a living. But unlike Birju in *Mother India* and Vijay in *Deewar*, Vicky shows a desire to come back to mainstream.'

Ironically, it was Sunjay Dutt who helped Mahesh Bhatt stay off his heavy drinking during the shooting of Naam. *In Sanjay Dutt's biography, Yasser Usman quotes Mahesh Bhatt talking about Sanjay Dutt: "He had just come back from de-addiction .... He had brought the book* Alchoholics Anonymous, *which he gifted to me."*[72]

In the 1990 *Agneepath*, the village of Mandwa is infected by drugs and liquor, owing to the handiwork of a slick don in a sharply cut suit called Kancha Cheena (Danny Denzongpa). Kancha Cheena purchases land rights to the village Mandwa from Dinkar Rao (Goga Kapoor), and then converts schools into liquor warehouses, gets children to brew liquor and forces the women of the village into prostitution, thus making Mandwa a source of dirty revenue for his empire. Said Danny, 'We made Kancha Cheena into a sophisticated guy. He is very well-dressed, suave and speaks like a civilized person. He never raises his voice. But underneath this demanour, he is a ruthless guy.' The contrast came out rather well, one must say.

As for most Bollywood villains, the name 'Kancha Cheena' has an interesting history. Shared Danny, 'Because of my features, and also out of love, people would call me "Cheena" wherever I went. Every time I drove from Shivaji Park, I remember this boy would run after my car calling out "Cheena bhai, Cheena bhai" all the way till the traffic light. If there was a red light, the car would stop there and he would bang on the window. I would open the window and he would shake hands with me. So, when we were discussing this role, we thought of Rana as the name of the character. But Director Mukul Anand wanted the name to match my features, i.e., somebody from Nepal or the North East, the identification would be easier. Then I thought about it and said, "Cheena, yaar. Kancha Cheena." And it stuck.'

Strangely, in his eighteen-year-old career, Danny had never been in the same frame with Amitabh Bachchan, refusing almost twenty films including *Coolie* and *Mard* because the roles offered weren't prominent enough compared to that of the main hero. Director Mukul Anand was to break the spell. 'I heard about the role from Mukul Anand and I said, "This is it",' said Danny. 'Before the shooting began, I was anxious. And so, I had asked for the dialogues to be delivered in my hotel suite beforehand because I want to be prepared. When I didn't get the dialogue sheet, I lost my cool at the assistant director who apologized and left my suite. Two minutes later, the bell rang and I shouted, "Who's this?" The reply came, "This is Amitabh." I did not know that Mr Bachchan was in the next room. When I opened the door, he asked, "Why are you losing your cool? I've got a copy of the dialogues. Let us rehearse together." We rehearsed for half an hour after which I felt totally relaxed,' said Danny.

Jewels, artefacts and drugs were not the only items these smugglers dealt in …. They would land up wherever they could smell money.

Kartavya (1979) is about poachers in Madhuban jungle who were destroying the ecological balance by killing elephants, tigers and rhinos and selling elephant tusks, tiger skin and rhino's teeth illegally abroad. These poachers also fell sandalwood trees illegally and smuggle the wood to other countries, causing financial losses worth crores to India. This gang of poachers and smugglers headed by a jagirdar (landlord) Dewan Dhanpat Rai (Utpal Dutt) and his son Dushyant (Vinod Mehra) also use a ruse of a mumbo-jumbo about the jungle being haunted by a ghost, to keep the forest officers and the villagers away.

> In a meeting with the author, actor Ranjeet who played Jacob, one of the members of the smuggler Dhanpat Rai, shared a scary incident during the making of Kartavya, 'During the shooting in the Mudumalai forest in Tamil Nadu, they would sew up the mouths of the lions and remove their claws. There was this shot in which I fall into a pit containing a lion. The mouth of the lion was not sewn up because I did not have to get close to the lion. But when the lion was being teased to rile it for the shot, it got so angry that it chewed off the rope. It was a very dangerous shot and a near miss.'

To add more variety to the smugglers' activities, we see two rival groups led by Wong (Rajan Haskar) and Wasco (Mohan Sherry) in *CID 909*

(1967) trying to steal a peaceful scientific formula from a Professor while Vikram (Danny) smuggles Uranium in *Ashiq Hoon Baharon Ka* (1977). 'Yes, when Natraj ki murti becomes very common, we try something new,' opined Danny.

There was a much-discussed strip poker scene in *Ashiq Hoon Baharon Ka* featuring Danny and Zeenat Aman. Said Danny, 'I do not recollect whether it was Zeenat herself or a body double. The scene was very aesthetically shot because a close-up shot zooming into the bosoms is more vulgar than someone in a bikini.' Zeenat Aman however, denied stripping for that scene. 'I have no recollection. There may have been a body double. For me there were always lines drawn,' she asserted, in an interview with the author.

Hiding and transporting smuggled goods is never easy. This is where the smuggler genre also introduced innovations that brought an extra edge to viewing.

In *Night in London* (1967), stolen gems are tied to pigeons and released into the skies just ashore Hong Kong. In *Jane Anjane* (1971), Miss Suzie (Helen) gets past Bombay Customs by hiding the diamonds inside a case of '555' cigarettes. In *Parvarish* (1977), children's toy cars prove handy to hide hashish and diamonds in, while Sahani Seth (Amjad Khan) in *Kaalia* (1981) smuggles gold bars underneath layers of textile mill products. Amjad Khan, on turning a director himself, came out with something unique in his *Chor Police* (1983)—hiding diamonds inside the false dentures of an old man; something he probably borrowed from *Diamonds Are Forever* (1971). In *Awwal Number* (1990), the air hostess Maria (Neeta Puri) tries to smuggle gold biscuits into the country by hiding them in the folds of her sari, her blouse and inside her bra. In an earlier Dev Anand film *Heera Panna* (1973), the diamond locket stolen by Panna (Zeenat Aman), a bikini model who got entangled in a smugglers' gang, is hidden inside the gasoline compartment of a car.

'*This ingenious idea of hiding the jewel in the gasoline compartment was Dev saab's, he had come upon it somewhere,' revealed Amit Khanna in an interview with the author. Khanna also remembered that the photography equipment used by Heera (Dev Anand) belonged to the famous glamour photographer Dhiraj Chawda. 'Dev saab bought two cars specifically for Heera Panna—one was an open MG and the other was a Vauxhall. Also, the party scene in which the diamond theft takes place—that was an actual party at Palace Grounds, Bangalore. And the people present were actual guests invited for the party. They were not told that a film shooting was on!'*

4

'D', *the* 'Supari' *Era*
The 1980s onwards

'*K*aam *to kaam hai na? Koi doctor hota hai, koi engineer hota hai. Main gangster hai* ... (Work is work. Someone is a doctor, someone an engineer. I am a gangster)'—Deshu in *D* (2005)

The city of Bombay has been the default backdrop of Hindi films. Thus, every Bollywood fan, regardless of whether they have ever lived in Bombay or not, is familiar with the names of Bombay's prominent localities. Versova beach is equal to the docking station for unlisted ferries carrying something fishy. Juhu and Malabar Hill meant the tony rich while Matunga and Kolivada were assumed to be low-income localities. And Khandala meant a getaway from the city. Churchgate and Bandra were lyrically included and even non-Bombayites knew that Gateway of India (with its perennial droves of pigeons) was in the vicinity of Hotel Taj International, while Marine Drive is that one long stretch for insatiable action. Bombay's local trains became the motif for any number of action sequences. In *Shalimar*, the horn of the Bombay electric train drowns out the sound of the shot fired from a telescopic gun. And the Bambaiyya accent with phrases like '*kya horeila hai* or *kya kar reila hai*', too, added a tangy flavour that the purist shunned. Actor Sharat Saxena who hails from the Hindi heartland of Madhya Pradesh clarified, 'The Bambaiyya dialect is spoken by certain groups in Mumbai and not everyone. So, it provided a variety. We must also remember that times have changed since the 1970s. Today many dialects of Hindi are spoken in Mumbai because of influx of people from all parts of India into the city'.

In Haath ki Safai *(1974), the suburban train scene in the climax provided enough off-screen drama as well. Said actor Ranjeet in a chat with the author,* 'Haath ki Safai *was getting delayed as it was proving to be very difficult to get Hema Malini, Vinod Khanna and Randhir Kapoor together this climax train scene. Then they came to know that I had a five or six-hour stopover at Bombay en route to London from Mauritius. They managed to convince the customs and immigration and brought me out of the airport. I was taken to Panvel Station 40 kilometres away. In the car, during transit, I shot for* Mastan Dada *by changing in the car itself! And, on reaching Panvel, I shot for* Haath ki Safai.'

When the mafia come … can the police be far behind? With Bombay as the smugglers' capital in the 1970s, the cops would obviously be called Inspector Shinde, Bhende, Wagle, Ambolkar, Patankar, Gupte, Sathe, Gawde, Bhosle, Gaitonde, Deshpande or Patil, played by Jagdish Raaj or Satyen Kappu. Sitting two levels up was Iftekar, the smart DCP who had to get smarter, too, to match their quarries.

Bombay/Mumbai would continue to be the focal point of the mafia films in the 1980s and 1990s too …. But it would be a different city altogether.[73]

Maharashtra emerged as the strongest Indian State with the state income growing by 3.5 times between 1981 and 1991.[74] Unfortunately, however, greater wealth meant bloodier crimes. And thus, the 1980s brought new kinds of organized crime like black marketeering, extortion, prostitution, betting rackets, supari (contract) killing, human trafficking, sale of human organs, protection money (hafta) from poor wage earners, eviction of tenants from their chawls (low-income community housing), or lending money for satta (gambling) or real-estate builders, and then being merciless on those who failed to pay back. Even the rich had little reprieve. They had to cough up money to one Bhai (Don, as he is called in the local lingo) in return for protection against kidnapping and ransom from another Bhai. Landowners were forced to sell their properties at gunpoint with the Bhai presiding over the mandwali (negotiation). Threatening calls and letters to anyone that had purchased a new flat or an expensive car became commonplace in the early 1990s. Film financing, too, quickly became a favourite of the mafia who saw exponential returns, with the association with the glitterati thrown in as a bonus. Film producers like Gulshan Kumar, who declined their financial help, were not looked at very kindly by the mafia.[75] And then there were the inter-gang rivalries, too. Mahesh Dholakia, the owner of the erstwhile Caeser's Palace hotel, was gunned down by Chota Rajan and his associates in 1987.[76]

Thus, from the mid-1980s, Bombay/Mumbai became a cauldron of crime a la Chicago of the 1930s. Daytime shootouts at traffic signals through rolled down car windows, throats getting slit in the by-lanes twining through chawls, contract-killing at highway petrol pumps by shooters in Maruti Omni vans and vehicles dressed as ambulances, audacious revenge killings at JJ Hospitals and other public places, murder of witnesses inside courtrooms—Bombay was under a virtual siege by the mafia. The Bombay police, despite its intent, was helpless because the mafia had key politicians and police on their payroll. Contrarily, the war on the streets got worse when the government gave a free hand to the police.

Smuggler movies of the 1970s were fun to watch because the common man on the street was relatively untouched by those activities. (The statue of Nataraj stolen from the museum didn't belong to anyone from the public anyway.) But these newer crimes of the 1980s and 1990s, when represented on-screen, made for disturbing viewing because God forbid, these could happen to you and me.

For story ideas, all that Bollywood had to do was read the daily newspapers. But where would Bollywood find the actors to play these roles? Remember, the films of the 1970s were still *actor*-centric rather than *reality*-centric ones. As a result, what we saw were figments of imagination masquerading as mafia—for example, apart from four scenes in the uniform of a coolie, Vijay of *Deewar* (1975) was not even close to Haji Mastan, on whose life the film was purportedly based. Likewise, the foodgrain hoarding mafia Don Lion, which is pronounced as 'Loin' in *Kalicharan* (1976), looked too refined and elegant. That was because the character of Lion had been scripted keeping *Ajit* in mind.

> *In Sidharth Malhotra's show* Ek Villain Ek Dastaan *on Zoom TV,* director Subhash Ghai *recalled: 'Hum bolte rah gaye ki "Sir 'Loin' aise mat boliye lekin wo unka andaaz tha. Urdu bolne wale log takriban English aise hi bolte hain. (We kept telling Ajit sahab the correct way to pronounce "Lion". But that was his style. Urdu speaking people tend to speak English this way).'*[77]

For a similar reason, Shakaal (Kulbushan Kharbanda) in *Shaan* (1980) as a hoarder and black marketeer with multiple godowns in Bombay under his command looked quite unconvincing. For one, he was sitting in a hideout 300 kilometres away from Bombay, whereas black marketeers are usually close to the action to be able to be in control. Secondly, even Shakaal's four henchmen (actually three, as one of them gets fed to the sharks) who manage his operations in Bombay are dressed in natty, pristine white suits and ties—not one of them look like they had ever visited a dusty godown. Shakaal looked closer to one of those villains in James Bond films—which made his appearance inconsistent with his activities.

To play authentic mafia characters from the Bombay underworld of the 1980s, Bollywood needed faces that looked like anyone one would meet in the bazaar, someone who spoke Marathi-accented Hindi and who was comfortable riding pillion on motorbikes (not left-hand driven imported cars) with a ghoda (horse, a local lingo for a pistol) tucked under their belts.

———

The new neighbour next door was a simple, studious-looking, bearded young bachelor. He was rather shy, soft-spoken and very helpful to elderly people. His neighbours knew that his name was Satya. What they did not know was that he worked for the Mumbai underworld and had seventeen murder charges against him.

In the 1980s and 1990s, there emerged maverick young film-makers like N. Chandra, Vidhu Vinod Chopra and Ram Gopal Verma with fresh ideas around a realistic depiction of the domestic mafioso. With that came a galaxy of never-before-seen and fine actors like Sadashiv Amrapurkar, Manoj Bajpayee, J.D. Chakravarthy, Pankaj Kapoor, Charan Raj, Mukesh Rishi and Nana Patekar.

Govind Nihalani, with a decade's experience in parallel cinema behind him, opened the doors to this realism in 1983. Nihalani's *Ardh Satya* (1983) was about the naked truth. For the first time we saw the true, unadulterated image of the Bombay mafia kingpin—the swarthy Rama Shetty, who spoke in a distinctly local dialect, played by debutant Sadashiv Amrapurkar. Rama Shetty runs a sizeable gambling racket in a low-income locality of Bombay. Shetty is also something of a kingmaker in the Legislative Assembly elections because he can influence the voters in that locality as he is sort of a godfather figure to the dwellers. He also wields significant influence over the police at senior levels, getting his goons released from lock-up by making a mere phone call to someone high up, making the police look stupid. Amrapurkar hailed from Ahmednagar and began acting in plays since his college days. By the early 1980s, Amrapurkar had become a well-established Marathi theatre actor.

Nihalani wanted a completely new face that had never been seen before as a villain or as a hero, 'a freshness that would add to the character'. And so, as suggested by Vijay Tendulkar, Nihalani met Amrapurkar. 'I liked his eyes and face, but I had never seen him perform,' Nihalani said.

In an interview with the author, Amrapurkar shared: 'I was playing a cop in Vijay Tendulkar's Marathi play called *Hands Up!* around that time. Govindji called me to his place the next day. I presumed that since I had played a cop in the play, I would get the role of a policeman in *Ardh Satya* as well! But guess what he offered me—the role of the mafia don Rama Shetty, adding that the role wasn't very big, but it was a very important one.'

What Nihalani saw in Amrapurkar playing the farcical cop was the actor's 'brilliant timing', which immediately assured the director of the latter's acting prowess. 'The character's name, originally kept as Krushna Shetty, was later changed to Rama,' Amrapurkar recalled. 'The dialogues were very strong, and the film and the character became famous for that. Without Rama Shetty, the film would have been incomplete. And I felt good at the importance that the role received. I was very nervous to start with. But it was a great experience working with these two great personalities Govindji and Vijay Tendulkar sahib.'

Nihalani was thorough with his homework. In a chat with the author he said, 'During that period, with the help of a police inspector, I also met some people. I went to their addas. So, I had a feel for this character though I did not want Sadashiv to imitate anybody. I allowed him to discover and evolve into Rama Shetty.'

And Amrapurkar remained indebted to Nihalani. 'It was just a two-and-a-half day shoot. And then I forgot about it. But when the film released, my performance was lauded highly. And because of that film *ab tak meri rozi roti chal rahi hai* (And because of that film, I am still being able to earn my livelihood to this day).'

Then, in the 1987 *Pratighaat*, there was the local extortionist and negotiator Kali Prasad, played by debutant Kannada actor Charan Raj.

Unlike Rama Shetty who takes nothing personally—not even his son getting thrashed in a police lock-up—Kali Prasad is a fool with a short fuse, who'd overreact. No mafia would disrobe a woman in public and attract needless attention the way Kali does. *Pratighaat* was newbie director N. Chandra's second consecutive successful reality check after *Ankush* (1986). *Ankush* is about a group of good-at-heart young coercers and tenant evictors led by Ravi Kelkar (Nana Patekar). In a 2017 television interview with Navniit S. Anand for *Fiji Times Australia* in Sydney, N. Chandra shared that the Worli Naka area of Bombay in which he grew up was home to the ten biggest slums of Worli area. Also, ten mills were located in the area.[78] Elucidated N. Chandra, 'There was a Worli Hill where the most affluent people used to stay. So, we had the disparity of extreme levels'. In the course of the interview, Chandra shared that the biggest mill strike in Bombay in the early 1980s in which 600,000 workers went on strike for two years, changed the face of Bombay. 'Everything was standstill. Then somehow it (the strike) was broken into pieces and then, from there the (Bombay) underworld started', he stated definitively.[79] Evidently, these events shaped Chandra's sensibilities when he made *Ankush* and *Pratighaat*.

But wait ... wasn't there a system to keep these mafia under check? What was the government doing? And here is the background of how the mafia found a very useful ally and sponsor—the corrupt politician. Here is the genesis of the corrupt politician, one of the most abominable villains of Bollywood.

Politicians with ambiguous intent had been around for a long time, e.g., the management stooge Pradhan (Rajinder) and the manipulative Das Kaka (P. Jairaj) instigating labour violence in *Baharon ke Sapne* (1967), the wheeler-dealer Lallu (Om Prakash) in *Aandhi* (1975) trying to outmanoeuvre his party chief Aarti Devi by having conversations with a rival party by the side. But these were either shrewd political manipulators or ideological fanatics—and not really into corruption yet. But within two decades of independence, established criminals figured out that the best place to camouflage their crime was under the seat of a public office. Arguably the first of this tribe was the adulterator and racketeer Jung 'JB' Bahadur (Jayant) in Mehboob Khan's last directorial venture *Son of India* (1962) who runs for elections. Soon, many like 'JB' followed. Dharamdas (Om Prakash) in *Apna Desh* (1972), an embezzler of public money, runs for the post of the Municipal Chairman. So does smuggler and hoarder Dharam Kohli (Utpal Dutt) in *Kotwal Saab* (1977).

Black money was one of the immediate benefits that the corrupt politician earned. Obviously, it had to be hidden away as unaccounted money cannot be deposited in bank accounts. In a story set in 1981, Member of Parliament Rameshwar Singh (Saurabh Shukla) of Lucknow, in *Raid* (2018), gets done in by someone in his own household who tips off the Income Tax department. The Department uncovers truckloads of unaccounted gold, currency and valuables in his mansion, and Rameshwar ends up in jail. *Raid* is based on true incidents. Saurabh Shukla shared deeper insights, '*Raid* was not based on a real incident. Bits of pieces were taken from some case and then some other case and then they (added up to) make a story of one guy (Rameshwar Singh). In some case of an IT raid somewhere (maybe not this exact case), somebody must have reached the capital and made way to the Prime Minister of India. It was just to have that authenticity and to just to make you feel that way (that the PM angle was depicted in *Raid*). In the film it never says "Indira Gandhi". But subconsciously it makes you believe.'

But this was kids' stuff. Far more serious offences by a Bollywood politician were around the corner.

Kissa Kursi Kaa (1977), with Gangaram (Manohar Singh) as the president of a fictitious country called Jan Gan Desh, is a fictionalized (and thinly disguised) account of the Allahabad High Court's annulment of the then Prime Minister Mrs Indira Gandhi's 1971 election victory and her subsequent ban from contesting elections for six years; in response to this Mrs Gandhi's imposed National Emergency in India in June

1975. The political murders, the overnight flattening of the Turkhman Gate slums and Sanjay Gandhi's 'small-car' Maruti programme during Emergency were all fictionalized in *Kissa Kursi Kaa*. It was naked abuse and misuse of the government machinery by President Gangaram of Jan Gan Desh. The film also laid bare organized bribery at official counters of government offices. A mute, helpless young lady called Junta (Shabana Azmi) is the allegory for the public at large. Driven by frustration, Junta commits suicide outside the 'Parliament'.

Kissa Kursi Ka was not a one-off. It was only a curtain-raiser.

Interestingly, in *Son of India* and *Kotwal Sahab*, the villain did not actually *win* the election—he was only an aspirant. But it gave their successors like Rama Shetty in *Ardh Satya* and Kali Prasad in *Pratighat* a good career option. In addition to the safety net that a political office provided them, the criminal-politician (yes, 'criminal', not merely 'corrupt') could not have hoped for a better shield than the police force. No wonder criminals-turned-politicians like Rama Shetty and Kali sniggered with glee. The very police who should have locked them up, were now duty-bound to protect them during their political campaigns.

The mid 1980s was also a period when core Marxist values like intellect and education were being threatened by new-age groups of loud-speaking militancy that lured workers by a show of braggadocio. Datta Samant was one of those militant trade union leaders who, in the early 1980s, mobilized massive support from Bombay's mill workers. Promising huge wage increases to mill workers, Samant convinced the workers of over fifty textile mills to go on a mass strike in 1982, crippling the Bombay textile industry. Militant trade union leader Rustom Patel (Naseeruddin Shah) in Govind Nihalani's *Aghaat* (1986) is modelled on Datta Samant. The arm-twisting and coercion of workers to join Patel's rival union was reminiscent of Datta Samant's aggressive posture to the Textile Mill management in 1981 and his rallying cry to derecognize the elected RMMS (Rashtriya Mill Mazdoor Sangh) as the representative union of the mill workers.[80] Patel's mouthpiece was the

goonda Krishnan (played by Malayalam actor Gopi) who spreads fear
by merely using Rustom Patel's name. Patel, the antagonist, makes his
physical appearance only in the last scene—and gets driven away by the
incumbent trade union members who, too, resort to violence. But clearly
the labour union mafia member Krishnan is employed by the politician
villain Rustom. The politician had begun to figure out how to use the
mafia. And reciprocally, the mafia could not have found a better shield
than an elected public servant.

In *Arjun* (1985), for instance, gambling den owner Anup Lal
(Paresh Rawal) and the extortionist mafia are owned by politician Deen
Dayal Trivedi (Prem Chopra). The politicians also had at their disposal
an inexhaustible band of unemployed, frustrated youth. Shivkumar
Chowgule (Anupam Kher), a rival politician of Deen Dayal Trivedi, is
one such villain who uses a disgruntled young man Arjun (Sunny Deol)
to gather evidences against Trivedi with the stated reason of bringing to
public notice Trivedi's illegal activities. But Chowgule's intentions are
very different. In an interview with the author, Anupam Kher spoke of
his role as the deceitful politician, 'Chowgule was a character which was
used at a time when the youth still trusted the politicians. But politicians,
whether they look clean or not, are politicians. They will not shirk
from ruining your happiness at any given moment. That's why they are
politicians.' After using Arjun to get evidence against Trivedi, Chowgule
uses it for bartering a political deal with Trivedi.

International terrorist Anil Raj (Tiger Prabhakar) in *Inquilaab* (1984)
is hired by Shankar Narayan (Kader Khan), the president of the political
party 'Garibon ki Party', to spread terror in the city by looting shops
and murdering and abducting people so that Shankar Narayan's rival
ruling party may be shown as ineffective. Another member of Narayan's
party, Sitaram (Utpal Dutt), is also involved closely with an international
smuggler Koya Koya Attache (Shakti Kapoor). In a master-stroke
political move, Narayan installs a former supercop, ACP Amarnath,
as the party president and paves the way for Amarnath to become

the chief minister of the state so that Narayan and Sitaram, shielded and protected by the puppet chief minister, may continue with their illegal activities. Narayan also fills up Amarnath's cabinet of ministers with individuals like food adulterator Vishwanath (Pinchoo Kapoor) as the Food Minister, the illiterate Saraswati Prasad (C.S. Dubey) as Education Minister, currency counterfeiter Kamaleshwar Rao (Ram Mohan) as the Finance Minister, goonda, blackmarketer, seller of illicit liquor Bhupat (Ranjeet) as Excise Minister .... In other words, the state cabinet is an ensemble of the city's mafia with Sitaram himself (and now the father-in-law of Amarnath) as the Home Minister. The coupling between the politicians and the mafia was now official. Meanwhile, N. Chandra delivered his third blockbuster in a row—*Tezaab* (1988). Unfortunately, Kiran Kumar's competent performance in the role of the extortionist Lotiya Seth got cannibalized by the film's other humungous attractions. In the *Ek Do Teen* countdown, Lotiya Seth got discounted.

Another question that demands an answer: what was law enforcement doing? Shouldn't the police be handcuffing these corrupt politicians along with the mafia? Yes, they used to. But then, even the men in khaki in Bollywood got compromised to form another genre of villainy—the corrupt policeman.

Arguably, the first ever corrupt policeman was observed in *Apna Desh* (1949) in which Sub-Inspector Bholanath (played by Chandrashekhar) accepts a bribe of an expensive wristwatch from smuggler Mohini's gang in return for allowing Mohini's gang to smuggle out goods from the harbour. In the same film, we observe with concern a corrupt Customs Officer Gulzar Singh who permits gold bars to get smuggled in through the air route. And guess what? Even a young official Jan Barbar at the Government Arms Depot is corrupt. He allows Mohini and Dhaniram's gang to steal a thousand guns from the Arms Depot because Jan Barbar owed a favour to Dhaniram. But *Apna Desh* was an exception. Apart from this film, one struggles to recollect even one corrupt policeman in films till the late 1970s. Forget corruption, even showing the policemen indulging in any form of vice was taboo. In *C.I.D.* (1956), the song *'Jaata Kahan Hai Diwane'* showing Inspector Shekhar (Dev Anand) getting drunk was edited out.

Another observation in the context of the genesis of the corrupt policeman is that, starting with *Jaal* (1952), the hawaldar (constable) has been the stock comedian of Bollywood—a lathi-wielding dimwit with that substantial belt perched clumsily on his belly. Film after film, comic cameos by Asit Sen, Agha, Rajendranath, Dhumal, V. Gopal, Asrani, Birbal, Anoop Kumar, I.S. Johar, Bhagwan and Keshto Mukherji resulted in the image of the policeman getting ridiculed. Even senior-ranking officials were caricatured. It was almost customary for the police to rush in at the climax scene, firing pistol shots in the air shouting, 'Hands up! *Koi apni jagah se nahi hilega* (Nobody moves)!' *after* the hero had polished off the villains. Peals of laughter would ripple across the auditorium at what had become a symbol of police ineffectiveness.

So, turning corrupt was a logical next step for the Bollywood policeman because the ineffective ones are the ones most susceptible. Inspector Thakur (Manmohan) in *Kotwal Saab* (1977) who keeps shielding the smuggler was one of the first something-like-corrupt policeman. Hawaldar Nekiram (Jagdeep) in *Do Hawaldar* (1979) was perhaps one of the earliest portrayals of a policeman accepting petty bribes.

Sometime in the early 1980s, the Bollywood policemen started accepting bribes to cover up crimes more serious in nature. *Andhaa Kanoon* (1983) is a fine example of bribery at every rung—from the traffic constable who accepts a bribe from a traffic violater right up to the retired jailor Gupta (Madan Puri) who distorts the police record of a rape and murder case in exchange for a fat retirement plan from the three villains Amar (Prem Chopra), Akbar (Danny Denzongpa) and Anthony (Pran). In *Dharm aur Qanoon* (1985), Superintendent of Police Kader (Danny) voluntarily partners with the smuggler Teja (Om Shivpuri) in his illegal business. In fact, Kader is the brains behind this odious partnership. Kader tells Teja, 'Ye *mat bhulna ke ye khel mera hai. Tum sirf mere haath ho aur mai tumhara dimag* (Remember, this is my game. You are just the hands, but I am the brains behind this).'

And soon, the inevitable alliance between the corrupt khaki and the corrupt khadi happened. For example, a popularly elected Member of the Legislative Assembly Gopal Chowdhary (Om Shivpuri) in *Shatru* (1986) publicly states that he found it incomprehensible that a policeman would *not* accept a bribe!

Said Danny about the scene in Dharam aur Kanoon *in which Kader murders Asha Parekh. 'I had to put the cord round Asha Parekh's neck but it depended on how I held it. Yes, my muscles flexed and so did the expression on my face and hers. The whole trick is—I hold the cord at her throat, not too loose (it won't look real) or too tight (as it can choke the person). Now I didn't pull the cord back towards her throat. I pulled it a couple of inches away from her throat.'*

Meanwhile more fresh blood in Bollywood film-making had arrived in the form of Vidhu Vinod Chopra who, right from his student days at FTII Pune, had a preference for dark films. His first two films—the suspense thriller *Sazaa-e-Maut* (1981) and the murder mystery *Khamosh* (1985)—were critically acclaimed commercial failures. But the pigeons brought good news for Chopra with his 1989 *Parinda*, a landmark film on the Bombay underworld. Nana Patekar stunned the industry once again in his role of the pyrophobic mafia don Anna Seth of South Indian origin who, shuffling around indecisively, often scratches or taps his head as if looking for ideas … and then, issues the deadliest of sentences with a deadpan expression, screechy laughter and jerky hand movements. In a very rare occurrence, Nana Patekar won both the Filmfare Award as well as the National Award that year. Few deserved it more.

The role of the Abdul Khan (Suresh Oberoi), Anna Seth's henchmen, was initially offered to Danny. Though Danny declined the role, he did make a contribution to Parinda. *Said Danny in an interview with the author, 'One evening as we were all sitting and having a drink, we started singing. There was a flute lying there and I started playing it. Instantly, Suresh got the idea that the character would be playing a flute and I was told to teach Suresh to play the flute. And since Vinod is a perfectionist, every evening I would teach Suresh to play the flute!'*

Having hit upon the formula Nana wasn't about to let go, returning an exceptional performance in *Angaar* (1992) as the land-grabbing Don Majid Khan, the rebel son of the patriarch Don Jahangir Khan (Kader Khan). By the mid-1990s, land grabbing had become one of the top priorities for the mafia. 'Yes,' agreed Danny, speaking of his role as the land mafia kingpin Chatursingh in *Krantiveer* who goes about inciting public disturbance in order to grab a piece of land to build a resort on. 'The writers pick up on incidents related to whatever happens in the society.' But then, the real-estate corporations could not afford to have their names get linked to the land mafia. Yet, those corporations needed the services of the very same land mafia to acquire land from house owners to build multi-storeyed buildings on. This corporatization and the legitimization of the real estate mafia is what Govind Nihalani depicted in *Thakshak* (1999). In a brilliant performance in *Thakshak* (1999), Rahul Bose plays Sunny, the scion of Bhavani Builders who is in the pursuit of his goal of becoming the real estate King of Mumbai. '*Hum is sheher par hukumat kar rahe honge...* (We shall rule this city)', Sunny spells out the strategic vision for his company, holding a pistol in his hand. In this endeavour, Sunny recklessly, remorselessly (and sometimes needlessly), eliminates all those who come in the way of his goal—be it people who refuse to sell their houses to his company or competitors to Bhavani Builders like Feroze Constructions. Sunny has no regard for relationships and is totally bereft of conscience. Yet he is able to don the veneer of a smart-suited corporate bigwig when needed. Despite the film's commercial failure, Sunny stood out as a good example of the corporatized land-grabbing mafia.

Prostitution, they say, is the oldest profession known to man. And if the smugglers could deal in national artefacts, drugs, tusks and animal skins, what was to stop them from entering the flesh trade? In Bollywood, prostitution as an organized crime trickled in with *Keemat* (1973), where unsuspecting girls were promised jobs abroad but ended up being doped and coerced into prostitution. While Inspector Balram in *Ram Balram* (1980) saved dozens of innocent girls from being smuggled away to Dubai to be sold as prostitutes, neo-pubescent girls like Lakshmi in *Giddh* (1984), under the excuse of an archaic devadasi custom, kept getting sold by pimps to brothels in Bombay. In her cult classic *Salaam Bombay!* (1988), Mira Nair traces the journey of a virgin, sixteen-year-old 'Solasaal' (Chanda Sharma), forcibly brought into a brothel in the infamous red light of Falkland Road and detained there till her sale at a premium to her first customer. *Salaam Bombay!* depicted Bombay's dark underbelly of slums with child abuse, child labour and their exploitation, with minors turning felons in no time. The city was a quick teacher. Far from facilitating the delinquent back to mainstream, the juvenile homes only helped the boys 'graduate' into criminality. Chaipau (Shafiq Syed) in *Salaam Bombay!*, all of thirteen, murders the drug dealer Baba (Nana Patekar). *Salaam Bombay!* is about the realities we all knew.

Homeless children, the mafia figured, can be used in multiple ways. Making destitute children a source of revenue by making them beg on the streets, for instance. The portrayal of the begging mafia had started as early as in the 1954 *Boot Polish*. With Bombay's population implosion, begging became a deep and dark network much like multi-level marketing, as was seen in a comedy-coated subplot in *Gardish* (1993). Harishbhai Manishbhai (Annu Kapoor) starts off as a beggar himself and soon builds a massive network of 20,000 beggars around the city who are his main source of revenue. Soon, Harishbhai Manishbhai owns a plush office, car and bungalow. And of course, part of the earnings from the 20,000 beggars under Harishbhai find their way to the local Bhai Billa Jilani (Mukesh Rishi).

But the raw fear that the prostitution mafia don Maharani in *Sadak* (1991) struck was singular. Played by Sadashiv Amrapurkar, Maharani (the name chosen by Mahesh Bhatt) was arguably the first hijra (eunuch) villain in Hindi films. Maharani runs a prostitution racket, enlisting helpless girls and renting them out to clients. The prostitution rackets of *Salaam Bombay!* and *Sadak* were very different compared to those in *Keemat* and *Ram Balram*. In *Salaam Bombay!* and *Sadak*, prostitution was part of an ensemble of crimes and criminals in which every foot-soldier was replaceable and dispensable. When Chillum (Raghubir Yadav) in *Salaam Bombay!* dies of drug abuse, he is replaced by another boy called—guess what—Chillum again. And unlike the conscientious law enforcers in *Keemat* and *Ram Balram*, Maharani in *Sadak* has the support of another 'prostitute' in khaki—Inspector Irani (Pankaj Dheer) who is on the payroll of Don Maharani.

In an interview, Amrapurkar shared about his role of Maharani, 'From the way we conceived it right from the first shot, the character would be about fear and not comedy. And I've seen bike-riding extortionists in sari and jewellery. The scenes were conceived broadly and then executed spontaneously. Dialogues were written but improvised on the spot as in the way the dialogue "*Billi boli meeaow, kahe ghabrao* (The cat says meow meow, why worry)" had to be delivered.' The actor credited Mahesh Bhatt for the way he laid out the role, 'like an open book', he said. The director gave Amrapurkar the full freedom to work the way he wanted to, and in return, the actor poured his mind and soul into it, thereby making the role the foundation on which the film was based. 'A writer friend of mine had created the character of a thug who had a fascination for wearing sari, kumkum, jewellery, talking like women, living amidst women like women and getting himself photographed in female outfits. I carried this in my memory and used it in the sari changing scene in *Sadak*,' said Amrapurkar.

Hitherto, a Bollywood villain has been a man or a woman. Maharani was something in between. Mahesh Bhatt, in a chat with the author, shared the origin of the paradigm-breaking villain character. 'Maharani was sourced from my memory of a person called Tikku. He was my hairdresser in Mahim, where I grew up. He was a tall and handsome hijra but very violent when cornered. I have seen him brutally beat men with the physical grace of a woman. I felt that, to create a character like Tikku would be a risk, but one worth taking. We wanted someone very earthy to play the role and hence we selected Sadashiv who had a theatre background in rural areas. Bollywood whispers said that this film would be a colossal disaster because you can't have the villain of the film who is a "hijra" because the term "hijra" is an embodiment of cowardice. But, people still remember Maharani.'

Director Mahesh Manjrekar brought out the best of Sanjay Dutt as Don Raghunath 'Raghu' Shivalkar in *Vaastav: The Reality* (1999); this film is once again about land mafia-dom. Raghu's story starts off as the son of a simple lower income group family who sets up an eatery shop and tries to earn an honest living. But he gets sucked into a street brawl with Fracture Pandya (Jack Gaud), the brother of a local goon. Pandya gets killed in the brawl, things spiral out of control and Raghu is forced to go underground and into the underworld in the gang of Vitthal Kaanya (Paresh Rawal). With time, Raghu grows in strength and influence, emboldened by the fact that a person no less than the Home Minister Babban Rao Kadam (Mohan Joshi) approaches Raghu through a middleman and assigns him the task of evicting a Parsi family from their ancestral house.

Contrary to popular belief, *Vaastav* is not a biopic on the life of the mafia king Chhota Rajan—a fact confirmed by Hussain Zaidi as well, in a chat with the author. This misconception could be because the film was produced by Chhota Rajan's brother Deepak Nikalje.

A year earlier, the truth of the Mumbai mafia was paraded by Ram Gopal Varma in his *Satya* (1998). Young Satya is an immigrant in Bombay and starts out by working as a waiter in a bar. Trouble starts when he gets humiliated by Jagga, one of the uncouth customers at the bar. The next time someone tries to bully him, Satya retaliates, lands up in jail and runs into Bheeku Mhatre, another underworld operator involved in extortion, film-financing and gambling. Satya starts working for Bheeku's gang and soon grows to become Bheeku Mhatre's most trusted man and Bheeku's strategist. Unlike Bheeku, Satya is unemotional by nature, making him deadlier.

But then, *Satya* was not about Satya alone. What Anurag Kashyap and Saurabh Shukla scripted was a ballet of characters that danced around Satya to accentuate his impact. The big don Bhau Thakurdas Jhawle (Govind Namdev) and a contestant in the upcoming municipal corporation elections, is Bheeku's boss and mentor. Given his long-standing respect for Bhau, Bheeku would not take any step that would upset Bhau. But Satya has no such loyalty towards Bhau and quickly (and correctly) perceives that Bhau was merely using Bheeku for the upcoming elections. And Bheeku's increasing dependence on Satya for strategic decisions makes Don Bhau Jhawle very uncomfortable about Satya. At Satya's prompting, Bheeku disobeys Bhau's orders and murders a buddy-turned-rival gangster Guru Narayan. And Bhau is furious with Bheeku for this.

On the one hand it is inter-gang rivalry and on the other Police Commissioner Amod Shukla (Paresh Rawal) lets loose his force on the mafia gangs. The city rains bullets and human blood flows into the gutter along with monsoon water while gangsters, in the face of custodial police torture, bleat for mercy like dismembered goats. Every bullet in *Satya* performed exactly the way it was supposed to—death in an instant.

Govind Namdev who played Bhau Thakurdas Jhawle ranked this role as one of his top five roles. In an interview with the author, he shared: 'When the story and character were narrated, I built a hazy shell of the character in my mind, i.e., in what way would he be bad, how heartless would he be, maybe he would sport a moustache, etc. These got refined out in discussions with director Varma. And then my search for such a character began within the society. Since I had not interacted with anyone from the underworld earlier, I collected fifty or sixty crime magazines, old and new, to study the pictures of real underworld criminals as a part of my preparation for the character of Bhau. And I showed those pictures to Ram Gopal Varma. Also, when I laid out the pictures of these criminals on the table, I observed that, for some strange reason, more than 50 per cent of them had a gap at the centre of their moustaches. For playing Bhau, I took the moustache from one of the characters in those pictures and the eyebrows from another. And finally, based on my observation of various people, we imposed a certain way of talking into the character of Jhawle, similar to the way a Marathi speaks Hindi. Post this, collecting magazines on real-life industrialists, politicians, policemen and studying their pictures became my way of preparing for my roles.'

All the mafia characters of *Satya* were newbies, the only exception being South Indian actor J.D. Chakravarthy. Post his debut in *Shiva* (1990), Chakravarthy had quite a few well-received outings in Tamil and Telegu films before coming back to Hindi with the biggest success of his career—in the title role Satya. According to Anurag Kashyap, co-writer with Saurabh Shukla on *Satya*, 'The film took on new dimensions. While the crew was excited during the making of the film, no one realized the extent to which it would go.'

In *Satya*, there were a few good men too. In a chat with the author, said Saurabh Shukla, who essayed the role of the avuncular member Kallu Mama of Bheeku Mhatre's mafia, 'I am sure there were reflections of many actors and great characters in my role, such as Luca Brasi in *The Godfather* or Paulie Cicero in *GoodFellas (1990)*.'

What made the characters in *Satya* memorable was their hilarious two-facedness. As Shukla revealed, 'In the scene after the "*Goli Maar*" song, one of the gang members throws a beer bottle from the balcony.

I berate him on his lack of civic sense and say that it could have hurt someone. It is pure irony that people who kill others are talking about civic sense.' There was a paradox even in their names. Neither Kallu Mama nor Bheeku Mhatre match their professions. Agreed Shukla, 'Yes, there is a saying in Hindi, "*Aankh ke andhe, naam Nayansukh.*" A man called Samrat (emperor) may be a labourer in a building, and Garibchand (a name including the word 'garib' meaning poor) would be the promoter building it.'

And then above all, there is Bheeku Mhatre, the underdog. Manoj Bajpayee, who played Mhatre, explained his character in an interview with the author: 'Bheeku is like a child, just as vulnerable, as emotional. He is a great husband, a great father. Bheeku too has a wife who nags him and scolds him for absconding from home'. And there's just one thing about him—he could not take betrayal. The child in him had to come out in his nervous laughter and the way he spoke. He had to look like someone who would ultimately die. He will rule but people like him are doomed.' Bajpayee's nervous laughter wasn't *acting*. Revealed Anurag Kashyap in a telephonic interview, 'Manoj Bajpayee kept laughing nervously during the shoot as he knew he had got a big break. His nervous laughter gave him a character. There was no choreographer. Ramu (Ram Gopal Varma) gave him the full freedom.' Another fun fact that Kashyap shared is that Bheeku was the name of Ram Gopal Varma's domestic help, and they decided to go with that name.

Satya brought forth a new paradigm. It was not just about power and money. It was more about survival, where violence was the need to combat violence. And quite disturbingly, both *Satya* and *Vaastav* showed the inseparable link between the political system and the underworld.

———

Criminals, as we have seen in Bollywood, have always sought to silence upright media men. An example of this was seen in an earlier film *Aarop*

(1974), where editor Subhash Tripathi (Vinod Khanna) of the firebrand vernacular daily *Mashal* rages a lone war against baron Mahkhhanlal Singh (Rehman) and gets framed for a murder that he did not commit. In *Benaam* (1974), the criminal Kishenlal goes a step further and tries to have investigative journalist Verma stabbed to death to prevent him from exposing Kishenlal's criminal activities. The fast-growing electronic media of the 1980s made the criminals, including the political criminals, more nervous. In Ramesh Sharma's *New Delhi Times* (1986), Vikas Pande (Shashi Kapoor), Editor of *New Delhi Times*, is confronted by all forms of intimidation including physical assault while investigating the mystery of a political murder in Uttar Pradesh. Aspirant Chief Minister Seth Gokuldas (Manohar Singh) in *Main Azaad Hoon* (1989) has no qualms about either manipulating the editor of his own newspaper company or firing him when the editor refused to comply with Seth Gokuldas. Things go a step further in *Jurm* (1990), in which editor Ritesh Nandy (Akash Khurana) gets liquidated in a murder sponsored by the Minister Kandelwal (Om Shivpuri) himself. Visionary media men like Vinod Dua, Prannoy Roy and Karan Thapar made television a public investigative agency by forcing politicians to sit on the hot seat and face the whole nation. It was only a matter of time before politicians like Chief Minister Balraj Chauhan (Amrish Puri) in *Nayak* (2001) would stand exposed. A riot breaks out in the city following a clash between students and a driver of the State Transport Corporation bus. The State Transport Corporation employees call for a Chakka Jam flash strike. Chief Minister Chauhan instructs the Commissioner of Police to take no action because one of the rioting drivers was a member of his party and another belonged to the caste which had voted Chauhan's party into power. Moreover, he cannot afford to lose the goodwill of the students either since they were his party workers. '*Yeh problems kabhi bhi solve nahi karni chahiye. Balki inka issue banakar Raajneeti khelni chahiye* (Never try and solve these problems. Instead, make an issue out of these and play politics),' instructs the Chief Minister.

Meanwhile, the Bollywood policemen had gone from corrupt to ridiculous.

The decades-old laughing stock image of the policemen got further cemented with the arrival of Inspector Giridhar and Havaldar Arjun in *Hum* (1991). The two venomous buffoons live under the largesse of the gangster Bhaktawar (Danny Denzongpa) who oppresses his dock laborers and dunks those who dare to dissent in his acid tank. Giridhar and Arjun then burn Bhaktawar's family to death and scoot with all his wealth. In an interview, Anupam Kher spoke about how the role of the corrupt Inspector Giridhar came about, 'When I reached the set at Mukesh Mills on the first day of the shoot, I told Director Mukul Anand, "Mukul, it is not working out. There is something missing in this character Giridhar. There is no colour to it." I told him that Annu Kapoor and I should shave our heads completely so that visually we would look different. I suggested a Himachali lingo to our dialogues. So whatever dialogues were given by writers, we used to adapt them into our language and deliver them.'

The Bollywood police had lost respect even for their uniforms. The cop slouching on his chair with his legs stretched out on the desk and the top two shirt-buttons of his uniform unfastened became a common sight in films. Their personal integrity had got diluted too. In an alleged murder case of a housewife Karuna Sharma (Poonam Dhillon) in *Police Public* (1990), the corrupt Senior Inspector Maha Singh Garhwal (Naseeruddin Shah) lecherously strips the dead victim's beautiful sister Usha naked with his eyes and makes dirty remarks about Usha right in her father's presence. And the family was still mourning the death of their daughter Karuna.

Even ex-policemen could not influence these cops anymore. A shattered *Indrajeet* (1991) waits patiently outside the cabin of Police Commissioner Shyam Sundar (Sadashiv Amrapurkar) for justice for his foster daughter who had been raped and murdered by Minister

Sadachari's (Kader Khan) rogue son. But Shyam Sunder, bought out by the Minister, calmly nibbles away at a biscuit.

———

In the new millennium, the flesh trade continued and flourished. By the time *Chameli* (2004) released, prostitution had become a pseudo-legitimate business in which all the 3 Ps—pimp, police and politician—were shareholders. Disclosed Sudhir Mishra, director of *Chameli* in a chat with the author, 'Anant Balani, inspired by my earlier *Iss Raat ki Subah Nahi* (1996), was making *Chameli*. But he passed away. And I took that idea and I rewrote the script.'

Interestingly, the villain in *Chameli* (and one of the causes of the all-night melee), Corporator Naik, isn't shown in the film at all. The dark interiors of the city continued to be a breeding ground of young criminals. Just the way that Chaipau in *Salaam Bombay!* stabbed Baba (Nana Patekar) to death, the bar dancer Mumtaz's (Tabu) fifteen-year-old son Abhay (Vishal Thakkar) in *Chandni Bar* (2001) coolly shoots dead two former remand home inmates as a revenge for having forcibly sodomized him when they were at the remand home. And, forced by financial circumstances, Mumtaz's daughter too starts dancing at Chandni Bar .... There was no escaping the vicious circle.

Business was there for the taking for the mafia at every *Traffic Signal* (2007)—beggars, prostitutes, tricksters and flower sellers that earn a living there. And there is a pimp called Silsila (Kunal Khemu). Lording over them was the mafia Bhai Haji Bhaijaan (Sudhir Mishra) who pockets hafta from all these workers. The underworld in *Ghajini* (2008) makes money by extracting human organs from living people. The gang whisks away young girls to Goa and surgically removes their kidneys to be resold for a heavy price.

In addition to all this, in the new millenneum, the corrupt politician and the corrupt policemen that were born in the 1980s grew in stature

and authority to become something far worse—the political *mafia* and
the police *mafia*. Their earlier 'alliance' now became an inseparable three-
way coalition—with the underworld as their third partner.

And thus, there was no difference at all between the politicians and
the mafia. Extortion, kidnapping, blackmail, intimidation, buying out
the police ... every activity of the mafia was copied by the politicians.
Between the politicians, deals would get struck in party sessions, over a
drink, while watching raunchy dances in lawn parties, in hospital ICU
wards and even on the chase with bullets were flying past their ears. In
fact, in some way, they were worse than mafia. Mafia is never into terror-
financing. But politicians dabbled in that too. In *Fiza* (2000), ahead of
an election, two party leaders negotiate thus:

'... *Is baar sarkar hamari hi banne wali hai kyunki majority hamare saath
hai* .... *Agar Musalman bhai bhi hamare saath aa jayen, to hamari party ki
secular chavi poori ho sakti hai* (It is almost certain that we will form the
government this time because the majority vote is with us. The support
from the Muslims will give our party a secular image),' says V.K. Singh
(Ravi Jhankal), leader of the Hindu party.

'*Chief Ministership to aap hamey offer karne se rahe. Home Ministry ke
barey me kya khayal hai* (I know you will not offer me the post of Chief
Minister. What about offering me the post of the Home Minister)?'
Sayeed sahib (Dinesh Thakur), leader of the Muslim party, states his
demand in return.

'*Mujhe sweekar hai* (I accept),' says V.K. Singh. Singh and Sayeed
stand up and hug each other.

V.K. Singh adds, '*Hamare iss gat bandhan se dangey phasad phir se ho
sakte hain* (This alliance of ours may spark off communal riots again).'
To which Sayeed responds, '*Is mein to hamara hi fayda hai na*? (Would
that not be to our benefit)?'

In Madhur Bhandarkar's outstanding *Satta* (2003), politicians like
Liyaqat Baig (Govind Namdev), Yashwant Varde (Atul Kulkarni), Vivek
Chauhan (Sameer Dharmadhikari), Mahendra Chauhan (Shrivallabh

Vyas) were worse than pimps, changing sides and allegiances as and when the situation demanded. What mattered was money, power and political expediency. Nothing else.

Another example of the political mafia was *Sarkar* (2005), in which the Don 'Sarkar' Subhas Nagre (Amitabh Bachchan) is on a first name basis with the Chief Minister Madan Rathore (played by Deepak Shirke). And there is another politician—the MLA Vishram Bhagat (Raju Mavani) who tries to eliminate Sarkar by teaming up with two rivals of Nagre. It transpires ultimately that the kingpin behind the plot to eliminate Sarkar was the Chief Minister Madan Rathore himself because so long as Sarkar was alive, Rathore would remain a puppet Chief Minister. Certain sequences in the film were clearly lifted from *The Godfather*. But at least Ram Gopal Varma was honest enough to admit in the opening credits that '*Like countless other Directors all over the World, I have been deeply influenced by "THE GODFATHER". "SARKAR" is my tribute to it*'.

This coalition between the political mafia, the police mafia and the underworld was active in rural and semi-urban India as well. *Gangaajal* (2003), *Apaharan* (2005), *Haasil* (2003), *Raajneeti* (2010), *Maqbool* (2003), *Gangs of Wasseypur* (2012) and *Udta Punjab* (2016) stand out as fine examples.

You could almost reach out and touch the central characters of *Gangaajal*. There was the local don of the Tezpur District Sadhu Yadav (played by Mohan Joshi) and his son Sundar Yadav (Yashpal Sharma). The two of them and their 'extended family' that includes the police force of the local Tezpur Police Station who are dependent on the largesse of the Yadavs, practically run the economy in the district. DSP Bhurey Lal (Akhilendra Mishra) smugly 'presides' over the daylight rigging of a government tender by the Sundar Yadav. No wonder the newly appointed Superintendent of Police Amit Kumar (Ajay Devgn) is angered at the way the police had sold themselves out to the local mafia. What didn't help matters was the same factor that we saw in the chapter on dacoits—caste. Caste is an important factor in rural North India. People of the same caste empathize with each other. The caste factor overrides profession. In *Gangaajal* (2003), because of the Yadav–Yadav link between Inspector Bachha Yadav (Mukesh Tiwari) and the criminal Sundar Yadav, Bachha has been quietly helping out Sadhu Yadav and Sundar Yadav for a long time. Amit Kumar figures this out and berates Bachha. When Bachha falls in line with his duties, and he gets killed by Sundar Yadav's men. Meanwhile, Sub-Inspector Mangni Ram (Daya Shankar Pandey) alleges that his Superior officer Amit Kumar was being unduly harsh with him because Mangni belonged to a backward caste. And amidst all this, a person of no less a stature than the DIG, Verma (Mohan Agashe) pockets INR 5 lakhs as his 'fees' for negotiating a bail for the murderer Sundar Yadav charged with the murder of Bachha Yadav. And the Home Minister Dwarka Rai (Vishnu Sharma) is literally directed by Sadhu Yadav to release Yadav's criminal son Sundar. A brilliantly disturbing classic by Prakash Jha, *Gangaajal* was based on the infamous Bhagalpur blinding case of 1979–80 in which the eyes of over thirty suspected criminals were gouged out by the Bhagalpur police using a 'takwa' (a long sharp needle used for stitching gunny bags) and then, acid was poured into the empty eye sockets.[81] The scene was replicated by Prakash Jha, the term 'gangaajal' (holy water) being a code name for sulphuric acid used in car batteries.

Actor Yashpal Sharma, who played the role of Sundar Yadav to perfection in *Gangaajal*, shared his insights in an interview with the author. '*Gangaajal* was a world in itself. Set in a small village in Bihar and in and around the police force, you get to see the whole world of the police force and all the happenings there. Half the work is done by the script and content itself, i.e., by Prakash Jha. The language in his script was very strong, too. The Bihari is not an affected one like "*Kaa kar rahe ho bhaiyya?*" It could be a simple, "*Kya kar rahe they tum?*" with the tone bringing out the Bihari essence. I have spent a lot of time with Biharis and UP-ites in National School of Drama (NSD), in Haryana, Mumbai.

That helped me pick up the Bihari tone and accent. I had worked hard mentally and physically on the body language and attitude of Biharis.'

Prakash Jha's *Apaharan* (2005) is about Tabrez Alam (Nana Patekar), a sitting Member of the Bihar State Assembly owning a kidnapping and extortion racket which is run on his behalf by his henchman Gaya Singh (Yashpal Sharma). The blatant involvement of top-ranked police officials like DSP Shukla and the Home Minister Dinakar Pandey (Chetan Pandit) with Tabrez Alam's extortion racket is shocking.

Said Yashpal Sharma, 'A jailed convict Gaya Singh in *Apaharan* who runs a kidnapping mafia sitting inside the jail under instructions from his boss Tabrez Alam (Nana Patekar) … all these are real.' It seemed that a few of our educational institutions were the 'birthplace' of gangsters. In Tigmanshu Dhulia's debut *Haasil* (2003), Allahabad University is a battleground between two gangs which has the backing of politicians as well. Ranvijay Singh (Irrfan Khan), the so-called student leader, could have been a role model for aspiring gangsters as he systematically leads gang fights against rivals. In his book *40 Retakes*, author and journalist Avijit Ghosh said, 'Tigmanshu says the film was inspired by a real-life incident narrated to him by a friend. "He had faced this crisis when a local goon became a threat to his relationship with a girl. But I did not want to make a tame love story. I wanted to pitch it against the volatile atmosphere of the region".'[82]

Few films demonstrated the likeness of the politicians to the mafia better than Prakash Jha's *Raajneeti* (2010). Largely modelled around the *Mahabharata*, it showed how easily they could kill, maim and frame as they pleased. The characters discuss political manoeuvres with the objective of upstaging political rivals—and not even once for the welfare of the people. It was all about holding on to their positions and toppling the next guy. In an interview with the author, said Manoj Bajpayee who played Veerendra Pratap, '*Kal Yug* (1980) was about corporate business whereas *Raajneeti* was about power politics. Duryodhan was a victim of his own mind whom we have always seen as a black guy. I had to look at the role as the most positive character ever—of someone who is victimized so that he evokes sympathy through emotion. Now, to get emotion out of this guy and to paint him as grey and not black, was the challenge for me as an actor. Veerendra is ambitious, suave. He does not aspire for wealth or women. The only thing he wants is power which he thinks is his birth right. Which is why, my interaction in the climax scene with Ajay Devgn was very emotional. When Veerendra crumbles he breaks down like a child.'

> Bajpayee said that Mahesh Bhatt had called him up to congratulate him. 'Black as black is boring. Your victory lay in winning the audience sympathy and making it grey. You brought out emotion from this character.'

Needless to say, this dirty power corrupted the politicians morally too, similar to the way the moral capital of the policemen had corrupted. In *Raajneeti* (2010), politician Babulal (Vinay Apte) getting filmed in bed with his male masseur in a rival-party-perpetrated sting operation was more of an embarrassment for him than a scandal. In *Dirty Politics* (2015), the sixty-plus politician Dinanath (Om Puri) gets honey trapped by Anokhi Devi (Mallika Sherawat) and their debauchery gets filmed on a VCD. Nothing new about this except that Anokhi Devi too is a candidate for the next elections! Irrigation Minister P.P. Rathore (Kulbhushan Kharbanda) in *Manorama Six Feet Under* (2007) had a similar appetite for sex … with a difference. He was a perverted serial child molester.

Anurag Kashyap did not mention any specific mafia don in his cult *Gangs of Wasseypur* (2012). But it could have been on any don in the rural coal mining mafia of Dhanbad and Wasseypur of Bihar. A background of the film's storyline: Sometime in the mid-1950s, the Coal Welfare Association was created, and from from this was born the National Trade Union. Taking advantage of this, the supervisors of the NTU gradually became the earliest avatar of the coal mafia. They became labour contractors who would enlist labourers into NTU and force them to pay subscription fees. The mafia lent money to the labourers and would withhold their wages against the exorbitant interest that the labourers owed to the mafia. We never missed any real-life rural mafia don in *Gangs of Wasseypur*. They all looked like anyone we would meet when we alight at Dhanbad Railway station.

The sordid story of this three-way coalition would be incomplete without a mention of Abhishek Chaubey's *Udta Punjab* (2016) in which we see pre-teen boys snorting, injecting themselves and suffering from seizures as a result of drug overdose. 'This is green revolution part two', chimes the rogue ASI Jhujar Singh (Manav Vij). Drugs like Pheniramine and Buprenorphine, which are supposed to be sold independently (and that too only under prescription), were being mixed and sold openly for as little as INR 50. There is also this fake company Deluxe Pharmaceuticals on whose name government-controlled opium was being sourced .... And obviously being misused. This fake company is owned by the Honourable Member of Parliament Maninder Singh Brar (Kamal Tiwari) who runs a state-wide narco-politics. And enormous quantities of contraband penetrate the interior districts of Punjab by bribing the police at the checkposts. 'Many Members of Parliament are drug dealers themselves,' reveals the honest ASI Sartaj Singh. Profanities, obscene, below-the-belt hand gestures and psychedelic images led to over eighty cuts by the censors. But they were all restored—*Udta Punjab* wouldn't have been what it is without those. The deep-rooted, cross-border smuggling-aided drug menace in Punjab was corroding the entire generation. The politician-police-underworld 'coalition' had surpassed conventional mafia dons like Don Vito Corleone and Dharamdas in notoriety and unscrupulousness many times over.

Sometimes one or two of the three cogs of this 'coalition' would be missing but the wheels of villany still turned.

Two policemen in the twenty-first century were equivalent to *three* witches in the 17th century! Vishal Bhardwaj recreated the three soothsaying witches in Shakespeare's *Macbeth* as Inspector Pandit (Om

Puri) and Inspector Purohit (Naseeruddin Shah) in *Maqbool* (2003). Pandit and Purohit were close confidants and facilitators of the Mumbai underworld dons Maqbool (Irrfan Khan) and his boss Jahangir Khan, nicknamed Abbaji (Pankaj Kapur). The two policemen regularly wine and dine with the gang members and are obviously the recipients of huge favors from the gang in return for police information. Abbaji is the khuda of the minorities. Any political party that associated with Jahangir Khan was guaranteed to win the elections. Unlike the two witches of Macbeth, Pandit and Purohit go beyond merely soothsaying that Maqbool would remove Jahangir Khan and take over as the don of the underworld. They actually influence the events to make that happen.

The professorial Head of Investigation Bureau Bhaskaran's (Dhritiman Chatterjee) act of selling highly classified data to various organizations in *Kahaani* (2012) is beyond all realms of imagination unpardonable. To further complicate matters, Bhaskaran's agent and conduit for smuggling out secrets, Milan Damji, turns a rogue agent, becoming something of a Frankenstein's monster for Bhaskaran. In an interview with the author, director Sujoy Ghosh shared the back story, 'When Damji turns a runaway rogue agent, it was too late for Bhaskaran who then had to abet Damji as otherwise, Bhaskaran would be dead too'. It was a classic tiger-by-the-tail case. Sujoy Ghosh used a false flashback concept, as in the film *Stage Fright* (1950), to double effect. Explained Ghosh, 'In my head it was always a game of chess using stories as pawns. Hence the title *Kahaani*. Firstly, Milan Damji's name was used throughout to create authenticity (and not just terror) about his existence. What Damji was capable of, given what the audience saw in the first scene inside the Kolkata metro (in which scores of people are killed by a poisonous gas), stayed cemented in the audience's minds than on the screen. And when Damji kicks Vidya in the stomach it reaffirmed the audience belief that Milan Damji was *indeed* a bad guy. Which is why the audience cheer when Vidya takes Damji out. And while I saw Milan as Vidya's queen piece, the non-existent Arnab Bagchi became the other MacGuffin of *Kahaani*.'

The few honest policemen that tried to sincerely discharge their duties were made victims of political backlash, e.g., Mathur (Kamal Haasan) in *Yeh Desh* (1984) gets ticked off by his superior for using force on a politically-backed raasta roko (road blockage). ACP Ashok Saxena in *Hiraasat* (1987) gets framed for drug-dealing by his one-time mentor politician Narayan Rao (Chandrakant Gokhale) for refusing to assist with the drug trade. Hawaldar Sathe (Amrish Puri) in *Gardish* (1993) gets transferred out because he had the 'temerity' to apprehend the MLA's son for a parking violation. DSP Aayan Ranjan (Ayushmann Khurrana) in Anubhav Sinha's *Article 15* (2019) gets suspended for his persistent investigation of the gang rape and murder of two low-caste village girls. Even the CBI wanted to hush up the case.

Sometimes the system becomes so rotten that nobody within it can be trusted. An outsider's help is needed to fix it. Which is what Retd. Colonel Pratap Bajpayee (Darshan Jariwala) in *Kahaani* (2012) did. He hits upon a novel idea to fix this systemic corruption in the police ranks by planting Vidya Bagchi to infiltrate his own corrupt system. Shared Sujoy Ghosh, 'When the metro rail gas tragedy happened and Vidya came to him, Bajpayee saw her as his only weapon to *infiltrate his own system*. Because Bajpayee was a specialist at hiring an average person and turning him/her into an agent.'

By design, the bureaucracy is meant to guide the government. But do they always? In the BBC television serial *Yes Prime Minister*, Civil Servant Sir Humphrey Appleby was the puppeteer that made the Prime Minister dance. In contrast, in Dibakar Banerjee's *Shanghai* (2012), Principal Secretary Kaul (Faooque Shaikh) was putty in the hands of the imperious Chief Minister (Supriya Pathak). The scheme to build an international business park in Bharat Nagar was enough to hold the attention of many a political honcho, the bureaucracy and the police. A Leftist professor and writer Dr Ahmadi (Prosenjit Chatterjee) who dares to speak up against the government is run over by a vehicle. What follows is the charade of an enquiry commission, an immoral police force, a tenuous coalition … and finally, the Chief Minister directing the investigating IAS Officer

T.A. Krishnan (Abhay Deol) to hand over the enquiry of the attempted murder of Dr Ahmadi to her as she would handle it directly. In other words, it was a hush-up, with Principal Secretary Kaul dancing to Madam Chief Minister's music. Dibakar Banerjee zoomed deep into the dark recesses of the power corridors, the suffused lighting and close-up shots of the hand-held camera opening up the truth behind their faces.

———

If the political mafia can make a business out of religion, then why would the mafia not make a business out of something which, in India, is as dear as religion? I mean cricket, of course. Big boys play at night—or rather, undercover. In 1997, former Indian cricketer Manoj Prabhakar made startling revelations that in 1994, he had been paid money to throw a cricket match against Sri Lanka. And the next three years sullied all that the gentlemen's game had come to stand for in its 120-year-old history. Hansie Cronje, Mohammad Azharuddin, Ajay Sharma, Mark Waugh, Shane Warne, Asif Iqbal … the skeletons march-past from inside the cupboard was endless. Life bans were slapped on Hansie Cronje, Azharuddin and Ajay Sharma, while fines and temporary bans were imposed on a few others. They had all become party to the betting mafia. In an article dated 19 January 2016 in the *Economic Times*, Shailesh Menon quoted FICCI estimates of the cricket betting market in India as INR 2,40,000 crore—a staggering $33 billion.[83] And all of it was illegal because, while betting on horses is legal in India, betting on cricket isn't. Why would the mafia not want to dip its beak in cricket betting?

And soon, a year after Manoj Prabhakar's exposé, the cricket-betting mafia arrived in Bollywood in *Ghulam* (1998), followed by *Supari* (2003) and in *Chamku* (2001). Kunal Deskmukh's *Jannat* (2008) showed a South African match-fixing don called Abu Ibrahim (Javed Sheikh) who uses the proceeds of betting money to finance terrorism and insurgency. Can one ever forget Pakistan's perplexing loss to Ireland in the 2007 Cricket

World Cup? Pakistan was suspected of deliberately losing that game. Worse was to follow. Within a few hours of Pakistan's loss, Pakistan coach Bob Woolmer was found dead in his hotel toom under mysterious circumstances.[84] *Jannat* picked up this story and showed an Asian cricket team's foreign coach catching the captain Shadab red-handed negotiating with the mafia. The coach is shot dead.

Finally ... the Bhaiopics

There was a don of South Indian origin whose father, a union leader, was shot dead by the police. The boy fled to Bombay in the mid-1940s and became the godfather and benefactor of South Indian slum dwellers of Dharavi. His name was Varadarjan Mudaliar. Velu Nayakan (Kamal Haasan), the don in Mani Ratnam's Tamil film *Nayakan* (1987), had very distinct strokes of Varadarajan including the backstory of Velu's father getting killed and Velu fleeing to Bombay. With his daredevilry and cunning, Velu Nayakan grows to become the godfather of the South Indian migrant slum dwellers in Bombay. Of course, rival mafia families try to usurp his power, and the inevitable bloodshed follows. Finally, Velu gets killed by someone very close to him.

Here again, the spirit of *The Godfather* lingered. Apart from the South Indian link to the real-life Varadarajan Mudaliar, Velu Nayakan bore strong resemblances to Don Vito Corleone. Director Mani Ratnam, however, subtly denied the link of *Nayakan* to *The Godfather*. A November 2013 article in *DNA* quoted Mani Ratnam: '... *Nayakan* was rooted to the Tamil culture and inspired by a character here.'[85] But strangely, in the same newspaper, lead actor Kamal Haasan sounded perplexed at Mani Ratnam's denial of *The Godfather* as the source of inspiration for *Nayakan*. Says Haasan, 'In fact, we were so conscious of our source material that we made deliberate efforts to make my character *dissimilar* to Marlon Brando in terms of the walk, the talk and attitude .... Hence the efforts to bring in a true-life Tamil gangster in Mumbai,' Hassan said. Feroze Khan had no such confusion when he remade *Nayakan* in Hindi as *Dayavaan* (1988), with Vinod Khanna in the title role. As it was a remake of *Nayakan*, the story and Velu's characterization were identical to the Tamil original. But the fact that *Dayavaan* was a Hindi language film diluted the very premise of a South Indian immigrant; and Vinod Khanna, with his distinct Punjabi features and desperately trying to make his flawless Hindi sound Tamil-accented, didn't help!

In Bombay there also emerged the Pathan mafia menace led by Karim Lala. The Pathans were basically moneylenders, who were always known to be fist-happy at the slightest of provocation. As Hussain Zaidi said in a chat with the author, 'The Pathans could not be disciplined. They had no respect for law and would stab debtors who couldn't return their money on time. Even the police could not control these Pathans.' In Tagore's *Kabuliwala*, Rehmat, the Afghani Pathan, stabs a defaulting creditor.

The benevolent Pathan mafia king Khushal Khan (Dharmendra) in J.P. Dutta's *Hathyaar* (1989), who was loosely based on the life and activities of Karim Lala, was not consistent with reality: the Pathan mafia was anything but benevolent.

Haji Mastan Mirza was said to be the first official Bhai of Bombay who arrived in the city from south India in 1934 and started his hafta racket at the Bombay dockyard. As we have already seen, *Deewar* was *not* based on Haji Mastan's life. Milan Luthria's *Once Upon A Time in Mumbaai* (2010), however, portraying Sultan Mirza's (Ajay Devgn) life story was more relatable to that of Haji Mastan Mirza—even though the opening credits carried a disclaimer to the contrary. But while the story was by and large consistent, the character of Sultan Mirza is far more glamorous than the real-life Haji Mastan. Said Hussain Zaidi, 'In reality, Haji Mastan was not as generous, intelligent or smart. He was a miser.' In *Once Upon A Time in Mumbaai*, Sultan Mirza sports tailored suits and expensive leather shoes. 'Haji Mastan used to wear chappals,' pointed out Piyush Jha in an interview with the author. But then, a Bollywood hero wearing chappals just woudn't cut it. Hence the inconsistency with the actual Haji Mastan. A flood destroys young Mirza's home in Madras and he is forced to relocate to Bombay. Being uneducated, he does menial work for survival. But his helpful disposition earns him respect among his fellow destitues and he becomes something of a leader in the ghetto. Mirza grows up to become an underworld don in Bombay who believes in peaceful coexistence of all the dons in the city. He also shuns the business of drugs. So, Mirza somewhere has his moral anchors intact and is portrayed throughout as being benevolent to the needy.

There was another character in *Once Upon A Time in Mumbaai* called Shoaib Khan (Emraan Hashmi). He was the son of a policeman and joins Sultan Mirza's mafia. Later he upstages Sultan Mirza himself and takes over as the unquestioned don of Bombay. Does the story sound familiar? Starting in the late 1970s, a policeman's son who used to live in the chawls of Dongri fast-tracked his way up the ladder of Bombay's organized crime. He was mentored by Haji Mastan but then stomped all over Haji to get ahead in life. His name was Dawood Ibrahim. Shoaib Khan of *Once Upon A Time In Mumbaai* is a thinly veiled portrayal of Dawood Ibrahim. Though primarily about Haji Mastan, the film shows the important transition in Bombay's mafia landscape from a Robin Hood-ian Haji Mastan to a mercenary like Dawood.

From the mid-1980s, Dawood Ibrahim had become numero uno in the Bombay underworld. His upmarket lifestyle and flamboyant attire were tailor-made for Bollywood. The Dawood stylization was first seen in *Salim Langde Pe Mat Ro* (1989). Pavan Malhotra once said that the slightly drooping moustache that he wore in the film while playing the role of Salim Langda was modelled on the sort of moustache that Dawood Ibrahim used to sport in the late 1980s and early 1990s.[86]

Which makes one wonder why it took so long to see Dawood portrayed on-screen. The first film to show Dawood Ibrahim was *Black Friday* which released in 2004—a full twenty-five years after Dawood

Ibrahim entered the world of crime. In a chat with the author, Hussain Zaidi analysed the reason: 'In his active days in India starting in the late 1970s, Dawood Ibrahim was perceived to be just another local Bombay goon. And when he left India, he was still entertaining film stars in Dubai and enjoying cricket matches at Sharjah .... It was only after his alleged involvement in the March 1993 Bombay blast that people realized what a mega don Dawood Ibrahim was. His stature continued growing in the 1990s and thus inspired film-makers starting the mid-1990s.' And post *Black Friday*, quite a few films showing Dawood Ibrahim or disguised versions of the Don have appeared. Right from the drooping moustache to the goggles to the portly body, Iqbal Seth (Rishi Kapoor) in Nikhil Advani's *D-Day* (2013) closely resembled Dawood Ibrahim. Iqbal Seth, too, was a Bombay-ite who had fled to Karachi, and he, too, was a prime suspect in major blasts in India right from the ones in March 1993 in Bombay to one in Hyderabad in 2013.

Dawood Ibrahim had built an ecosystem commonly referred to as the 'D Company' consisting of associates like Chhota Shakeel, Chhota Rajan, Abdul Latif, the BRA trio (Babu Reshim, Rama Naik, Arun Gawli), Abu Salem and others. But, fuelled by ambition, some of them started fanning out, forming 'companies' of their own. Some like Chhota Rajan broke away from Dawood in 1993 and became his rival. Biopics on these individuals, too, have hit the screens in the last thirteen to fifteen years.

Ram Gopal Varma's *Company* (2002) is one such film and had Ajay Devgn, playing the role of Malik, who is a camoflauged version of Dawood. In the film, Malik wants a pie in every construction and stock market business till the 'gang' morphs to a legitimate 'company'. He begins to control his overseas businesses sitting in Hong Kong, which was perhaps a reflection of Dawood's migration to Dubai and then to Pakistan. And Malik's fallout with comrade Chandu (Vivek Oberoi) in the film, once again, carries shades of Dawood's fallout with his erstwhile close aide Chhota Rajan.

For some misplaced reason, *Gangster* (2006) was rumoured to be based on Abu Salem's life—maybe because Gangster Daya Shankar's (Shiney Ahuja) girlfriend Simran (Kangana Ranaut) plays a dance bar girl. And the real-life Abu Salem's partner was Monica Bedi, a former actor. But there was no other connection to Abu Salem. Daya is a gangster who breaks free from his boss Khan (Gulshan Grover) following a dispute. Daya flees to Seoul with Simran and what follows is pretty much the fugitive Daya's saga and a love triangle between Daya, Simran and Aakash (Emraan Hashmi), an old friend of Simran who creeps into her life again in Seoul. Aided by Simran who has been convinced by the police to cooperate with them to help capture Daya, the law catches up with Daya. Interestingly, Pakistani fast bowler Shoaib Akhtar was offered the titular role by Mahesh Bhatt, which Shoaib declined. If Shoaib had accepted the role, he would have been the second Pakistani cricketer after Mohsin Khan to star in a Bollywood film. In the 14th May 2005 edition of BBC News, scribe Zubair Ahmed quoted Mahesh Bhatt making a Corleone-sounding claim, 'Once he hears the story, he cannot refuse it.'[87] But Shoaib Akhtar did refuse the role of Daya Shankar, making way for Shiney Ahuja.

Sharique Minhaj's 2014 film *Lateef: The King of Crime* was based on the life of Abdul Latif, another member of the Dawood ecosystem. Latif was a Gujarat-based bootlegger and rose to commit other crimes. He was said to be the only Gujarat-based associate of Dawood. While Minhaj's effort sank into oblivion, the more celebrated *Raees* (2017), with Bollywood superstar Shah Rukh Khan playing Abdul Latif, raked in good money. In the film, the titular Raees Alam is a bootlegger who was active from the 1960s till his death in the early 1990. He smuggles spurious liquor in the state but is a Robin Hood within his community, providing employment to many. Where the story of Raees differed with that of the real-life Abdul Latif was that the real-life Latif was believed to be a willing accomplice in the 1993 bomb blasts. As we would have guessed, there was off-screen controversy with Abdul Latif's son sending a legal notice to the film's producers for using his father's life story without permission.

Ashim Ahluwalia's *Daddy* (2017), a period film set in mid-1970s, was based on the true story of the BRA trio of Babu Reshim, Rama Naik and Arun Gawli. The son of a labourer, Arun Gawli (Arjun Rampal) starts his career of crime with petty hold-ups and thefts. He later graduates to smuggling transistor radios, VHS players and perfumes—an activity he describes as 'import-export' to his girlfriend. And then one day Arun discovers that he was able to get away after committing a murder because one Maqsood Bhai (a fictionalized version of Dawood Ibrahim, played by Farhan Akhtar) of Dongri had helped him get a reprieve. But Gawli wishes the BRA gang to operate independently and not under Maqsood. *Daddy* traces Arun Gawli's rise through the 1980s, his fall and imprisonment and then eventual transition to politics.

Sanjay Gupta's *Shootout at Wadala* (2013) is a stated hybrid of fact and fiction on gangster Manya Surve (John Abraham) and is partly inspired by Husain Zaidi's book *Dongri to Dubai: Six Decades of the Mumbai Mafia*. *Wadala* included fictionalized versions of Dawood Ibrahim and his brother Shabir. For some reason, director Apoorva Lakhia denied any connection of *Shootout at Lokhandwala* (2007) with the police siege and killing of gangster Mahindra (Maya) Dolas (Vivek Oberoi) in a real-life police shootout in November 1991.[88] But in an interview with the author, Zaidi confirmed that '*Lokhandwala* was based on Maya Dolas.' Just the way that the incidents and characters in *Haseena Parkar* (2017) by Lakhia were unmistakably about Haseena Parkar, Dawood Ibrahim's sister.

Despite the disclaimer to the contrary in the opening credits, the story of *Mumbai Saga* (2021) is a near replica of the life and notorieties of gangster Amar Naik who operated in the 1980s and till mid-1990s. The Bhai in the film is Amarthya Rao (Arjun Rampal), a veiled version of Amar Naik. In the opening scene of the film set in the mid-1990s, the owner of Khaitaan Mills, Sunil Khaitaan's Mercedes is waylaid on

Mumbai's main throughfare and he is shot dead through the shattered windowpanes with a Zoraki 917-T semi-automatic by Amarthya and his three associates on two-wheelers. This was exactly how Sunit Khatau, owner of Mumbai's Khatau Makanji Spinning and Weaving Mills, was assassinated on 7 May 1994.[89] Amarthya's rival is Gaitonde (Amole Gupte) who runs his gang from his 'fortress' in Arthur Road prision, just the way that Amar Naik's sworn enemy Arun Gawli used to run his gang from Aurangabad prison. Even some of the real-life names like Nari Khan, a friend of Amar Naik, were retained in the film with Gulshan Grover reprising the role. In the finale, Amarthya is eliminated by encounter specialist Vijay Savarkar (Emraan Hashmi). Savarkar was a fictionalized version of Vijay Salaskar, Sub-Inspector of Mumbai police.[90]

Amole Gupte shared, 'When I played Gaitonde in *Mumbai Saga*, I thought I should break the stereotype, and Director Sanjay Gupta allowed me to do that. I became a cackling person, made the character like a joker. And suddenly the menace comes in between a line or two and again it is back to repartee and jokes. I might be making a biopic but personally as an actor I would imagine that I am myself standing there armed with the knowledge of cinema and playing a character differently.'

Gupte shared an anecdote, 'Prior to Covid, save for two hours of work, I had completed my entire work. In mid-Feb 2021, after the break due to Covid, I went back to the set to shoot in mid-Feb 2021 with 300–400 junior artistes in a mill in Thane for a death scene. No Covid protocol was followed because we needed to take off our masks. And sure enough, I came from the set and got Covid. I lost twenty kilograms in seven days. I had preserved myself for one year and in one day which was not in my control, I went and got the return gift of Covid. But I recovered using alternative therapy. And Gaitonde survived to see the final cut.'

There have been biopics on the rural mafia too. Director Kabeer Kaushik must consider himself unfortunate that his *Sehar* (2005) got a left-handed deal at the box office. But it remains one of the most authentic films on the menace of the Eastern Uttar Pradesh (UP) mafia ever made. The antagonist Gajraj Singh (Sushant Singh) is a fictionalized version of Shri Prasad Shukla, a dreaded gangster of Bihar and eastern UP in the 1990s. Shukla was shot dead by the Special Task Force in Delhi's Ghaziabad area. Actor Sushant Singh once said, 'I come from Bijnore in western Uttar Pradesh. I could easily understand how goondaism is a soft ladder to a political career. Shri Prakash Shukla, on whom Gajraj was based, had both flamboyance and ambition. The challenge was to find this delicate balance. From the research notes, I found out that after committing a murder, he had immediately shopped for clothes. That gave me more insight to his personality.'[91]

The web series called Rangbaaz *(2018), too, is based on Shri Prakash Shukla.*

5

Dhoom Macha Le
The Trickster-thieves

At the turn of the millennium a special brand of trickster-thieves seemed to jump out of the pages of Indrajal Comics or Diamond Comics into Bollywood. The plots were too fantastic to be credible, and yet, told with amazing confidence.

Arguably, Krishna Shah's *Shalimar* (1978) may be termed as one of the precursors to these millennial tricketer-thieves. *Shalimar* was a delightful galaxy of 'artist' safe-crackers, each unique in his or her own way, none of whom had ever been caught. The line-up consisted of the lame and dumb Columbus (John Saxon), who has flicked an expensive diamond. And then the seductive Countess Rasmussen (Sylvia Miles) who is a star trapeze artiste, and to her credit, has stolen seven Van Gogh paintings and three statues. The near-blind Dr Dubari (Shammi Kapoor) who embraces all religions of the world, has visited Jerusalem as a delegate of the Conference of Religions and made away with the cross of St. Timothy by hiding it inside his religious book. The modest South Indian K.P. Iyengar (O.P. Ralhan) who, unknown to the world, was the brain behind acts like the gold heist from Bank of Singapore and lifting of a precious knife from a museum in France. And above all, there was the ailing Sir John Locksley (Rex Harrison) who had in his procession, the 1,214 carat ruby called Shalimar worth INR 135 crores—the ruby whose origin can be traced back to the times of Alexander the Great and down to the Mughals when it was located at Shalimar Bagh. The Portuguese take procession of the Shalimar from the Mughals but lose it to the British in 1796. It goes missing for a hundred years before surfacing in a museum in America, and somehow, comes into the possession of Sir John. Sir John invites Iyengar, the Countess, Columbus and Dr Dubari to his expansive private island, Saint Dismas, and challenges them to steal the Shalimar from its bulletproof enclosure guarded by a cynosure of CCTV cameras, explosives, alarms and armed guards. Pretty Sheila Enders (Zeenat Aman) is Sir John's live-in nurse and confidante.

Shared Zeenat Aman in an interview with the author, 'Shalimar was shot in two versions simultaneously—one each for the English and the Hindi versions, just like Guide. *Now, I was convent educated and not very well versed in Hindi which is criminal, given that my father wrote* Pakeezah *and the screenplay and dialogues of* Mughal-e-Azam. *During* Shalimar, *we had this very interesting situation where Dharamji (Dharmendra) would be sitting with his English language coach and I would be sitting with the Hindi dialogue coach. The voices of Rex Harrison, John Saxon and Sylvia Miles were dubbed in the Hindi version.'*

Come to think of it, Zeenat Aman happened to be part of quite a few international gangs in several films, e.g., *Paapi, Shalimar, The Great Gambler, Aashiq Hoon Baharon Ka.* The actress believed that her Westernized looks and overall anglicized persona had a lot do with the kind of roles she was being offered in those films.

For the stock Hindi film viewing public, *Shalimar*, with a screenplay dominated by this villain assemblage, may have appeared unconventional. But the time for films like these would come in a little over twenty years.

An attempted clean-up of INR 18 crore New Year Eve collections from the basement vaults of Goa's Taj Exotica Hotel by Kabir (John Abraham) in *Dhoom* (2004) ... raids-from-the-sky on Namibian deserts by 'A' (Hrithik Roshan) in *Dhoom 2* (2006) ... a 200-million-dollar-insurance fraud plotted by Rajiv Singh (Akshaye Khanna) in *Race* (2008) that involved Rajiv killing his stepbrother Ranvir (Saif Ali Khan) ... a racket of laundering 'fake currency' by Ranvir Singh (Saif Ali Khan) and the attempted theft of the *Shroud of Turin* in the ruins of Antalya (Turkey) by Armaan Malik (John Abraham) in *Race 2* (2013) ... theft of the priceless 'Rose of Samarkhand' necklace from a jeweller in Amsterdam by Charlie (Abhishek Bachchan) and Riya (Bipasha Basu) followed by the robbing of a train on the Russia–Romania line containing INR 10,000 crore worth pure Romanian gold by a handsome gang in *Players* (2012) ... robberies inside art galleries to an underwater treasure hunt in the Bahamas in *Blue* (2009) ... centuries-old diamonds excavated in Southern India in *Cash* (2007) ... these robbers and conmen were the unabashed 'heroes', reducing the police to helpless, gawking admirers.

In *Bunty aur Babli* (2005), the con-pair (Abhishek Bachchan and Rani Mukherjee) actually 'sell' the Taj Mahal (And some stupid oaf actually 'buys' it). In *Prince* (2010), the squabble is over a memory-altering computer chip hidden inside a 3,000-year old coin of Sri Lankan origin. Karan (Shahid Kapoor) and a few other smart-asses in *Badmaash Company* (2010), taking advantage of the economic liberalization during 1991, are equally innovative in their machinations; that too in a foreign land. Ricky (Ranveer Singh) in *Ladies vs Ricky Bahl* (2011) pulls off three high-ticket con jobs—a real estate one in Delhi, a fake M.F. Hussain painting one in Mumbai and a garment business-related one in Lucknow—all by himself. *Special 26* (2013) is a film inspired by true incidents. It is about a group of four conmen led by Ajay 'Ajju' Singh (Akshay Kumar) and the elderly Sharmaji (Anupam Kher) who, sometimes posing as CBI officers, sometimes claiming to be from the Income Tax Department and sometimes from the Anti-Corruption Bureau, conduct 'raids' at the homes of businessmen and politicians and make off with the loot. The victims do not report these to the press as this would expose their black money. This emboldens the gang for them to carry out thirteen 'raids' in two years in various cities in India. (The actual count of loots is forty-nine, admits Sharma). CBI Officer Waseem Khan (he is a real one, by the way), played by Manoj Bajpayee, tasked with cracking this gang, manages to close in on them. Well almost. In the climax scene, Waseem Khan realizes that he has all along failed to recognize the mole planted in his team by Ajay Singh. But too late. Ajay and gang have already given Khan the slip with their largest loot and and all Khan can do is laugh at himself. The finale of *Special 26* is as classy as any we can find in world cinema. In *Bang Bang!* (2014), the invaluable Kohinoor diamond is apparently stolen from the Tower of London and brought back to India by an 'invisible' thief who has left behind no fingerprints. Neither have the CCTV cameras manage to capture a single picture of him. This unkown thief becomes an instant celebrity, with his act being justified in the Parliament because the Kohinoor belonged to India anyway, and even grannies falling in love with this new jewel thief. Well, the 'theft' in itself is a ploy by the British MI6 and Internal Secret Service to extradite a wanted terrorist. And the 'thief' Jai Nanda (Hrithik Roshan) isn't really a thief. But, for a significant portion of film, the audience witnesses what they *believe* is a super thief in all his super-heroic glory.

By now, all relationships are impersonal. Nobody mourns for anyone. In *Players* (2012), within days of being widowed, the young Shayla (Shweta Bhardwaj), in a bikini, teases her late husband's friend. If Tara (Padma Khanna) did a striptease in *Johny Mera Naam* to save her boyfriend's life, Aaliya (Katrina Kaif) does one in *Dhoom: 3* (2013) to clear an audition for a circus artiste.

Some of the plotlines of these films were borrowed from Hollywood, e.g., replacing the stolen diamond with a laser light in *Dhoom:2* was a take-off from a Lex Luthor scene in *Superman 2* and the train-top fight sequence resembled those in *Matrix*; the trope of a bomb hidden in the car used in the three *Race* franchises was inspired by *Speed* (1994). While *Players* was an honest remake of *The Italian Job* (1969/2003), *Prince* (2010) was a take-off on the Bourne series. This category of films is also a label parade with premier accessories like Winch 6000, Apple Mac laptops, Tanishq jewellery, Surfer brand skullcaps, Batman face masks, Suzuki bikes, biking accessories like Venom, Yamaha, Alpinestars, Airoh. Micro-sensor fitted playing cards and display-screen embedded goggles in *Race 2* helped tycoon Armaan Malik purchase casinos on the Altamash waterfront in Turkey.

Far from the silly beards of older films, 'Mr A' in *Dhoom:2* is a master of disguise. Unresearched generic terms like 'pistaul', 'revolver' and 'bandook' had gotten replaced by specifics like '44 Magnum with hollers point slugs' in *Kaante* (2002). Corporate-sounding phrases like 'Please see the bigger picture', 'I'm in' and 'It's time to win' sat comfortably with the personality of these new characters.

And there was a promise of 'watch-this-space-for-more'. Kabir leaps off the cliff on his bike in *Dhoom* but no dead body is found. We knew the franchise would continue. And it did. In *Race 2*, Armaan winks at the audience in his parting shot, '*Race jahan khatam hoti hai, shuru bhi wahin se hoti hai* (The race begins where it ends).' *Race 3* (2018) signs off with, 'So there will be one more race?' In the last frame of *Cash* (2007), the thief discloses that he is already planning his next heist.

There was a modicum of a demarcation between the policeman Jay Dixit and the thief Kabir in *Dhoom*. But soon, in *Bunty aur Babli*, *Dhoom 2*, *Cash* and *Badmaash Company*, the lines are not only blurred, but actually crossed over with certified heroes Abhishek Bachchan, Hrithik Roshan, Ajay Devgn and Shahid Kapoor playing cool thieves. The glamorization and legitimization of crime was now official. By *Dhoom:3*, the policeman was reduced to a comedian for all practical purposes. 'He is the perfect thief,' ACP Jay Dixit's statement about Mr A in *Dhoom:2* has a tinge of admiration. 'Chor ek tarah ka artist hota hai (The thief is an artist),' advises the hardened convict Victor Dada (Vinod Khanna) in *Players* to the entire posse of policemen as they listen respectfully with bowed heads.

Also, starting in the late 1990s, a noteworthy trend emerged in the smuggler/gangster genre with films like *Is Raat ki Subah Nahin* (1996), *Ek Chalis ki Last Local* (2007), *Sankat City* (2009), *Kaminey* (2009), *Ishqiya* (2010), *Delhi Belly* (2011)—something often funny but invariably violent.

A young Maharashtrian mulgi (girl) needs to get urgently married that evening at 8 p.m. as she has gotten pregnant by her timid boyfriend. But then, they get entangled with the cocaine mafia and ... 'Dhan Te Nan' ... it is mirth and murder all the way.

An unfaithful husband distressed at an impending break-up with his lovely wife, a minor argument with a gangster over a public telephone usage, a slap, a supari contract, and it is a night of wit and violence ....

A young BPO staffer misses the last local train at 1.40 a.m. from Kurla to Vikhroli and contrives to get involved in inter-gang rivalries .... And it is guffaws and gruesomeness from there on.

Evidently inspired by the punchy crime-comedies like Quentin Tarantino's *Pulp Fiction* (1994), Guy Ritchie's *Lock, Stock and Two Smoking Barrels* (1998) and *Snatch* (2000), these were something of an 'ominous comedy' in which a deathly twist could be just round the corner while you're laughing. Be prepared for nasty surprises. In *Kaminey*, the gangster Mikhail and the rogue politician Bhope horse around, parody each other and point a pistol at the other pretending to pull the trigger. And then without a warning, Bhope shoots Mikhail dead. Just like that. Just the way that the gangster Jules Winnfield (Samuel L. Jackson) in *Pulp Fiction* casually guns down two adversaries while discussing big Kahuna burgers with one of them. In Pankaj Advani's *Sankat City* (2009), a film about financing by the mafia, while we are laughing at the rotund film producer Gogi Kukreja's (Manoj Pahwa) clumsiness, without a warning, the hero of Kukreja's film Sikandar Khan (Chunkey Pandey) is blown to smithereens in a van explosion. Kukreja had teamed up with the moneylender Faujdar (Anupam Kher) to get rid of Sikandar so that Kukreja's under-production film may rake in profits by cashing in on the sympathy wave for the dead hero. For Kukreja, the decision to have Sikandar killed is an easy decision. As easy as it was for the arms dealer Boris in *Snatch* to put a bullet through Franky and then hacking Franky's forearm off with a handy chopper. Said Kay Kay Menon who plays the car-thief Guru, '*Sankat City* was a fun movie. It is very dark, similar to *Jaane Bhi Do Yaaro*—topsy-turvy, slapstick with very complex screenplay and characters.'

There is another curious similarity between *Kaminey* and the films by Tarantino and Ritchie mentioned above. In *Pulp Fiction*, the gangster Wallace fixes a boxing bout and his instruction to the boxer Butch (Bruce Willis) is clear: 'In the fifth (round) your ass goes down.' But Butch double crosses Wallace and knocks his opponent dead. Likewise, in *Snatch*, Mickey (Brad Pitt) knocks his opponent out cold when he has been paid to do exactly the opposite. Similarly, in *Kaminey*, the trouble starts with the race jockey double-crossing the bookie Charlie (Shahid Kapoor). The horse that was fixed to lose ends up winning, setting Charlie back by INR 1 lakh.

Said Amole Gupte of his role as the rogue politician Sunil Bhope in *Kaminey*, 'Casting Director Honey Trehan came to my office and showed me all the homework he had done about my roles in films like *Kafila* and *Abhisarika* at the Film Institute in the diploma films as an actor. Those were the films in which I had discovered that I could play bad characters. So Trehan led me into the role of Bhope softly. And because I loved what Vishal Bhardwaj did right from his early films like *Makdee* and *Omkara*, I said okay. The character Bhope was in my DNA because I am from Maharashtra, born and brought up in Mumbai. I knew the entire valuation of the character—how strong it could be played by being minimalistic. It is atypical, not stereotypical. It came naturally to me, using my natya shastra of ten years in theatre and ten years of films at the film institute. And I have to thank Vishal for that because he was also looking for new things. I built the diabetes into the character to make him palpable. I was well armed to play Bhope and to give the character a certain amount of kinkiness and a certain unpredictability—a manipulator, mercurial (laughs at times, and gets angry sometimes). So, you don't know exactly how to read him. But I think it went through with the audience. The first approval that Vishal got was from Naseeruddin Shah who said, "Yeah, this is a fine casting that you have done."'

Sanjay Khanduri's *Ek Chalis ki Last Local* (2007) is much darker with no fewer than a dozen deaths involving a variety of gangsters and corrupt cops—again, most of them sandwiched between comic scenes.

But the climax scene is an exhibition of corpses, reminiscent of the scene in *Lock, Stock and Two Smoking Barrels* in which a pile of corpses is all that is left after the deadly shootout between Rory's and Dog's gangs.

Pankaj Advani's *Urf Professor* (2001) could never have released in India. Not just because it shows an explicit sexual intercourse scene or a man masturbating ... not even because the nymphomaniac bride reels off her sexual exploits to her bridegroom on their wedding night ... but because Advani gave no hint of when a man's face would be hideously disfigured ... or that Lily's sex partner would be smothered to death even as she was approaching her orgasm ... or the perverse glee in watching an asthma patient wheeze to his slow death ... The laughter on our faces freezes in nauseating revulsion any moment while watching *Urf Professor*. And it is nothing like what was ever seen before in Bollywood.

Film historian Kaushik Bhaumik explained, 'There is a cartoony pastiche feel to these films heightened by quirky action, characterization, dialogues and situations. In as much they are a comment on the absurdity of life and death and criminality in contemporary capitalism, especially city life, they are also marked by the joy of cinema's power to show anything goes. Style for the sake of style is a hallmark of these films, the pure joy of perfectly and sharply employing cinema's genre conventions for their own sake irrespective of the story's emotional or moral implications. Hence these films portray imagery that is primarily iconic and not realistic.'

There is another film that exemplifies Bhaumik's analysis. In his luxurious hotel room in Delhi, Vladamir (Kim Bodnia), a supplier of illegal diamonds, is tortured by Cowboy (Vijay Raaz) and his gang of four who pound Vladamir's face, thrash his head repeatedly with a steel tray and jam a live firecracker into his anus. Vladamir screams pitifully for mercy, pleading ignorance about the whereabouts of the missing diamonds. Believe it or not—this is a *comedy* scene from Abhinav Deo's *Delhi Belly* (2011), epitomizing these crime-comedy films. The film is about a smuggling racket being run at Delhi's Indira Gandhi International Airport, allegedly in connivance with immigration and an Intelligence Bureau Official. A duty-free shopping bag containing diamonds gets mixed up with a bag containing stool samples of a young man. Upon non-receipt of the diamonds, Cowboy and gang swing into action. On the roads of Delhi and with collapsing ceilings, the chase continues. Through hotel walls and toilets, the bullets fly and crimson blood soils the plush carpets in the climax scene as all four gangsters lie dead. The release of *Delhi Belly* was preceded by a controversy over the lyrics of the theme song which, pronounced backwards, sounded like an expletive very liberally used in urban India.

Shared Bhaumik, 'The comedy is as much in the quirky film action and dialogue as much as in a quirky lighting, music/songs but above all in camera angles and cutting. One may say the comedy in these films really lies in the manner in which they are edited.'

And there is a pervasive 'chase' motif throughout in some of these films—police chasing gangsters or gangsters chasing rival gangsters. *Is*

Raat ki Subah Nahin (1996) is based on a real-life incident involving the film's director Sudhir Mishra's younger brother Sudhanshu in the latter's student days at FTII in the 1980s. Said Mishra, 'Sudhanshu had slapped an eve-teaser who turned out to be the brother of an underworld Bhai. Sudhanshu was on the run for three days. Later, based on this experience, he had written a script titled *"Bhaag Vijay, Bhaag!"'* The film is about sub-plots that daisy-chained into each other. Aditya's (Nirmal Pandey) wife Pooja (Tara Deshpande) catches him having an affair with another woman and threatens to throw him out. Accidentally, Aditya ends up having a minor scuffle with a member of Ramanbhai's (Ashish Vidyarthi) gang over the use of a public telephone. But Ramanbhai is being pursued by another gangster Vilas (Saurabh Shukla). And there is a corrupt policeman Inspector Patankar (Ganesh Yadav) who keeps switching sides at will. It is an all-night chase with non-stop action.

Said Sudhir Mishra, 'The possibilities of things getting snuffed out in Bombay interested me. I shot *Is Raat* ... all over the city. Except for the hero Nirmal Pandey's residence, all the rest were shot on locations like Grant Road, Bandra, Hanging Gardens, Naaz Café, Colaba. The shooting cost about 25% extra because it was all night shoots.'

Kaushik Bhaumik made another sharp observation, 'These films are structured like slapstick chase comedy films. People chasing each other endlessly and coming up against strange and outlandish impediments which abruptly halts their forward movement, highlighting the comic absurdity.'

Despite the evident inspiration of Tarantino and Ritchie, what talented film makers like Bhardwaj, Advani, Deo and Khanduri created were their own originals. Their individualities are visible in their usage of women characters. *Pulp Fiction, Snatch* and *Lock, Stock and Two Smoking Barrels* were targeted predominantly at a male audience. As expert quizzer and film buff Joy Bhattacharjya put it, 'These were the men's "beer club" movies, with very few women characters who would pass the Bechdel test. In other words, the women were mere props.' But in *Kaminey, Sankat City, Ek Chalis ki Last Local, Is Raat ki Subah Nahin* and *Delhi Belly*, there was at least one woman character playing a pivotal role. In fact, in the tangy comedy *Ishiqya* (2010), it was the other way around. Krishna Verma (Vidya Balan) was the kingpin who used the two men Khalu and Babban to kidnap KK and through him, to her estranged gun-running husband.

This was something fresh by the younger band of Bollywood film makers.[92]

VI

TUM LOG MUJHE DHOOND RAHE HO …
The Anti-heroes

In a book on villains, why are we discussing heroes? Here is why ….

Until about the early 1940s, Indian film heroes were usually virtuous like Lord Ram. But then something changed. There surfaced a variety of heroes who were no longer epitomes of honesty and simplicity; they began to show shades of grey, without being outright two-dimensional villains. We can term them 'anti-heroes'. As film-maker Shyam Benegal pointed out, 'The differentiator between a villain and an anti-hero is in the motive. The villain has a *bad* motive. The anti-hero has a *good* motive with improper means to achieve it.' So, the anti-hero may skirt, bend or even break the law to achieve a good motive, whereas a conventional hero would follow the law. But since the anti-hero's means are technically illegal or unethical, he merits a discussion in a book of villains.

1

Dreams and the City
The 1940s and the 1950s

In a conversation with the author, scenarist Sachin Bhowmick remembered actor Ashok Kumar telling him: 'I would only get to do roles of "postmasters", "station masters" or "schoolmasters" who would come to a village dressed in a Nehru jacket and Gandhi cap. They would fall in love with a village belle and get separated from her and sing melancholic songs. And finally, they would get married despite the odds. It was getting all too boring and predictable. So, in 1942, when Gyan (Mukherjee) narrated to me a story in which a hero would be doing a negative role for the first time, it sounded good.'

The film was *Kismet* (1943), with Ashok Kumar playing Shekhar, a pickpocket and a conman who is generous to two sisters stuck in a deep financial crisis. *Kismet* was an exception to the stock fare because the majority of the audience was the hoi polloi. As Bhowmick pointed out, 'More than 90 per cent of the movie-going public was rustic and with low IQ levels.' And yet, riding on the hitherto un-benchmarked image of an anti-hero in Ashok Kumar, *Kismet* rewrote box office fortunes.

It ran from 15 October 1943 to 17 April 1947, a total of 183 weeks at the Empire theatre (later renamed Roxy), Calcutta, a record which was broken three decades later by *Sholay* (1975) at Minerva, Bombay.

Four years after *Kismet* was released, India achieved freedom. But very quickly, another harsh truth dawned. As the late Shammi Kapoor pointed out in an interview with the author, 'The 1950s was a realization of a "Now what?" dilemma.' Independence brought with it colossal expectations for the youth, one of them being the notion of a romanticized life in the big city. The cities in focus at the time were Calcutta and Bombay.

> *Calcutta was the country's film capital till the mid-1940s. Post the Bengal famine of 1943 and the shutting down of New Theatres, the Calcutta film industry took a downturn and Bombay took over as the country's film and business capital.*

Our film scripts, too, mirrored this mindset. Bombay was the new Port of Hope of a free India resulting in a large number of city-based scripts in the 1950s like *Awara* (1951), *Baazi* (1951), *Humsafar* (1953), *Taxi Driver* (1954), *Shree 420* (1955), *Funtoosh* (1956), *Bombai ka Babu* (1960), *Kala Bazar* (1960) which are punctuated with images of a burgeoning metropolis with construction workers, noisy traders and scurrying office goers, busy streets and buses, the frenetic commercial stock exchange and pockets of the city for leisurely after hours, like the cafes, bars with live brass bands and red light areas.

In *Shree 420*, Raju arrives in Bombay all the way from far-off Allahabad in search of livelihood. In *Bombai ka Babu*, too, Babu (Dev Anand) hails from a small town and lands up in the Big City. However, it is not that these youngsters were always rootless. It is just that the storylines chose not to dwell on their roots, merely making a fleeting suggestion of their origins.

They came, they saw, they ghettoized. The stock dwelling of the young jobseeker of the 1950s was the noisy chawl with a babel of Marathi and Hindi (like Lalita Pawar's character switching between the two languages in *Shree 420*), scarce privacy and the seemingly ever-present clatter of utensils at the water line and of the homeless sleeping inside huge pipes amidst pelting rain, like we see in *House No. 44* (1955). The dream job for these migrants was a white collared one in an office. The next acceptable level was the brown-collared jobs like in *Taxi Driver* (1954).

In their book, Chetan Anand: The Poetics of Film, *authors Uma Anand and Ketan Anand share an anecdote about the shooting of* Taxi Driver. *'Having little scope for elaborate sets, Chetan took the camera out of doors, strapped to the bumper of a taxi. Almost the entire story is shot in the streets, on the beaches, through the palm groves and gullies of a remarkable character; the city of Bombay circa 1954.'*[93]

This cramping represented the dark underbelly of the city into which the unemployed youth had been pushed. The ever-present street bulb at night was a testament to a city that slept very little. The city, in fact, ended up being more than a backdrop. It was an experience. 'The streets on which he sleeps at night along with the homeless is where his social identity dissolves,' pointed out film historian Kaushik Bhaumik. And the differences between the 'haves' and the 'have-nots' quickly boil to the surface. The wealthy, like Judge Raghunath (Prithviraj Kapoor) in *Awara*, fine-dine and shop for jewellery, while Raj (Raj Kapoor), half hidden behind a pillar, simmers at the inequality. His lusty drag at the cigarette is a metaphor for the fire burning within him.

Raj's sense of deprivation in *Awara* is even more acute because he is the son of the wealthy and respected Judge Raghunath, and has been unfairly pushed into the underbelly of the city because his mother, suspected of infidelity, had been discarded by Raghunath. And then, the twelve-year-old Raj is thrown out of school because the authorities disapprove of his working as a part-time shoeshiner. Pushed into extreme penury, Raj is coaxed by the the goonda Jagga (K.N. Singh) to enter the world of crime. Shammi Kapoor said in an interview with the author, '*Khoon ki baat aa gayi thi* (it was about his legitimacy). Raj was a judge's son but grows up in the kichad (cesspool) with Jagga and hence became like Jagga.'

Circumstances had clearly not been fair to the other young men either. Madan (Dev Anand) in *Baazi* (1951) desperately looks for proper work and returns home every evening disappointed to his tuberculosis-ridden sister Manju. To be able to raise funds for her permanent cure, Madan is forced to join the notorious gambling den Star Club, where his job is to ensnare people fond of gambling and bring them to the club where these unsuspecting customers are cheated of their money. Star Club is under constant police surveliance for its suspected illegal gambling activities.

Journalist Noshu (Dilip Kumar) in *Footpath* (1953) is penniless and is compelled to join an illegal outfit involved in the selling foodgrains in the black market. The penurious Raju (Raj Kapoor) in *Shree 420* makes all attempts to earn an honest living in Bombay. But the city teaches him that dubious means can fetch much more money; more easily and sooner. Raju succumbs to the lure and gets into a gambling racket and a fraud ponzi housing scheme. In *Kala Bazar*, Raghu (Dev Anand) loses his job as a bus conductor because he accosts a passenger who abuses Raghu. And all Raghu was doing was urging the passenger to get off the bus because the seats were occupied. Thrown out on the streets, Raghu's mind staggers at what he sees and hears around him: the beggar asking for a paisa, the shoeshine boy living for a nickel, the rich man with a wad of banknotes, the black marketeer Kalu selling cinema tickets for a premium. It appears to him that the city can survive without oxygen, but not without money. The background score of '*Paisa, paisa, paisa babu paisa, paisa babu paisa…*' builds into a deafening, mocking crescendo. Raghu, too, takes to black marketeering cinema tickets.

In an ostensible show of defiance, our anti-heroes also carry themselves with a haughty swagger: their hands dug into their pockets, sporting knee-length trench coats or sporty berets, as well as a two-day stubble and an outlandish scarf. The attire and Westernized demeanour of the anti-heroes of the 1950s was undoubtedly copied from the Film Noir genre of Hollywood of the 1940s and early 1950s, where the lead characters tended to be morally flawed and suffering from some internal conflict. And perhaps due to this Hollywood influence, the 'good Indian man' was demonstrating habits that were taboo in Indian society—cigarette smoking, for instance. Although conventional sense dictates that good men do not indulge in vices, the anti-hero smokes and drinks because, by definition, he is an *anti*-hero—someone who goes against the convention.

The anti-heroes of the 1950s are well nuanced too. Dev Anand, with traces of the Cary Grant persona, is a softie gone astray, Raj Kapoor is the sympathy seeker, while Dilip Kumar in *Footpath* is the educated man. Kunwar R.K. Singh (Ashok Kumar) in Gyan Mukherjee's *Sangram* (1950) and Tony Fernandez (Dev Anand) in *Jaal* (1952) are very different from the other anti-heroes. Neither of them was pushed into crime by the force of circumstances. Spoilt by his father's excessive love and affection, Kunwar takes to bunking school, gambling and getting into scuffles with the good-for-nothing neighbourhood boys at the age of twelve. On growing up he runs a casino, pulls off a gold heist and flees the city. He was simply born with a penchant for wrongdoing. '*Kanoon bujhdilon ko darata hai. Mai kisise nahi darta, kisiko nahi manta* (Law scares only the cowards. I am not scared of anyone),' Kunwar brags. Tony Fernandez (Dev Anand) in *Jaal* (1952) is a strong, smart, young man. But instead of working hard and earning honest money like hundreds of other fishermen in Goa, he chooses to be a thug because he has observed quick money being made by smugglers' middleman on the coast.

Sachin Bhowmik shared: 'Awara *was inspired by a book called* Knock on Any Door *(a novel by Willard Motley). K.A. Abbas had read the book.* Knock on Any Door *was made into a film of the same name in 1949 and was an American court room trial film noir starring Humphrey Bogart and debutant John Derek.*'

The misdemeanours of most of these anti-heroes are pardonable as they are able to reverse their lives to an honest course. Raghu in *Kala Bazar* is back on track (including changing from Western clothes to a white Nehru jacket) once he realizes that he could lose his lady love if he doesn't. He serves a mild jail sentence and gets the reprieve of a happy ending. Likewise, Noshu in *Footpath* (1953) submits to an arrest along with his accomplices in black marketeering. His heroine too is waiting outside the prison for him to get married. Shekhar in *Kismet* reunites with his long-lost family in the end. Madan in *Baazi* is made to serve a mild sentence and released. In *Awara*, a contrite Judge Raghunath (Prithviraj Kapoor) finally accepts Raj as his son. With the root causes of the loss of social status having been restored, Raj will serve out the three-year jail sentence and return to being a conventional hero again.

Tony in *Jaal* knows that he wants to turn a new leaf. '*Jo aaj bura hai woh kal accha ho sakta hai* (A bad man can turn into a good one),' he tells his lady love Maria. He bows in supplication to the Almighty and reforms.

As Shyam Benegal sums up: 'If you study those films, they (the heroes) seem to have qualities of anti-heroes, but they are not so. Eventually they are still shining good men.'

Kunwar in *Sangram*, however, has gone too far down the road of crime to come back. Death is his only escape. But in his dying moments, he admits that this was the punishment he deserved.

2

The Angry Young Generation
The 1960s and the 1970s

In the 1960s, economic stagnation, social malaises like bribery, babugiri and rising unemployment had begun to set in, leaving the youth disappointed. In *Paigham* (1959), engineer Ratan Lal (Dilip Kumar) joins the labour union in their revolt against the factory owner (Motilal) who metes out an unfair treatment to his factory workers. This was arguably the first time that labour unrest was portrayed in Bollywood films. The power of the student union was on display in *Nai Umar ki Nai Fasal* (1965) even as elders dissuade the hot-blooded Rajeev (played by Ashok Chandra) from joining politics. Satyapriya Acharya (Dharmendra) in Hrishikesh Mukherjee's *Satyakam* (1969) is a young graduate with a dream of contributing to a new, independent India. But in his first job, he is asked by his employers to endorse a faulty project plan in return for an 'honorarium' which is nothing but a bribe in disguise. Very soon his bitter disillusionment at the corruption at every step becomes a perennial wellspring of a frustration. In fact, Acharya is arguably the first significant 'angry young man' in Hindi films.

Narayan Sanyal's novel Satyakam *was based on his real-life experiences at the Public Works Department (PWD). Hrishikesh Mukherjee adapted the story for his film of the same name, and* Satyakam *was his favourite film.* Satyakam *was actually a period film with the story set between 1946 and the late 1950s. But the issues and conflicts were relevant to any era—especially the 1960s.*

Whatever the degree of their frustration with the defective system, characters like Acharya could not do anything to fix it. But sooner or later there had to be a bias for action for these angry heroes. In other words, the *angry* hero would transition into the *anti*-hero who would break rules and laws.

As Shyam Benegal emphasized, 'From a clear morality tale we shifted gears to a more sophisticated, a more complex and a more difficult one.'

Also, around the mid- to late-1960s, the Naxalite movement involving the peasants, the educated and the intellectual young had commenced in various parts of the country. Violence in the streets, violence in mofussil areas, violence against the police and violence against the landowners were now regular news headlines. So, would physical force be the only available option for these youngsters to fix unjustness?

It was against this backdrop that at the turn of the decade, came Gulzar's directorial debut *Mere Apne* (1971) with a bunch of bright, educated young boys, for whom the real world did *not* turn out the way their textbooks had shown. Frequent strikes disrupt their college classes, examinations were not announced, the college itself turns into an 'akhara' (sandpit) for politicians to fight their battles and the college principal is an insensitive man who calls in the police to apprehend the students instead of placating the boys. The angry students vandalize the college and drop out. With no jobs and a general sense of being rejected—by family and society alike—the boys Kabir, Shyam, Sanju and gang are bound to act, rather react, and non-violence would not be a part of their reaction.

———

In *Mere Apne*, Gulzar infused shades of *West Side Story*-like inter-gang rumbles (rather unusual for a Gulzar film)—and the film arguably became the first instance of a gang war in Hindi films with countrymade bombs, hockey sticks, cycle chains and crude pistols. Gang members take sadistic relish in punishing their rivals, waterboarding them and being cruel in creative ways. Embedded in their actions is hatred, with an intent to maim, cripple and publicly humiliate the victim. Blunt weapons connect with skulls, swinging hockey sticks land on mouths. While the injured with bleeding faces roll on the streets bleating in pain, there is no dearth of acid bombs exploding around them. Danny Denzongpa, who played the puppet-carrying Sanju in *Mere Apne*, recalled, 'We all agreed that the fight sequences in *Mere Apne* should not look like one involving the typical *dhishum dhishum*. Everyone contributed to the discussion because we have all gone through gang fights in college and schools. That's why you will see that the fights choreographed by Ravi Khanna had more of pushing, pulling and struggling, which made the scenes look very real—exactly like a real fight.'

Danny Denzongpa shared some interesting trivia. 'I did not know how to operate a puppet. I needed a teacher to teach me how to operate it because it should not look as if I was trying too hard. There was a puppeteer that lived somewhere in a shanty in Bandra East. When I reached this man's place it seemed as if, for the first time the urchins had seen some "chinky" guy, as they gathered around me to look at me very closely. The door was locked and I sat in there all afternoon waiting for him. He finally returned and apologized for having made me wait. He proceeded to show me how to operate the puppet and manipulate it. I then requested him to come to my place in Shivaji Park which he did.'

And then, in 1973, arrived a new variety of anti-heroes—one for whom livelihood wasn't a problem at all. He had a respectable job; of a law enforcer, no less.

———

In Hindi films, the police had never had to use their physical power or take the law into their hands. Their uniform and authority were enough to apprehend criminals. But this new vigilante policeman who arrived in 1973 took it upon himself to mete out on-the-spot punishment to criminals. Power was going to be his; he would ensure that it would be his. But since he was taking the law into his own hands, technically he was breaking the law. Therefore, by definition, this young man too was an 'anti-hero'.

The character of this male lead scripted by Salim–Javed was a surly and angry young man called Vijay Khanna, haunted by a traumatic past. Despite being warned of his behaviour repeatedly, Vijay doesn't change. He manhandles a lorry driver brought in as a suspected culprit of rash driving that results in the death of children. Vijay Khanna also thrashes the gambling den owner Sher Khan (Pran) to make him shut shop. Vijay's behaviour was partly a result of his frustration at the system. For example, the lorry driver may have escaped arrest on some technicality of vision-impairment. Also, it is implied that Sher Khan enjoys the protection of some politician or the police themselves. How else would someone have the temerity to stride confidently into the police station when summoned? But, apart from this frustration, Vijay sees his parents' killers in every criminal in town, and therefore, seems to have a personal vendetta against each of them with a suicidal streak in him, entering the rogues' ghettos unarmed and alone.

The problem confronting Producer-Director Prakash Mehra was— where in the world was he going to find the actor to play this role?

It was while actor Pran and Prakash Mehra were watching the 1972 film *Bombay to Goa* that in one of the scenes, they both instinctively knew that they had found the male lead for Mehra's project. After five flops, a semi-hit and a film in which he was acclaimed for a side-role, the character of an angry, young, brash policeman would be the last throw of the dice for the almost thirty-one-year-old lanky Amitabh Bachchan.

Did the character Vijay Khanna draw its inspiration from the role of Inspector Harry Callahan played by Clint Eastwood in Dirty Harry *(1971)? 'Not really,' says Diptakirti Chaudhuri. 'The script for* Zanjeer *had already been written in 1970.* Dirty Harry *released in late 1971 and would have hit the screens in say, March 1972.* Zanjeer *was released a year later, in May 1973. So, at best, any likeness of Vijay Khanna to Harry Callahan would have been a mid-script influence.'*

The spurious liquor gang that Vijay Khanna was trying to apprehend in *Zanjeer* frames him in a fake bribery case. Vijay Khanna loses his job and gets jailed. But, on getting released from jail, he figures out that he can effectively punish those who had framed him by staying outside the system; and being a law unto himself. And thus, two years later, came Salim–Javed's next anti-hero, Vijay Verma of *Deewar* (1975) who stays on the wrong side of the law from the outset, with no half-measures such as pickpocketing. He joins a smuggling gang and moves straight up the ladder. Vijay Verma's reasons for negative behavior are similar to those of his 1950s' predecessors—the bitch of a system. Someone tattoos '*Mera Baap Chor Hai* (My father is a thief)' on young Vijay's forearm and this ignominy scars Vijay psychologically for life. Then Vijay's father deserts the family leaving them as destitutes. Vijay's mother is forced to work as a meneal labourer, where she is harassed and abused. All these culprits get away without punishment. Vijay Verma's trauma is worse than that of *Zanjeer's* Vijay Khanna. In *Zanjeer*, it was but a solitary murderer (and also the same person who frames Vijay in the fake bribery case) who was the problem. But immediately after his parents' demise, Vijay Khanna gets a loving foster home, education and a respectable career.

But *Deewar*'s Vijay Verma gets neither education nor a career. He has to drop out of school, work as a shoeshine boy, later graduating to a coolie. And so, when a 'kindly' smuggler provides a lucrative job to Vijay Verma, it never bothers Vijay that he is entering the chasm of organized crime. Because, his end game is to shower his mother with riches, *regardless of the means*. And this is why Vijay Verma is the quintessential anti-hero—good end, bad means.

And because their childhood traumas were dissimilar, the two Vijays are very different. Outside of work, Vijay Khanna of *Zanjeer* is sensitive, soft-natured. Deep down he is a romantic and can forge friendships for life. Vijay Verma of *Deewar*, on the other hand, is a hard-as-nails, friendless loner. Vijay Khanna starts out by having belief in the system. But Vijay Verma of *Deewar* never had any faith in the system and is a pariah right from the get-go.

At some level, *Deewar* was perhaps a story of unemployment and other societal ills that lead to good young men losing their way. But interestingly, in a session with the author at the Kolkata Literary Meet in 2016, Javed Akhtar dispelled this commonly held perception around the origin of the angry young man. He said, 'We (Salim–Javed) had none of the (prevalent) social and political situation in mind at all while crafting the Angry Young Men. We were not even aware of those to any great extent! Maybe it was good that we were not so close to the situation. Because we could write as writers.'

In 1978, Salim–Javed and Director Yash Chopra created another anti-hero called Vijay Kumar (Amitabh Bachchan) in *Trishul*. Vijay Kumar is born a bastard after a young businessman R.K. Gupta (Sanjeev Kumar) abandons his mother after making her pregnant. Unlike *Zanjeer* or *Deewar*, *Trishul*'s Vijay's revenge strategy isn't physical. He ambushes R.K. Gupta's mammoth construction business using corporate espionage, among other tactics, reducing the Gupta empire to near-bankruptcy. Corporate espionage acts like bribing a rival organization's employee to disclose competing tender bids and then underbidding by 1 rupee lesser than the competitor is considered unethical. Vijay does all this to avenge his mother's humiliation. And that is why Vijay is an anti-hero; good motive, improper means.

On the heels of *Zanjeer* and prior to *Deewar*, Salim–Javed had crafted another anti-hero—Shankar (Dharmendra) in *Yaadon Ki Baaraat* (1973). Shankar is similar to Vijay of *Zanjeer*—a man seeking out his parents' killers. Again, as in *Zanjeer*, popular wisdom would suggest that Shankar is a true hero as he was avenging his parents' murder. But Shankar's end game is to kill the murderer even if it meant the gallows for himself. So, here again, 'murder' as a means to a heroic motive of avenging his parents' murder makes Shankar an *anti*-hero. Because two wrongs don't make a right.

The angry young man and the anti-hero of the 1970s were conceptualizations of Hrishikesh Mukherjee and Gulzar in *Satyakam* and *Mere Apne* respectively. And Salim–Javed seem to have perfected the trope. Shyam of *Mere Apne* still carried the Gulzaric elements of romance, whereas Salim–Javed removed the niceties off the characters and made them unadulteratedly macho.

They had created a brand for posterity.

3

Anti-hero Pe Mat Ro
The Legacy

In the post-*Zanjeer* world, examples of the vigilante policeman-hero thrashing suspected criminals without a proper warrant became so common that we, as the audience, almost started believing these anti-heroes were legitimate. Govind Nihalani's *Ardh Satya* (1983) serves as an example of how Inspector Anant Velankar (Om Puri) feels about the impotence of his powers in the face of a corrupt system. As he is about to arrest the mafia don Rama Shetty (Sadashiv Amrapurkar), he gets a call from his superior officer asking him to vacate Rama Shetty's place. 'In *Ardh Satya*, it is the anguish and frustration of a person who is educated and empowered. And yet, he is a part of the police force ...' Govind Nihalani pointed out in an interview with the author.

Nandita C. Puri, in her biography on Om Puri, discloses that Om, excited at bagging the role in Ardh Satya, *prepared extensively for it. She says, 'For the first time Om joined a gym at the producers' expense at the Holiday Inn Hotel to tone up his otherwise lean frame. Like a typical cop he also learnt to ride a motorbike …' She adds, 'As a preparation for the role, Om also visited a couple of police stations, Mahim and Girgaum, to observe the behaviour of policemen when they were away from public scrutiny and to soak in the general ambience. One evening he was offered a drink called Maramari, which is half lemonade and half soda, so that the cops with their poor pay-packets get a taste of the fizz without having to pay for a full soda bottle. It was at the police station that he first heard about "zero police", an unofficial police person, who sometimes doubles as a peon and an informer or* khabri.'[94]

The policeman continues to feel frustrated in the new millennium. The hard-hitting policemen Chulbul Pandey (Salman Khan) in *Dabbang* (2010) and Baji Rao Singham (Ajay Devgn) in *Singham* (2011) do not bother about political correctness, thrashing criminals, dragging them to the police station by their collars, plucking street lights out of parapet walls and beating up the goons using those as weapons …. These actions are very similar to those of Vijay Khanna and Anant Velankar. But a scene later, Chulbul Pandey and Singham are romancing their women or dancing with the town belles, diluting the essence of ingrained anger intrinsic to an anti-hero.

———

In *Andha Kanoon* (1983), *Ankush* (1986), *Aakhree Raasta* (1986) and *Ghayal* (1990), anti-heroes, young and old alike, are convinced that their definition of justice is the truest and best. *Ankush* (1986) carried forward *Mere Apne*'s legacy of the bright, young educated boys who, denied of employment, took to petty crimes. In *Ankush*, N. Chandra's directorial debut, a band of disgruntled boys are led by Ravindra Kelkar (Nana Patekar) for whom the medical college is the 'institution' that has inducted him into the world of felony. When Ravindra protests against rampant cheating going on with the full collusion of the 'invigilators', he is falsely accused of creating disturbance on campus and rusticated. It was a near replay of the scene in *Mere Apne* in which the boys' pleas for proper classes and timely examinations are met with rebuttal and police action. In *Mere Apne*, the old naani (grandmother, played by Meena Kumari) is the saner voice trying to calm down the misguided boys. In *Ankush* it is the young Anita (Nisha Singh), a Labour Relations Officer. As in *Mere Apne*, the *Ankush* boys too are the do-gooder, compassionate boys who demonstrate an openness to come back to the mainstream. But when Anita, after being raped by her employers, commits suicide, the boys pick up arms and butcher her killers.

These boys are not mercenaries. Revenge for justice was the motive of the anti-hero led drama. In Aditya Bhattacharya's *Raakh*, Aamir Khan plays Amir Hussein, a twenty-one-year-old boy from a well-to-do family, who is shooed away by the police when he approaches them for justice for his friend Neeta (Supriya Pathak), who gets raped by the member of a family of rogues. Hussein find an unlikely sympathizer in a cop P.K. (Pankaj Kapur) who has been fired from the police force unfairly. Hussein and P.K. set about eliminating the members of the rogue family one by one.

The scripts were written in a way that the audience's sympathy lay with the anti-heroes, as their retaliation was understandable. The titles *Aakhree Raasta* and *Andhaa Kanoon* themselves suggest that turning vigilante was the last resort for the anti-hero protagonists since the law is blind. As Govind Nihalani emphasizes, 'When you write a script, you are carrying in you the anger of society, the anger of the writer *and* also the anger of a film-maker. How the film-maker expresses his anger is the key.'

The Naxalites that we spoke of earlier in this chapter are another example of the angry youth who wanted to fix a flawed system not by participating in the democratic process but by using brute force *against* it. Govind Nihalani's *1084 ki Maa* (1998) is about the Naxalite activist Brati Chatterjee (Joy Sengupta). Says Nihalani, 'The Naxalites were intellectuals who wanted to impose a different ideological system by overthrowing a lawfully elected one. For them Naxalites, the Indian State, which was not able to deliver, became the villain.' Their intention of fixing the system may have come from a good place but since their means were violent, Brati and his comrades are anti-heroes. They get killed and Brati is reduced to a mere number—'1084', the number assigned to his dead body at the mortuary.

———

But fixing a systemic problem is not always as easy as the mainstream masala films made it out to be. Take the example of the young, uneducated tapori slum-dweller named Salim Langda. He sits by the Marine Drive at night and looks longingly at those Bombay skyscrapers. But why was Salim unable to get a proper job in the first place?

Director Saeed Mirza spoke about his classic 1989 flick *Salim Langde Pe Mat Ro*: 'In Mumbai, a fairly large percentage of the underworld are Muslims. Why do they quit studies? Why can't they be in a 9 to 5 job? But then, who the hell gives them jobs? It is an underlying message passed on to Muslim youth—"Education isn't going to work because you will never get a job." Then what does he do? He creates jobs with his hands—electricians, mechanics, plumbers. Or he joins the underworld.'

Decade after decade, strong young men like Salim Langda have idolized the most unlikely of heroes. In a chat with the author, Pavan Malhotra who played Salim Langda traces the genesis of the role. 'In Hyderabad and Bangalore, everyone wants to join IT because they see successful IT heroes around them. Likewise, in Bombay, people from film industry join the film industry because for them, the heroes are the directors and actors .... Now when Salim is growing up in an area which is famous for its goondas, he looks at the senior smugglers around him and actually *aspires* to be like them.' For Langda, idolizing Ibrahim Malbari (Sudhir Pande), an illiterate who has risen from the gutter to become a prominent smuggler, is also propelled by the fact that he is undereducated and is frustrated over not being able to secure a job for himself. Salim Langda's idol is Ibrahim Malbari (Sudhir Pande), an illiterate who has risen from the gutter to become a prominent smuggler.

One wonders what the difference between the petty goondas and anti-heroes is. After all, both take to crime because of their poverty and circumstances. The answer is that there possibly is no difference, except that the anti-heroes are author-backed and these petty criminals aren't. As Kaushik Bhaumik summarized, 'The anti-hero is the one we instinctively identify as the hero thanks to the way the script is written.'

Actor Pavan Malhotra shared some trivia, 'Co-actor Makarand Deshpande and I had spent time in that Chor Bazaar area where I was shooting for another film. I drew from things in the recesses of my mind. My father's machine tools business was in Old Delhi. We had so many Muslims as friends. My father's best friend was a Muslim. So, there are so many things that I was able to bring out from my memory bank.'

Salim Langda exemplifies the hundreds of others who keep fighting this quicksand all their lives, and, in most cases, sink. Their ends are quite anti-climactic. Says Mirza, 'Salim comes in contact with another erudite young Muslim and the way forward dawns upon Salim; he too tries to get a respectable job as a mechanic. But it is too late.' Unlike Vijay of *Deewar*, Salim Langda does not win a hero's death. While celebrating his sister's engagement, he is stabbed to death by a member of Ibrahim Malbari's gang because Salim had refused to carry out a supari (killer) contract for Ibrahim. Salim's dead body is eventually disposed of, and nobody sheds tears for him.

Somewhere in his journey of struggle, Salim Langda had assured his friends that hopefully, '*Apna bhi* time *ayega* (My time too will come).' But it never does.

———

The other change in the anti-hero image has been the arrival of the 'acceptable grey' hero image. For example, Shankar (Dharmendra) in *Sitamgar* (1985) is a smuggler who loots from other smugglers and distributes the wealth to the poor, i.e., a typical anti-hero. He indulges in paid sex; but neither the character nor the scriptwriter is apologetic about it. Dev's (Abhay Deol) love for Paro (Mahie Gill) in *Dev D* (2009) is indistinguishable from his explicit lust for her. 'Paro, do you touch yourself? *Bol na,*' Dev asks her over phone from London. He convinces Paro to click a topless picture of herself and email it to him (Those were the pre-WhatsApp days). Shyam Benegal said, 'It is only in the last thirty-forty years that the Indian audiences have come to accept a much more sophisticated rendition of characters *without labelling them immoral.* For example, *Dev D* (2009) is an *amoral* hero, not an *immoral* one.'

This is the newest shade of 'grey' in the anti-hero palette.

VII

JAANE BHI DO YAARO ...
Crime and Punishment

The difference between cinema and real life is that a movie has one/two villains, whereas in the real world, we encounter an ensemble of them at various points in life. A few intelligent film-makers thought about this. As we approach the final lap of the rogues' gallery, we observe that, at a subterranean layer of mainstream cinema, there has existed a genre of thoughtfully made films with an *ensemble* of dark characters in an ecosystem that may be the home or the world. It can be urban India or rural India; and this ensemble of dark characters represented the defects in that ecosystem. In an interview with the author, film-maker Sudhir Mishra said, 'These were pessimistic, dark films and took an outside-in view rather than an inside-out view. These had a moral centre and posed questions which, in turn, posed more questions, without assigning themselves the job of finding solutions. These films lamented that this was not the best possible world and that we are only looking at the realm of what is possible.'

Jaagte Raho (1956) was arguably the first ever dark ensemble with a gallery of antagonists residing in various flats of a housing society, each representing a societal ill. There was a sly astrologer, a dipsomaniac wife-abuser, a thieving husband, a fake doctor, a spurious-liquor brewer and a fake currency counterfeiter. Each gets unmasked one by one when the residents of the housing society are busy looking for—guess what—a thief! *Jaagte Raho* was like an abridged version of a book on villains.

Two more films that followed—*Pyaasa* (1957) and *Parakh* (1960) were examples of dark ensembles of opportunists. In *Pyaasa*, the poet Vijay (Guru Dutt) is a crestfallen common man. After having walked everywhere from the underbelly of red-light areas to the pseudo erudition of mushairas to high society parties, and having his thought-provoking, truthful poetry getting silenced and his siblings indecently negotiating royalty amounts with the publisher over Vijay's poetry, Vijay has given up hope of anything genuinely honest in this country or even in the world. His theatrical rhetoric in the finale song, '*Ye duniya agar mil bhi jaaye to kya hai* (Who wants this irredeemable world)?' sums up the story. There is no one specific villain—yet they are everywhere. *Parakh* (1960) is set in a small village in which there are four antagonists—the wealthy zamindar Rai Bahadur Tandav (Jayant), the village doctor (played by Rashid Khan), a temple priest, Panditji (played by Kanhaiyalal), and an old and obese Bhanj Babu (Asit Sen) who, even at his age, is desirous of marrying a young girl. One day a letter arrives from a former resident of the village, stating that he wishes to entrust INR 5 lakhs towards the progress of the village to that one person who is the most honest and most capable of utilizing the money for the welfare of the village. The panchayat decides that the recipient should be chosen by popular vote. Immediately, all the four antagonists turn into virtual saints, bending over backwards to help villagers, as each aspires to receive the money which they undoubtedly intend for their personal use. They are chameleonic in their shiftiness and progressively slide from saam (cajole) to daam (compensate), and then accelerate to dand (punish) and bhed (blackmail) as tools to coerce people to vote for them. It was more of a cultural defect than the fault of those four individuals. Manoj Kumar's star-packed *Roti, Kapada aur Makaan* (1974) is something of a modern-day *Parakh* with three antagonists. A grocer, a tailor and a landlord are the metaphors for the three all-powerful basic needs of man that control and drive things—food, clothing and shelter. From the honest, unemployed Bharat (Manoj Kumar) to the slum-dwelling single unwed mother Tulsi (Moushumi Chatterjee), every common man is impacted by the lack of one of more of these three basic needs. We may not remember those dark characters vividly, but we remember very well what they stand for. As Sudhir Mishra analysed, 'From a person centric cinema, the dark ensembles zoomed out into a broader frame that encompassed a large group of people, their situations taking the whole story forward rather than *a* larger than life hero or *a* large than life villain.'

These dark ensembles, as we would have observed, are about conflict. Director Sudhir Mishra too brought in the conflict angle delectably in in *Hazaron Khwahishen Aisi* (2005), in addition to a 'betrayal' aspect. The story is set during the peak of the Naxalite movement from 1969 onwards. The lead character Siddharth Tyabji (Kay Kay Menon) is an avowed believer of the Naxalite doctrine whereas his Hindu College classmates Geeta Rao (Chitrangadha Singh) and Vikram (Shiney Ahuja) are more materialistic. Sidharth leaves for Bihar to work towards bringing social equality and justice in a village. Within a few years the ambitious Vikram turns an entrepreneur who 'fixes' key people in the government to get results. In his own words he is a fixer, dealer, broker, pimp. Geeta gets married to a bureaucrat but cheats on her husband with Sidharth. All the while Vikram has secretly loved Geeta, despite being married to someone else. Vikram also disapproves of Sidharth's activities, terming him a coward and an escapist. And thus, the three central characters keep appearing in various shades of grey as the story progresses. At the end of it all, in the face of severe adversity, Sidharth abandons the Naxalite movement and his comrades and scoots to London to pursue medicine. Was Sidharth indeed the coward that Vikram termed him? Or was it Sidharth's disillusionment with the Naxalite movement? 'Maybe the mysteries of the human bodies will be less confusing,' he writes to Geeta, who has meanwhile, borne Sidharth's child out of wedlock. In an interview said Kay Kay Menon who played Siddharth, 'I depended a lot on Sudhir Mishra's inputs since he had witnessed much of the movement himself. I understood the fallacies, the contradictions and the uselessness of this whole movement .... Sidharth was symbolic of the disillusionment resulting from the unimplementability of the Naxalite concepts that I don't think human beings can ever achieve.'

A similar dual conflict—one in the external world and one in the inner lives—was leveraged by Vishal Bhardwaj in *Haider* (2014). Based on Shakespeare's Hamlet, *Haider* is set in Jammu and Kashmir and the cross-currents of situational conflicts locals are caught in. Young student Haider Meer's (Shahid Kapoor) doctor father Dr Hilaal Meer gets rounded up because he had treated a Kashmiri militant for appendicitis. Dr Meer goes missing and is later found dead, after extensive torture by the Army and the police. So, the Indian Army and their use of the dreaded Armed Forced Special Powers Act (AFSPA) to round up suspected Muslim militants and make them disappear is the villain as far as the innocent people of J&K are concerned. But, in the face of cross-border insurgency, what options did the Army have? The Judas, it turns out, is Dr Hilaal Meer's brother Khurram Meer (Kay Kay Menon) who had informed the Army that terrorists were hiding in Dr Meer's place. But then, by cooperating with the Army and law enforcement, was Khurram not doing his duty as a citizen? Remember, Haider had joined a terrorist group and was hours away from crossing the border to Pakistan. Did Khurram not place his country's interests above even blood relationship? Further, young Haider is traumatized to see his mother Ghazala (Tabu) in a relationship with her brother-in-law Khurram Meer. But did Ghazala not have a right to seek a new life? It can also be argued that to save her young son of the trauma, Ghazala could have ended the relationship with Khurram. The characters of Haider were all about their respective points of view. There was no right or wrong.

Kay Kay Menon spoke about his role as Khurram Meer in *Haider*, 'It was the most complex role in the film. Khurram had three aspects to carry with him that were pulling him in three different directions. One—his ambition, two—his guilt and three—his love for Ghazala (Gertrude in Shakespeare's *Hamlet* from which *Haider* was adapted). Khurram Meer, at every point, has to carry these three pointers together which became a complex form of performance. And then I had to speak Kashmiri Hindi without sounding as if I've learnt it recently. I don't know whether the audience or even the movie pundits understood or realized this complexity.'

Another blotch on our society is the way we have dealt with issues like homosexuality. Professor of Marathi Srinivas R. Siras (Manoj Bajpayee) of Aligarh University in *Aligarh* (2016) gets suspended by the university and expelled from his quarters. His fault? He is reportedly gay as evidenced by the fact that he was filmed in bed with a male partner. And Prof. Siras being gay is seen by the university as a matter of shame. 'He has violated the moral code of his employees,' argues the legal counsel for AU, claiming that the victim was AU and not Prof. Siras. Further the university argues that Prof. Siras's act was un-Islamic. Whereas the truth is that, at that time in 2009, Article 377 was decriminalized. In other words, being gay was not a crime anymore. So, AU's act was illegal. Moreover, Prof. Siras was denied the rights provided by Article 21 of the Constitution which gave the right of dignity and privacy to every individual because, a couple of reporters from News 100 channel forcibly entered Prof. Siras's house and filmed him and his male friend Irfan in his private moments, and beat the two of them up. The court hearings clearly bring out that two 'reporters' were sent by the AU top officials and video footage clearly suggest that the 'reporters' had forced Siras and Irfan to get into compromising positions.

Another centuries-old shame is the way Indian society has looked at female children. The arrival of a male child was a reason for rejoicing, whereas the household would go into mourning if the newborn was a female, with the mother being blamed for giving birth to a female child. It is unthinkable, but there are households and communities that have murdered newborn female children. Just like any other crime, the law against female infanticide is not always a deterrent. '*Betiyaan bojh hoti hai* …. *Agar tere baad meri das betiyaan aur hoti to mai unhe bhi jaan se maar deta!*' thunders Ranveer Chopra (Kamal Chopra) in *Tamanna* (1998), addressing his long-lost daughter who had been abandoned in a half-dead condition in a dumpster in the slums of Mumbai as soon as she was born.

In a chat with the author, Mahesh Bhatt spoke about his film *Tamanna* (1998) (a film based on a real-life story of a eunuch who had rescued a girl child from a garbage dump). 'That was a rare and unusual villain. The villain was not somebody with fangs but the grandmother (played by Zohra Sehgal), the maid (played by Sulabha Deshpande) and the father who are the symbols of your home of security becoming your threat, making the home the most dangerous place for a woman. It is the grandmother—a woman—who tells her son to get rid of the girl child. And it's the maid—a woman again—who throws the child into a garbage bin.'

Did they realize what these systematic killings of baby girls would lead to? *Matrubhoomi: A Nation Without Women* (2003) shows the future horror through a despicable custom in a Bihar village in which a newborn girl child is drowned in a container of milk by the child's father himself. Fast forward to 2050 CE, we see a dance show happening in that village one evening—with a male dancer dressed up as a woman. The menfolk are sexually deprived, and hence, frustrated because there are very few young women left in the village. Their systemic murder of girl children had created a society of gays, cross-dressing men and eunuchs. To release their sexual frustration, they watch poor-quality pornographic films in groups. And even the posterior of a cow can turn these desperate men on. A villager Ramsharan (Sudhir Pandey) brings home a bride, Kalki, from a neighbouring village for his five sons who take turns to sleep with her. And even Ramcharan gets to sleep with her—yes, his own daughter-in-law. Soon, Kalki gets caught in an inter-community war and she gets gang-raped by men belonging to a particular caste. She becomes pregnant and more violence ensues over who the father of Kalki's child was. Here, the entire village comes to represent the sordid and hugely problematic mindset of our society that sees women as dispensable, only to be used as a means to sexual gratification and procreation; the villain in *Matrubhoomi* is the society at large, more so, its mindset.

But wait—there are lighter ways of telling dark stories about our society ....

The municipality rules do not permit a twenty-fifth storey to be constructed. So, the real-estate tycoon Tarneja (Pankaj Kapur) corrupts the Municipal Commissioner D'Mello (Satish Shah) with a hundred thousand rupees, a woman and ... a Swiss cake. Suddenly in 1983, out of the blue, there arrived a revolution in the history of Indian cinema. Kundan Shah's *Jaane Bhi Do Yaaro* (1983). It strips the entire system naked. Below the delicious toppings of dark wit, satire, adult humour and good old slapstick comedy is an ensemble of spineless public servants, adulterous real-estate tycoons, sabotage, bribery, corruption, conspiracy and daylight murder, with only the intensity of blackness separating each black character from the other. D'Mello is so corrupt that he accepts bribes for awarding the contract for a new flyover to both Tarneja and another real estate company owned by Ahuja (Om Puri)—and actually awards the contract to a third company. Peeved at losing the lucrative contract, Tarneja gets Commissioner D'Mello murdered. Meanwhile the newly built flyover collapses due to spurious cement used by Tarneja. Even the one person we trust all through—the upright, bold Shoba Sen, editor of the *Khabardaar* magazine, turns out to be two-faced. Having used the two nincompoop photographers Sudhir (Ravi Baswani) and

Vinod (Naseeruddin Shah) to gather evidence against Tarneja with the
stated intention of exposing him to the public, Shoba actually negotiates
a deal with Tarneja.

Said Sudhir Mishra, 'I was twenty-two when I co-wrote the script of
Jaane Bhi Do Yaaro along with Kundan Shah who was my mentor. He
was gracious enough to give me a chance to write with him. *Jaane Bhi Do
Yaaro* was my film school. It was not based on anyone in particular. But it
was about idealists betrayed by the nexus and truth getting snuffed out.
In Kundan's view the newspaper woman Shoba Sen was the proverbial
femme fatale.' Except Naseeruddin Shah, there were no stars in the crew.

> *One can find a stark resemblance of the Draupadi cheerharan sequence with
> the Jekyll and Hyde play sequence starring Orson Welles in* The Thirteen
> Chairs *(1969), a film with an unusual star cast, also famous as Sharon
> Tate's last film.*

———

Sudhir Mishra went a few more lanes downtown to end up at *Dharavi*
(1992)—the world's most populous slum. Another naked truth of our
society. It spans a mere 2.1 square kilometres but its population is over
7,00,000. The Dharavi slum came up in the late 1800s. Yes, for over a
hundred years, while Bombay's high-rises have multiplied many times
over, Dharavi has remained a slum. Not only that, the place is believed
to be a hotbed of crime and prostitution. But let alone uplift Dharavi, we
have not even tried to decipher the truth of what that place is all about.
In an interview with the author, Sudhir Mishra shared, 'In my forty days
there during the shoot, I never saw prostitution and drugs out there.
There is much more prostitution in the so-called respectable localities.
It's a shame that the municipal authorities still have not regularized the
houses and treat them as unauthorized. A lot of people think of Dharavi
as a place of crime, but it is actually a small-scale industrial area with
entrepreneurs and taxi drivers who contribute a lot to the society. A lot

of the papad and achhar you eat in Bombay gets made there. Dharavi is a poor man's multiplex.'

Dharavi is the tragedy of the migrant.

> *Sudhir Mishra shared insights about the making of* Dharavi. *'Shabana Azmi used to come to Dharavi every day for forty days without grumbling and used to eat at the stalls there. All her costumes were stitched by tailors in Dharavi itself. Om Puri saab used to blend in so well that at times, people would come and ask me who the hero was. I used to point to him and the people refuse to believe me! So much had he become one of them. We never stopped the residents from walking and carrying on their day-to-day activities during our shoot. After a while they learnt not to look up at the camera when the shot was being taken.'*

———

Thankfully, by and large, Bollywood still believes in karma: what goes around comes around. These few bad men ultimately did meet their deserved punishment.

In *Doosri Sita* (1974), unable to agree to her husband's (played by Kuljeet) repulsive act of asking her to sleep with another man, Sita kills him.

> *Kuljeet's story is interesting. He was one of the contenders shortlisted in the Filmfare Talent show in 1967. But Lady Luck never smiled on Kuljeet and he had to accept side roles like the villain's henchman, the most well-known of which was as Peter in the famous fight sequence with Amitabh Bachchan in* Deewar. *In later years, he had a sports outfit at Chowringhee Road, Calcutta.*

Likewise, the bai in *Arth* knifes her wastrel husband (played by Suhas Bhalekar) to death for stealing the money she had saved for her child's education. In *Insaaf ka Tarazu*, Bharti Saxena's rape case is quashed in the court. She gets no justice. Further, her younger sister Neeta (Padmini Kolhapure) also gets raped by the same rapist Ramesh Gupta (Raj Babbar). Bharti Saxena takes the law in her own hands and shoots Ramesh Gupta to death. In an interview Zeenat Aman said, 'The first rape of Bharti was perhaps about lust. But the second rape act of Bharti's younger sister Neeta (Padmini Kolhapure) was about lust and domination. It was his brag that he could get away with again just the way he had done it and gotten away with it earlier. Obviously the sister is so much younger and more vulnerable. The second rape act gave Bharti, the main protagonist the reason to seek the revenge and she does.' Bharti shoots Ramesh to death.

Tapan Sinha's Bengali Adalat O Ekti Meye *was similar enough to* Insaaf ka Tarazu *for B.R. Chopra to not favour its selection for the National Award. B.R. was overruled by Ashok Kumar (the head of the Jury that year) and* Adalat O Ekti Meye *did eventually win the National Award for the Best Bengali Film in 1981.*

Sometimes the bad guys would make that one careless error that would trigger the police's suspicion and lead these men to their punishment. For example, in *Inkaar* (1978), the kidnapper Raj Singh (Amjad Khan) makes the fundamental mistake of putting his wallet in his left trouser pocket when he has disguised himself as a man with no left arm! Sometimes their emotions get them ensnared. Man Singh (Utpal Dutt) in *Shaque* (1976) is an emotional wreck. Having managed to keep his little secret of having murdered his boss and scooting with Rs 50,000 for ten long years, he needlessly returns to the scene of his crime ... and gets captured by the police. Said Kolkata based consultant psychologist, Dr (Mrs) Paromita Mitra Bhaumik, in an interview with the author, 'Some sort of guilt drives these culprits to return to the scene of the crime they commit. The unconscious guilt feelings of the criminal make them leave behind trace evidence—and that is where they mostly get caught.'

The other factor that led to their downfall was greed. In the climax scene of *Yaadon ki Baaraat*, when the hero closes in on Shakaal, Robert urges Shakaal to abandon the quest of the final loot (Irani jewellery) and board Robert's private aircraft. 'Come on Shakaal! There is no way out. And there is no time,' Robert shouts at Shakaal. That flight would have helped Shakaal escape the dragnet of the Indian police and flee India forever with his money safely stashed away in banks abroad. But Shakaal does not listen to Robert who takes flight sans Shakaal and his son Rupesh (Imtiaz Khan). Shakaal gets crushed to death by an oncoming train; but it was not Indian Railways that killed Shakaal, it was his greed.

In fact, while shooting this climax scene in *Yaadon ki Baaraat* in which which Shakaal's foot get caught caught between the railway tracks and a speeding train runs over him, actor Ajit playing Shakaal almost met with the same fate himself. Actor Tariq revealed in an interview with the author what he had been told by the assistants and the cameramen about the shooting of that scene, 'The railway track scene was shot in Panvel Uran which is frequented by good trains. The assistants were all hiding behind the bushes and they saw that Ajit sahib was not moving away even as the train got closer. The cameraman and Nasir sahib were inside the train thought, "*Ye to mar gaya* (he is gone)." Nasir sahib *ke paseeney chooth gaye* (Nasir sahib broke into cold sweat). Ajit sahib tried to let the train come right close and shifted just when the train was a mere two feet away! What if his shoe had really got stuck? The train was cruising at 25–30 kmph—fast enough to kill. Ajit sahib, when asked later, said that he wanted to give a realistic shot. There was no need for that risk. It could have been edited later.'

In *Shalimar*, in addition to his crime, it was his insecurity that did Sir John Locksley (Rex Harrison) in. Worried sick about being dispossessed of the priceless Shalimar, Sir John invites to his island the four master thieves who, he feels, may be best equipped to steal the ruby from him. Sir John's stated intent was to give those four a chance to steal the jewel; but his actual objective was to kill them so that he may not have to worry about the Shalimar getting stolen from him thereafter. A CBI Officer Kumar sneaks in as a fake invitee and proves to be Sir John's nemesis.

In *Gaddaar* (1973), a gang of seven crack open the sensor-controlled vault and steal INR 40 lakhs of cash. One of their own gang members Kanhaiya (Madan Puri) betrays them and vanishes with the entire loot to the snow-filled Kufri. They locate Kanhaiya but the gang members do not trust each other anymore. Three of the seven members get killed by each other and other two kill themselves, while the last two get captured by Inspector Raj Kumar who infiltrates the gang in the guise of a safe-cracker. In the entire death-fest, the ill-gotten bank notes serve only one useful purpose—suffering from severe fits of cough continuously, the gang leader B.K. (Pran) decides to burn some of the bank notes to give his throat some warmth in that extreme cold.

Some punishments are so painful that even the audience wishes for some leniency if not a quick death. Karan Sing Rathod in *Ek Hasina Thi* (2004) is in a relationship with the young and pretty Sarika (Urmila Matondkar). Unknown to Sarika, Karan is a part of an underworld gang. One afternoon Karan plants a consignment of illegal firearms at Sarika's place and gets her arrested. He had used her as a mule in his gun-running racket. Advocate Kamlesh Mathur (Aditya Srivastata) convinces Sarika to plead guilty, assuring her that the judge would serve her a mild sentence, maybe even a pardon. Sarika does as advised but she realizes to her horror that she has been deceived when the judge hands her a seven-year sentence. Kamlesh is a friend of Karan and was sent at his behest to give Sarika the idea of pleading guilty. The prison term destroys Sarika's career and personal life. Said Director Sriram Raghavan in an interview, 'The first fifty to sixty pages where the girl falls in love and gets cheated was similar to the Sidney Sheldon novel, *If Tomorrow Comes*. But from the escape onwards it was different film.' All Sarika now wants is revenge.

'It had to be a cathartic revenge', said Raghavan, in an interview with Rajeev Masand, of the grisly punishment to Karan. 'Putting a bullet through him or pushing him down a cliff or handing him over to the cops wouldn't have been satisfying enough.'[95]

Further, Sriram Raghavan shared in the interview with Masand, 'In the original script Sarita takes Karan to an abandoned mine and traps him 2,000 feet underground. When we were down in the mines, someone remarked that the place must be full of rats. And that is where we got the idea of the climax. The exteriors were shot in the outskirts of Khargar during monsoon. The insides of the cave was a set in Chandivilli Studios.'

Raghavan and Pooja Ladha Surti, the co-writer, shared more details in an interview with the author, 'We fetched two/three junglee rats and the rest were white mice (two dozen of them) that were coated black with charcoal powder. The white mice were quite docile. The rat which went up his trousers was a mechanically operated rat.'

The rats chewed up Karan to death. 'Saif Ali Khan was aghast at my idea but he decided to go ahead with it,' said Raghavan whose masterstroke lay in the choice of Saif Ali Khan as the villain.

Punishment need not be only corporal. Tej Puri (Rajat Kapoor) in *Monsoon Wedding* (2001) used to molest Ria (Shefali Shah) when she was in her pre-teen years, many years ago. Ria had not disclosed this to anyone but she grows up with that trauma. But now, years later, amidst the merry wedding gathering, Tej tries to seduce ten-year-old girl Aliya. But Ria prevents that from happening; Tej's shady history spills out into the open and he is asked to leave the wedding.

The 'villains' in comedy films were obviously let off with much milder sentences. In *Padosan*, Master Pillai (Mahmood), a strong aspirant for Bindu's (Saira Banu) hand, gets his competitor Bhola (Sunil Dutt) beaten up by goons. But this has just the opposite effect, as Bindu starts deeply sympathizing with the wounded Bhola. She nurses him back to health, falls in love with him and decides to marry him. Master Pillai is entrusted with the responsibility of playing the nadashwaram (a woodwind instrument used in Carnatic music) at Bhola and Bindu's wedding.

The police and the administration may let the people down, but the Courts don't. In *Jolly LLB*, Tejinder Rajpal's face gets contorted with anguish when Justice Sunder Lal Tripathi (Saurabh Shukla) hands a seven-year imprisonment to Rajpal's client Rahul Deewan for running his Land Rover over pavement dwellers and killing them. There was more drama in the finale of *Jolly LLB 2*. Just past 3 a.m. at the end of a marathon hearing session spread over two calendar days, the PIL (Public Interest Litigation) petitioner Jolly Mishra (Akshay Kumar) pleads with tears in his eyes with Justice Tripathi (Saurabh Shukla again) to allow him to ask the fake Pandit Saraswat (Enaamul Haque) a few final questions. Weathering vociferous objection from the defence lawyer Pramod Mathur, Justice Tripathi contemplates for several seconds during which justice hangs on a string. Saurabh Shukla spoke about those moments philosophically, 'That moment was very carefully crafted in the film. I played that decisive moment that way understanding what is written in the script. Please understand that we can take a stance and justify saying, "this is the way things work". For example, we are going through the greatest misery of humankind. From a scientific and clinical point of view, it is very simple to say that every species has a life span and that maybe our species is reaching the end of the life span and nature will create another life form which will perish us. But the interesting thing is—when your loved one dies, you get a shock. You go through that misery. That is what human life is. We are not some God sitting up there and seeing this whole chess game. We are human beings living it. If Tripathi had said, "According to the Law, this questioning cannot happen. The case is over", this would not have made a story worth telling. But Tripathi gets into the conflict of being either a judge or a human being. He had to take a side at the cost of his own professional ethics and he jumped that line. And that is what made it a story worth telling.'

At the end of those breathless moments, Justice Tripathi allows the witness. Lawyer Jolly exposes the identity of the fake Pandit as being the notorious militant Iqbal Qadri and establishes the guilt of the rogue Police Inspector Suryaveer Singh who, accepting an INR 50 lakh bribe from Qadri to be set free, had murdered an innocent man in a fake encounter. The teddy bearish Justice Tripathi hands out life imprisionment sentences to the rogue cop Inpector Suryaveer Singh and his cronies, leaving the defence lawyer Pramod Mathur's face drooping like a withered banana leaf.

In *Ankur Arora Murder Case*, a sting operation on a Blackberry mobile camera films Dr V. Asthana confessing his negligence during the surgery of the young boy. Shekhawat General Hospital is ordered to pay up a compensation of INR 10 crores to Ankur's mother and Dr Asthana is punished with a three-year prision term. A few of them managed to get away. And strangely, they happened to be murderers.

Ittefaq (2017) is one of those rare instances. Crime fiction writer Vikram (Sidharth Malhotra) from London murders his wife. He manages to cremate the damning evidence along with her dead body. In a gripping hide-and-seek game of minds, the Investigating Officer Dev Verma (Akshaye Khanna) deciphers that Vikram is the murderer. He succeeds in closing in on Vikram, but misses him by a whisker as the murderer boards a late-night flight to London—and freedom, as it would be near impossible for the Mumbai police to get Vikram extradited to India.

Another one that got away was Susanna (Priyanka Chopra) in *7 Khoon Maaf* (2011). She had got all her six husbands killed. And then she does something novel. Says Kolkata based author Urvashi Mukherjee, 'Susanna confesses her guilt at the church and becomes a nun, thus making Jesus Christ her seventh husband. As we all know, the Lord Jesus had taken all the sins of mankind upon himself. His crucifixion cleansed his "wife" of her sins too.' And thus, Susanna uses religion to escape the Law. Arguably, the most tragic denouement was in *Jaane Bhi Do Yaaro*. We howl with laughter at Charlie Chaplin's antics in *Modern Times* (1936) till Chaplin's sordid message sunk in—industrialization was turning men into machines. Similarly, we convulse with laughter at the comic acts in *Jaane Bhi Do Yaaro* (1983) till comes the stinging slap on our faces in the last scene. Cornered by damning evidence of the murder of Commissioner D'Mello and the collapse of a newly built flyover, the Assistant Municipal Commissioner Srivastava (Deepak Qazir) convinces Tarneja, Ahuja and Shoba that the only escape route is for them to sink their differences. Deals are struck on the spot and Srivastava fabricates a false inquiry report. Not only do the criminals slip away, innocent Vinod and Sudhir are made the fall guys and are implicated in the flyover collapse. They are last seen in prison clothes. Agreed Sudhir Mishra, 'It is a very sad film, actually. That was the genius of Kundan Shah.'

Sometimes their contrition is their punishment. Profit-crazed businessmen never quite realize how much harm they are causing to others. Till their own children teach them a much-needed lesson, as Lucky Singh (Boman Irani) in *Lage Raho Munna Bhai!* (2006) learnt. Lucky Singh is a real estate dealer and uses the services of the local thug Circuit (Arshad Warsi) to evict a group of senior citizens from their old age home 'Second Innings Home'. But then Lucky Singh's daughter Simran (Dia Mirza) for whom Lucky had acquired the old age home, leaves his palatial home and announces on FM Radio to the whole of Mumbai, 'I hate my father! .... He *was* my hero .... My father is a cheat ...' There can be no greater punishment than public humiliation and to be disowned by one's children.

> *In an interview Boman Irani talked at length about how he prepared for the role. 'There was this motor dealer on Lamington Road run by a sardar. I just sat at his shop and kept observing him, sometimes minding the shop store when the Sardarji would have gone to the bathroom. Then people started coming and giving me free advice, which is a damn good thing to happen because they are not teaching you to act any more. I learnt to wear the pugri, made sure that my body language was correct and that any word that I used colloquially was not something that a sardar would not use. I learnt Punjabi, had a dialect coach on the set and with me throughout the dubbing.'*

Said Irani to the author, 'The Sikh community was a bit apprehensive that we would made a mockery of the community. But when the film released, they were in for a pleasant surprise because Lucky Singh was not doing the same old *balle balle*. They did not feel offended at Lucky Singh being an underhanded guy because in every community you have people like that. In fact, after the film released the Sikh community honoured me at the gurudwara and give me a talwar. I was touched by that.'

———

We have reached the end of the rogues' gallery. Weren't the villains contemptible? Absolutely. But, as stated at the outset, one cannot deny that a big part of any film's entertainment would be incomplete without them. And, after providing all the entertainment for a better part of the show, they have almost always gotten beaten to pulp by the hero or gotten killed, so that the audience may go home satisfied at the *Ravana* getting burnt in the Ramlila.

And the few bad men have also left behind a proud legacy ....

They have given birth to their own brand of humour. 'Ajit' jokes are as popular as Khushwant Singh's Sardarji jokes with '*Ise liquid oxygen me daal do. Liquid ise jeene nahi degi aur oxygen ise marne nahi degi*' being worthy of a Nobel Prize in Chemistry. Teja and Shakaal became more than mere villain characters. And Ajit became much more than just a smuggler villain.

Prem Chopra's entry line '*Prem naam hai mera, Prem Chopra* (My name is Prem, Prem Chopra)', can stake claim to be the Indian cousin of 'The name's Bond, James Bond'. Mime artists have made careers out of aping Shakti Kapoor, Kader Khan, Ajit, Prem Chopra and others. A few of them are still trying to perfect K.N. Singh's pout and nose twitch. Advertising content writers have pocketed hefty bonuses thanks to Gabbar Singh. And the expectations of the audience have only gone higher on this count.

And much as we hate and loathe the characters they played in these films, we will remain in awe of their performances for a long, long time ....

Acknowledgements

Every major project needs an experienced guide. My most sincere note of gratitude to film historian and Associate Professor, School of Arts and Aesthetics, JNU, Delhi, Kaushik Bhaumik for his guidance, direction, invaluable knowledge and mentorship throughout, without which I doubt I would have been able to complete the manuscript at all.

I am very grateful to National Award winning author Anirudha Bhattacharjee for providing several critical inputs to the manuscript. I can't thank you enough.

To celebrated film-maker Sriram Raghavan for kindly consenting to writing the Foreword for the book—Thank you so much sir!

During the course of authoring the book, I deferred to a few individuals for their sharp insights and perspectives, and for their pointing out the gaps in the story that helped me get critical mental breakthroughs. They are—Amitava Chatterjee, Joy Bhattacharjya, Pavan Jha, Rajesh Jha, Shantanu Raychaudhuri and Supratik Gangopadhyay. Thanks so much!

Between 2009 and 2021 I conducted interviews with a little over fifty actors, scriptwriters, film-makers and individuals associated with the film industry. Unfortunately, some of them have left this world. I bow my head in respect to Late Basu Chatterji, Late Kader Khan, Late Sadashiv Amrapurkar, Late Sachin Bhowmick and Late Shammi Kapoor.

Veteran film historians, script/dialogue writers, biographers, poets, journalists and film producers played a critical role in lending substantial depth to the manuscript. For this, I owe a debt of gratitude to Amit Khanna, Baradwaj Rangan, Hussain Zaidi, Javed Akhtar, Ketan Anand, Madhura Jasraj, Piyush Jha, Pooja Surti Ladha, Ruskin Bond, Sanjit Narwekar and Suresh Jindal.

It was very important that, as a part of my research, I learn from film-makers their sense on the changing face of villainy in Hindi cinema. I am highly grateful to film-makers Anurag Kashyap, Govind Nihalani, Mahesh Bhatt, Mansoor Khan, Shyam Benegal, Saeed Akhtar Mirza and Sudhir Mishra for sharing with me their words of wisdom.

And of course, an equally big thanks to milestone-setting film-makers—Chandra Barot, Brahmanand Siingh and Sujoy Ghosh for their sharp observations and the backstories of how specific villain characters were conceptualized.

No book on villains can be written without speaking with the actors that actually essayed these roles. I am indebted to the following actors for granting me interviews and for sharing their experiences and behind-the-scene stories—Amol Palekar, Amole Gupte, Ananth Mahadevan, Anupam Kher, Ashish Vidyarthi, Bindu Zaveri, Boman Irani, Danny Denzongpa, Govind Namdev, Kay Kay Menon, Kulbhushan Kharbanda, Manoj Bajpayee, Pavan Malhotra, Prashant Narayanan, Prem Chopra, Ranjeet, Rohini Hattangady, Sanjeev Jaiswal, Saurabh Shukla, Sharat Saxena, Sharib Hashmi, Simi Garewal, Tariq Khan, Tisca Chopra, Yashpal Sharma and Zeenat Aman.

Some of my friends, colleagues, family members of film personalities and professionals from other fields provided very useful inputs, like sharing names of a few important films, pointing out certain aspects of villainy, narrating interesting anecdotes or helping me get connected with important people in the industry. A big 'THANK YOU' to: Andalib Sultanpuri, Akshay Manwani, Alaka Sahani, Arindam Majumdar, Arunita Mukherjee, Atri Bhattacharya, Dr Binayak Sinha, Devdan Mitra, Diptakirti Chaudhuri, Jai Arjun Singh, Indranath Mukherjee, Joydeep Roy, Kabir Roy Choudhury, Kishor Bhargav, Mousumi Sengupta, Dr Mukesh Hariawala, Partha Guha, Dr (Mrs) Paromita Mitra Bhaumik, Priyanka Bhatt, Rajesh Kannan, Rakesh Anand Bakshi, Shikha Biswas Vohra, Sumanta Ganguli and Urvashi Mukherjee.

Many thanks to Malavika Banerjee and Jeet Banerjee for giving me the opportunities over the past seven years to moderate prestigious talk shows. I am indeed honoured. A toast to my dear friends from India, Dubai, Singapore and the UK for making me a part of their wonderful events and for believing in me. I treasure those events and moments.

I take this opportunity to thank the assistants, PR personnel and friends and relatives of celebrities who helped me in getting appointments with them—Abhinav Singh, Ayaz Ansari, Christopher Dalton, Dakshesh Desai, Herman D'Souza, Madan Arora, Rakita Nanda, Rupali Guha, Sachin Tailang, Sajid Rizvi, Shailaja Desai Fenn.

I thank Simmam Raghu, Chennai, for converting the audio tapes into digital.

I am a second-generation Calcuttan with my roots to the city dating back to the late 1940s. To all my Kolkata friends I grew up with and refuse to grow up even today—you and the city inspire me to write every day. This 'villain' loves you all!

I could never have gotten into film-based writing if it were not for the quizzing fraternity of my alma mater Jadavpur University, Kolkata. Those four years in the hallowed institution sowed within me the seeds of inquisitiveness. Thank you, JU and all the people who became fast friends in those years!

To anyone writing on or about films, the National Film Archives of India (NFAI), Pune is indispensable; the hours I spent there researching proved to be hugely insightful.

The HarperCollins team—I am ever so grateful to the wonderful editorial team of Rinita Banerjee, Simar Puneet and Pooja Sanyal at HarperCollins India. What can I say about you? You got the book back on track with your editorial skill and experience. Can't thank you enough! And, of course, many thanks to Udayan Mitra for being a pillar of support.

Finally, I owe much to my wife Vandana, my mother Shanthi Vittal, my daughter Ashapoorna and son Akhilesh. They put up with my long absences necessitated by the work involved in this book; I was there yet not there. But for you all, I am always there.

Notes

1. From 'Swarajache Toran kyon bana Uday kaal', in V. Shantaram, *Shantarama*, V. Shantaram Foundation, April 1986, in *Documentary Today*, August 2007 edition, Films Division, pp. 46–47.

2. Jeannine Woods, *Visions of Empire and Other Imaginings: Cinema, Ireland and India 1910–1962*, Peter Lang AG International Academic Publishers, 2011, p. 98, https://books.google.co.in/books?id=Jw-2w-SpuZMC&pg=PA98&redir_esc=y#v=onepage&q&f=false, accessed on 8 July 2021.

3. Ashish Rajadhyaksha and Paul Willemen, *Encyclopaedia of Indian Cinema*, British Film Institute and Oxford University Press in association with the National Film Archives of India, 1994, p. 278, https://www.google.co.in/books/edition/Encyclopedia_of_Indian_Cinema/rF8ABA AAQBAJ?hl=en&gbpv=1&printsec=frontcover, accessed on 8 July 2021.

4. See p. 5, as available on https://archive.org/details/filmindia193804unse/page/n143/mode/2up?q=Sep+1938, accessed on 8 July 2021.

5. Prem Chowdhry, 'The Drum (1938): The Myth of the Muslim Menace', in *Colonial India and the Making of Empire Cinema: Image, Ideology and Identity*, Manchester University Press, 2000, p. 57, https://www.google.

co.in/books/edition/Colonial_India_and_the_Making_of_Empire/uE
nbnfVCHZYC?hl=en&gbpv=1&printsec=frontcover, accessed on 8
July 2021.

6. Leeladhar Mandloi, '*Empire Cinema ka Bharat Virodhi Chehra*', in
    Documentary Today, August 2007 edition, p. 41.

7. K.N. Subramaniam with Ratnakar Tripathy, *Flashback—Cinema in the
    Times of India*, a *Times of India* Sesquicentennial publication, 1990, n.p.

8. From 'Filming', in *My Adventures with Satyajit Ray: The Making of
    Shatranj ke Khilari*, HarperCollins, 2017, p. 99.

9. Asif Kapadia, 'Aamir Khan: Questions from the Floor', *The Guardian*,
    27 October 2002, https://www.theguardian.com/film/2002/oct/27/
    bollywood.features, accessed on 8 July 2021.

10. Satyajit Bhatkal, 'A Million Things to Do', in *The Spirit of Lagaan*,
    Popular Prakashan, 2002, p. 83.

11. Bhatkal, 'The Die is Cast', in *The Spirit of Lagaan*, p. 87.

12. Ibid., p. 94.

13. Bhatkal, 'Climbing a Mountain', in *The Spirit of Lagaan*, p. 166.

14. Bhatkal, 'The Die is Cast', in *The Spirit of Lagaan*, p. 95.

15. Avishek G. Dastidar, 'The Delhi Show, on since 1930s', *Hindustan Times*,
    28 April 2011, https://www.hindustantimes.com/delhi/the-delhi-show-
    on-since-1930s/story-MTmPe9yjwe5lAA6jI2cahJ.html, accessed on 8
    July 2021.

16. Anirudha Bhattacharjee and Balaji Vittal, 'Khemkaran Sector', in *S.D.
    Burman: The Prince-Musician*, Tranquebar, 2018, p. 248.

17. Avijit Ghosh, '"1971" (2007)', in *40 Retakes: Bollywood Classics You May
    Have Missed*, Tranquebar, 2013, pp. 247–48.

18. Amrish Puri with Jyoti Sabharwal, 'Act of Showbiz', in *The Act of Life*,
    Stellar Publishers, 2006, p. 213.

19. Ibid., pp. 216–17.

20. Ibid., p. 214.

21. Ibid., p. 222.

22. See 'Kabuliwala's Bengali wife Sushmita shot dead in Afghanistan
    by militants', *The Telegraph Online*, 5 September 2013, https://www.
    telegraphindia.com/india/kabuliwalas-bengali-wife-sushmita-shot-
    dead-in-afghanistan-by-militants/cid/259082, accessed on 8 July 2021.

23. See 'RGV zeroes on his onscreen Kasab', NDTV, 16 March 2012, https://www.ndtv.com/entertainment/rgv-zeroes-on-his-onscreen-kasab-624000, accessed on 17 July 2021.

24. '"Madras Café" not based on Rajiv Gandhi: Shoojit Sircar', *India Today*, 21 August 2013, https://www.indiatoday.in/movies/bollywood/story/madras-cafe-not-based-on-rajiv-gandhi-shoojit-sircar-174436-2013-08-21, accessed on 8 July 2021.

25. *Yeh Woh Manzil To Nahin* released in very select theatres. But incredibly, within a year of its being made, the Mandal Commission agitation began in college campuses across India.

26. Pavan Jha, '6 things you need to know about Bimal Roy', *The Hindu*, 10 January 2016, https://www.thehindu.com/news/cities/mumbai/entertainment/6-things-you-need-to-know-about-Bimal-Roy/article13992062.ece, accessed on 17 August 2021.

27. Dilip Kumar (as narrated to Udaytara Nayar), 'Colleagues and Friends', in *Dilip Kumar: The Substance and The Shadow*, Hay House, 2014, pp. 241–42.

28. Tisca Chopra, 'Baap bada na bhaiyya … Money matters and professionalism', in *Acting Smart: Your Ticket to Showbiz*, HarperCollins, 2014, p. 123.

29. From Ghosh, 'Aavishkar (1973)', in *40 Retakes*, p. 91.

30. Samira Sood, 'Gumrah, BR Chopra's tale of a woman's desire that challenged conventions back in 1963', *The Print*, 25 April 2020, https://theprint.in/features/gumrah-br-chopras-tale-of-a-womans-desire-that-challenged-conventions-back-in-1963/408477/, accessed on 17 July 2021.

31. From Yasser Usman, 'Love Triangle', in *Rekha—The Untold Story*, Juggernaut Books, 2016, p. 131.

32. See Bachi Karkaria, 'Sylvia's Story Beyond the Scandal', *LiveMint*, 2 May 2017, https://www.livemint.com/Leisure/OGsgT6hkkniURonylB2uXK/Sylvias-story-beyond-the-scandal.html, accessed on 8 July 2021.

33. The story was inspired by Agatha Christie's play *The Unexpected Guest*.

34. Madhura Pandit Jasraj, 'When Films Began to Talk', in *V. Shantaram—The Man Who Changed Indian Cinema*, Hay House, 2015, p. 83.

35. Poulomi Banerjee, 'Why Chambal's dacoits didn't ride into the sunset', *Hindustan Times*, 7 December 2017, https://www.hindustantimes.com/india-news/we-wouldn-t-come-charging-on-horses-like-they-show-in-bollywood-films-former-chambal-dacoits-remember-time-spent-as-bandits/story-1V8dXgX7BR50weQbN1VorJ.html, accessed on 19 July 2021.

36. Rauf Ahmed, 'Back to the Future', in *Mehboob Khan, The Legends of Indian Cinema*, ed. Aruna Vasudev, Wisdom Tree, 2008, p. 39.

37. Ahmed, 'The Magnum Opus', in *Mehboob Khan*, p. 83.

38. Uma Anand and Ketan Anand, '*Neecha Nagar* and the Poetics of Film', in *Chetan Anand: The Poetics of Film*, Himalaya Films, Media Entertainment, 2007, p. 35.

39. Kairvy Grewal, 'Vinoba Bhave, the Walking Saint who "talked" bandits of Madhya Pradesh into surrendering', *The Print*, 15 November 2019, https://theprint.in/theprint-profile/vinoba-bhave-the-walking-saint-who-talked-bandits-of-madhya-pradesh-into-surrendering/320600/, accessed on 8 July 2021.

40. Bunny Reuben, 'Jis Desh Mein Ganga Behti Hai: Understanding Raaka', in ...*And Pran: A Biography*, HarperCollins, 2011, p. 189.

41. Ibid., 189.

42. From 'The Travails of Film Making: Gunga Jumna and After', in *Dilip Kumar*, p. 199.

43. Ibid., p. 197.

44. Ibid., pp. 195–96.

45. Mahendra Sandhu, who plays Jwala, is again, a doctor forced to take up arms to defend his family.

46. In Anupama Chopra, 'Bahut Yaarana Lagta Hai', in *Sholay: The Making of A Classic*, Penguin Random House India, 2000, p. 104.

47. Ash Kotak, 'Mala Sen Obituary', *The Guardian*, 13 June 2011, https://www.theguardian.com/world/2011/jun/13/mala-sen-obituary, accessed on 8 July 2021.

48. IANS, 'Shekhar Kapur: Bandit Queen is my best film. Hope I can make another like it', *India Today*, 25 April 2019, https://www.indiatoday.in/movies/bollywood/story/shekhar-kapur-on-bandit-queen-it-is-my-best-film-1509706-2019-04-25, accessed on 19 July 2021.

49. Nasreen Munni Kabir, 'Conversations', in *Conversations with Waheeda Rehman*, Penguin Random House India, 2014, p. 81.

50. Madhavi Pothukuchi, 'Mujhe Jeene Do: When Sunil Dutt shattered inter-faith marriage taboo while playing a dacoit', *India Today*, 26 May 2019, https://theprint.in/features/reel-take/mujhe-jeene-do-when-sunil-dutt-shattered-inter-faith-marriage-taboo-while-playing-a-dacoit/241145/, accessed on 8 July 2021.

51. Chopra, 'Mujhe Gabbar Chahiye—Zinda', in *Sholay*, p. 54.

52. Chopra, '*Is* Story *Main* Emotion *Hai*, Drama *Hai*, Tragedy *Hai*', in *Sholay*, p. 161.

53. Chopra, '*Loha Lohe Ko Kaatata Hai*', in *Sholay*, p. 34.

54. Chopra, '*Loha Garam Hai - Maar Do Hathoda*', in *Sholay*, pp. 85–86.

55. IANS, 'Father was never credited for dacoit films: Jaya Bachchan', *The Indian Express*, 25 January 2015, https://indianexpress.com/article/entertainment/entertainment-others/father-was-never-credited-for-dacoit-films-jaya-bachchan/, accessed on 8 July 2021.

56. See Mark Olivier, 'Death of A Demon', *The Guardian*, 19 October 2004, https://www.theguardian.com/world/2004/oct/19/india.markoliver; and Pankaj Jaiswal, 'Reel life of UP's ex-bandit queen: Seema Parihar bites the bullet, helps ballot', *Hindustan Times*, 13 February 2017, https://www.hindustantimes.com/india-news/reel-life-of-up-s-ex-bandit-queen-seema-parihar-bites-the-bullet-helps-ballot/story-0tkgrDMtuMhgnRkugVhYYP.htm, both accessed on 8 July 2021.

57. See '*Is* Story *Main* Emotion *Hai*, Drama *Hai*, Tragedy *Hai*' in *Sholay*, p. 176.

58. See Rajadhyaksha and Willemen, *Encyclopaedia of Indian Cinema*, p. 286.

59. See 'Director Kardar gives his best picture!', in *Film India*, p. 20, https://archive.org/stream/filmindia194006unse#page/n465/mode/2up/search/Pagal, accessed on 8 July 2021.

60. Scott A. Bonn, 'Serial Killer Myth # 1—They are mentally ill or evil geniuses', *Psychology Today*, 16 June 2014, https://www.psychologytoday.com/intl/blog/wicked-deeds/201406/serial-killer-myth-1-theyre-mentally-ill-or-evil-geniuses, accessed on 8 July 2021.

61. TNN, 'The Only Other Time India Hanged 4 People', *Pune Mirror*, 20 March 2020, https://punemirror.indiatimes.com/pune/others/the-only-

time-india-hanged-four-people/articleshow/73211847.cms, accessed on 8 July 2021.

62. Scott Bonn, '5 Myths about serial killers and why they persist', *Scientific American*, 24 October 2014, https://www.scientificamerican.com/article/5-myths-about-serial-killers-and-why-they-persist-excerpt/, accessed on 8 July 2021.

63. See Faridoon Shahrayar, '7 Khoon Maaf', *Bollywood Hungama*, 2011, https://youtu.be/_gx3XaikEo0?t=109, accessed on 8 July 2021.

64. Poonam Saxena, 'Inside the mind of Raman Raghav, Mumbai's serial killer of the 60s', *Hindustan Times*, 14 June 2016, https://www.hindustantimes.com/bollywood/inside-the-mind-of-raman-raghav-mumbai-s-serial-killer-of-the-60s/story-LaA01MtT0wrAM0ZprCoLYJ.html, accessed on 8 July 2021.

65. Bob Christo, 'Part III - India', in *Flashback: My Life and Times in Bollywood and Beyond*, Penguin Books, 2011, p. 191.

66. Keshub Mahindra, as told to Vinod Mahanta, 'ET@50: 1961-70: After the Raj, it was Licence Raj', *The Economic Times*, 8 May 2010, https://economictimes.indiatimes.com/et50-1961-70-after-the-raj-it-was-licence-raj/articleshow/5907079.cms?from=mdr, accessed on 9 July 2021.

67. See Kamal Sadanah in an interview with Vishwas Kulkarni, 'Kamal Sadanah remembers the shootout', *Mumbai Mirror*, 4 October 2009, https://timesofindia.indiatimes.com/entertainment/hindi/bollywood/news/Kamal-Sadanah-remembers-the-shootout/articleshow/5086216.cms, accessed on 9 July 2021.

68. Keith D'Costa, 'Ajit - Memories', *Cinepolot*, 1991, available on https://cineplot.com/ajit-memories/, accessed on 9 July 2021.

69. 'Greed, politics, bribery, dirty money: India rated among the most corrupt in the world', *India Today*, 3 July 2006, https://www.indiatoday.in/magazine/cover-story/story/20060703-india-rated-among-most-corrupt-in-the-world-785043-2006-07-03, accessed on 9 July 2021.

70. See J. Ramakrishnan, 'The Lord Returns to His Abode', *Madras Musings*, Vol. XXVIII, No. 23, 16–31 March 2019, accessed on 9 July 2021. Also, for details of the trial Ram Lal Narang vs Union of India and Ors, 5 February 1982, see Records of Delhi High Court Proceedings,

as available on https://indiankanoon.org/doc/1439657/, accessed on 9 July 2021.

71. See Siddharth Malhotra, 'Ek Villain Ek Dastaan—Ajit', on Zoom TV, <https://youtu.be/scNLPtu89pE?t=63, accessed on 9 July 2021.

72. Yasser Usman, 'Naam', in *Sanjay Dutt: The Crazy, Untold Story of Bollywood's Bad Boy,* Juggernaut 2018, p. 90.

73. Books like *Dongri to Dubai—Six decades of the Mumbai Mafia* (Roli Books, 2012), *Byculla to Bangkok* (HarperCollins, 2014) and *Mumbai Avengers* (HarperCollins, 2015) authored by crime writer Hussain Zaidi (*Mumbai Avengers*, with Gabriel Khan), and personal conversations between Zaidi and me, helped reveal valuable insights about the Bombay underworld.

74. Directorate of Economics and Statistics, Planning Department, Govt. of Maharashtra, Mumbai, 'Maharashtra at a Glance', in 'Economic Survey of Maharashtra 2018–19', 2019, https://mahades.maharashtra.gov.in/files/publication/ESM_18_19_eng.pdf, p. 3, accessed on 9 July 2021.

75. IANS, 'Mumbai cops had intel on killing of Gulshan Kumar: Former top cop Rakesh Maria', *The New Indian Express,* 21 February 2020, https://www.newindianexpress.com/nation/2020/feb/21/mumbai-cops-had-intel-on-killing-of-gulshan-kumar-former-top-cop-rakesh-maria-2106634.html, accessed on 9 July 2021.

76. M. Rehman, 'Dholakia brothers: Mahesh Dholakia shot dead near his apartment', *India Today,* 30 April 1987, https://www.indiatoday.in/magazine/crime/story/19870430-dholakia-brothers-mahesh-dholakia-shot-dead-near-his-apartment-798817-1987-04-30, accessed on 9 July 2021.

77. See https://youtu.be/scNLPtu89pE?t=63.

78. See interview on https://www.youtube.com/watch?v=3KAM5_ub9UU&t=4s, accessed on 9 July 2021.

79. Ibid.

80. Arati Kade and Tathagatha Sengupta, 'The Strike that Never Ended', *GroundXero,* 12 June 2019, https://www.groundxero.in/2019/06/12/the-strike-that-never-ended-episode-4-1980s/, accessed on 9 July 2021.

81. Farzand Ahmed and Dilip Bobb, 'Bhagalpur blindings represents one of the darkest chapters in India's history', *India Today*, 31 December 1980, https://www.indiatoday.in/magazine/special-report/story/19801231-bhagalpur-blindings-represents-one-of-the-darkest-chapters-in-indias-history-773650-2013-11-29, accessed on 9 July 2021.

82. See 'Haasil (2003)', in *40 Retakes*, p. 233.

83. See 'The case for legalized cricket betting; it's not what you think', *The Economic Times*, 19 January 2016, https://economictimes.indiatimes.com/news/sports/the-case-for-legalized-cricket-betting-its-not-what-you-think/articleshow/50631879.cms?from=mdr, accessed on 9 July 2021.

84. Mark Townsend, 'The Murder That Never Was', *The Guardian*, 1 July 2007, https://www.theguardian.com/sport/2007/jul/01/cricket.features, accessed on 9 July 2021.

85. Subhash K. Jha, 'Was "Nayakan" inspired by "The Godfather"?', *DNA India*, 16 November 2013, https://www.dnaindia.com/entertainment/report-was-nayakan-inspired-by-the-godfather-1920072, accessed on 9 July 2021.

86. 'Pavan Malhotra - My Look As Salim Was Inspired From Dawood Ibrahim', *Mid-day*, 28 July 2016, https://www.mid-day.com/articles/pavan-malhotra--my-look-as-salim-was-inspired-from-dawood-ibrahim/17475179, accessed on 9 July 2021.

87. Zubair Ahmed, 'Bollywood offer for Shoaib Akhtar', BBC News, 14 May 2005, http://news.bbc.co.uk/2/hi/south_asia/4546945.stm, accessed on 9 July 2021.

88. M. Rahman, 'Shoot-out gives bloody nose to Bombay's underworld', *India Today*, 15 December 1991, https://www.indiatoday.in/magazine/crime/story/19911215-shootout-gives-bloody-nose-to-bombays-underworld-815180-1991-12-15, accessed on 9 July 2021.

89. Hussain Zaidi, *Byculla to Bangkok- Mumbai's Maharashtrian Mobsters*, HarperCollins India, 2014, p. 152.

90. Ibid., p. 203.

91. From Ghosh, 'Sehar', in *40 Retakes*, p. 240.

92. PTI, 'I&B asks Censor Board, How DK Bose song was cleared', India TV, 17 June 2011, https://www.indiatvnews.com/entertainment/

bollywood/i-b-asks-censor-board-how-d-k-bose-song-was-cleared-2484.html, accessed on 9 July 2011.

93. Uma Anand and Ketan Anand, *Chetan Anand: The Poetics of Film*, Himalaya Films—Media Entertainment, 2007, p. 57.

94. Nandita C. Puri, 'Ardh Satya', in *Unlikely Hero: Om Puri*, Roli Books, 2009.

95. Sriram Raghavan in an interview with Rajeev Masand, '*Ek Hasina Thi*—The Anatomy of a Scene', CNN News-18, https://www.youtube.com/watch?v=TuUIRkUnp_Y, accessed on 13 December 2020.

About the Author

Balaji Vittal is the co-author (with Anirudha Bhattacharjee) of *R.D. Burman: The Man, The Music*, which won the National Award for Best Book on Cinema (2011), *Gaata Rahe Mera Dil: 50 Classic Hindi Film Songs*, which won the MAMI Award for Best Book on Cinema (2015), and the highly acclaimed *S.D. Burman: The Prince-Musician*.